2009.01.03

☆☆COMBAT COMMANDER

COMBAT COMMANDER

AUTOBIOGRAPHY OF A SOLDIER

☆ ☆

MAJOR GENERAL E. N. HARMON

(...et.)

...ith

E

...d

E

...
...J.

DEMCO

D - 11 - 71

COMBAT COMMANDER: Autobiography of a Soldier by Major General
E. N. Harmon, with Milton MacKaye and William Ross MacKaye
© 1970 by Major General E. N. Harmon, Milton MacKaye, and
William Ross MacKaye
ISBN 0-13-152421-6
Library of Congress Catalog Card Number: 74-100630
Printed in the United States of America   T
Prentice-Hall International, Inc., London
Prentice-Hall of Australia, Pty. Ltd., Sydney
Prentice-Hall of Canada, Ltd., Toronto
Prentice-Hall of India Private Ltd., New Delhi
Prentice-Hall of Japan, Inc., Tokyo

FOREWORD by General Omar Bradley

Ernie Harmon and I were cadets together at West Point. Our friendship and close association was renewed during World War II in North Africa, and continued throughout the European Campaign. General Harmon was a combat commander during World War I and I believe history will most certainly tag him as one of our outstanding and most productive leaders of World War II.

One of the characteristics of the American soldier is that he fights best when he understands *why* he is fighting. As the readers turn the pages of *Combat Commander: Autobiography of a Soldier,* it will become evident that General Harmon clearly knew the "why" of every action in which he was involved. It is this understanding which was, I believe, the pivotal reason for his unique ability as a leader.

In addition to a superb study in leadership, *Combat Commander* offers an excellent clinical analysis of the Italian Campaign with a particularly lucid explanation of the facts and circumstances surrounding the action at the Anzio beachhead.

Ernie Harmon has earned my gratitude many times through the years. This time I am particularly grateful to him and his co-authors, Milton and William R. MacKaye, for providing an exceptionally fine contribution to the written accounts of our times.

Contents

ONE
★ ★
Beginnings

GENEALOGICAL RESEARCHERS REPORT that the Harmon family came from "sturdy" English and Scottish stock, and I have no doubt this is true. But I sometimes wonder whether those early English or Scottish yeomen were any sturdier than their descendants. To be sure, there were some spirited people in the ghostly Old World procession: a bishop of the Church of England, an admiral in the British Navy, and seagoing Captain Thomas Harmon who was killed fighting Algerian pirates off the coast of Africa. Captain Harmon was "wounded by three musket balls but still continued in command and died three days after."

Certainly the Harmons who settled in the New England wilderness were sturdy enough. They were Indian fighters and State of Maine skippers and my great-great-great grandfather, Josiah Harmon, enlisted in George Washington's army as a fifer in 1775. He was then 12 years old.

My mother's family, the Spauldings, seem also to have been an adventurous lot. The first shot at Bunker Hill was fired, reputedly, by an impetuous kinsman, Joseph Spaulding, and that shot killed Major Pitcairn, the brave and able professional British soldier who faced the colonials at the Battle of Lexington and gave the famous order: "Disperse, ye rebels, disperse."

A professional soldier myself, I have always deplored my kinsman's impetuosity. General Israel Putman, who was in command behind the American earthworks, did more. He smacked Joseph Spaulding on the head with his sword and threatened profanely to cut down any other man who wasted a musket shot before the Redcoats started up the hill. There were nine other Spauldings at Bunker Hill; one was killed and two were severely wounded.

My original Spaulding ancestor in this country was Edward Spaulding who came to Jamestown, Virginia, in 1619—a year before the Mayflower dropped anchor at Plymouth, Massachusetts. He and his family are listed in Virginia Archives as among the fortunate people who survived the Indian massacres after the death of friendly Chief Powhatan. Edward is believed to have lived a few years in Bermuda before joining the Massachusetts Bay Colony at Braintree in 1634. Later he moved to Chelmsford, Massachusetts, a town founded by five of his sons and a grandson.

On my mother's side of the family, there were other restless people who married into the Spaulding clan, particularly the Days and the Turners. Peletiah Day fought in the Revolution and later helped to write the Constitution of the State of Massachusetts. He was a great-great-great grandfather. So was Daniel Turner, who moved to Pennsylvania where he set up as a land speculator. A contemporary record says he "had many conflicts with Indians but was a bold, daring, and powerful man." This comment seems to be verified by an account of his exploits I was fortunate to find in an obscure volume, the *History of Clearfield County, Pennsylvania*:

"One day in the year 1813 while hunting . . . . he had a rough and tumble conflict with a panther, but succeeded in getting the animal by its hind legs and holding on in such a manner that it could not bite him, until Joseph Turner came and dispatched this dangerous foe with a tomahawk. At another time he wounded a panther and the animal retreated to a cave-like place, between two large rocks. Turner followed

2

and by attaching a sword-like bayonet to the muzzle of his gun, stabbed the panther to death. Few men would care to tackle a wounded panther in a place like that."

To a casual reader, this background might seem to provide an explanation of my choice of a military career. Nothing could be more wrong. As a young boy I never heard of my colorful ancestors. My own immediate family had more important things to think about: we were proud, we were respectable, we walked a mile-and-a-half to church every Sunday, and we were poor—struggling poor. My father and mother worked hard to pay for a new house they built in Pawtucketville, a suburb of Lowell, Massachusetts. I was born there February 26, 1894, the youngest of four surviving children.

The eldest was my brother Charles. Then came sisters Etta and Mabel at two year intervals, and then me. I can remember that we were a warm, tight, loving community. But my early memories are fragmentary because that happy community proved to be singularly impermanent. Sister Mabel died when I was six. My father died when I was eight.

Mother and I took Father's body to Unity, Maine, where he was buried in the family plot. I had never been away from Pawtucketville before, and was pleased to meet relatives at the old home place. Uncle Charles quickly became my hero. Uncle Charles was County Road Commissioner and a real Down East politician, the first of my acquaintance. One day he took me hunting and I shot a rabbit. Uncle Charles called in neighbors to celebrate his nephew's hunting debut. There was a barrel of hard cider in the barn, crackers and cheese, and sheer delight for me.

The grandmother I met there was not actually my grandmother by blood; she had been Grandfather Josiah's second wife. Grandfather Josiah, who died before I ever met him, had two families. He was a graduate of Colby College, a Free Baptist minister, and a teacher in various academies and secondary schools. My father, also a Josiah, and his two

3

brothers belonged to the first family and I assume they hustled out of Unity to make a living for themselves when the second family (to which Uncle Charles belonged) came along. Their schooling must have been limited, for they worked at undistinguished jobs: my father was a night watchman in a lumberyard at the time of his death. I am sure they were victims of the economic upheaval that sent thousands of young men from New England's unproductive farms to the industry of mill towns. Incidentally, I recall my step-grandmother with great affection. She was kind, she spoke with a hypnotic Scotch burr, she smoked a small clay pipe, and she tried, without much success, to inoculate me with pride in Harmon forebears completely shadowy to me.

Times became difficult when Mother and I returned to Pawtucketville. Mother had known trouble before. Her adventurous father had moved out to Iowa just before the Civil War and located at La Claire, a village on the Mississippi River. His twin daughters were born there. He gave them the Indian names of two small streams which met the Mississippi there: Mother's twin sister's name was Tacy Alpharetta; Mother's name was Mary Junaetta. Grandfather Spaulding took ill and returned with his family to Massachusetts, where he died of tuberculosis when my mother was twelve.

Probably friends and relatives rallied around to help my mother keep her family afloat after my father died. I just don't know. But I know about her courage and independence. She took in washing, went out to do housework by the day; she kept us clean and tidy and sent us to school. I know I was hard for her to handle because I was full of devilment and got into all sorts of small difficulties. Older boys in our neighborhood had the ancient, perhaps prehistoric, custom of blooding the young; in the evening they would form a ring around the gaslight at the end of my street and force the pee-wees to fight each other. I was naturally combative and found this experience valuable later, but it worried my mother. Frequently after a hard day she would come to ringside and escort me

4

home. This maternal interference was never challenged in our neighborhood, so perhaps our street society was not as tough as I thought.

Mother died of cancer when I was ten, and that was the end of the family. Brother Charles was eighteen; he left school to go to work and stayed in Lowell. My sister Etta went to live with friends of the family in Worcester, Massachusetts. I was taken to be raised by a particular friend of my mother's who lived on a small farm at West Newbury, Vermont.

She was Mrs. John Durant, the former Minnie Bell Brock, who was to be (for me) Aunt Minnie, and a second mother. She was a well-educated woman for her time, a former teacher who had been graduated from what was then called a normal college. Her husband was a hard-working and conscientious man, but considerably below her level in imagination and intelligence. Both were markedly religious; family prayers were regularly held and a chapter of the Bible was read at each meal and at bedtime. I believe I am correct in saying that, in this way, we went through the Scriptures fourteen times, never missing a chapter, or verse, and nary a tiresome Old Testament begat. In later life, it took a good deal of beguiling to get me back to Holy Writ.

The little school in West Newbury, where all grades were taught in the same room, came as something of a surprise. I believe I must have been somewhat farther along than the other children my age, for I remember standing to recite with boys who seemed to tower over me. Of course, I was too dazed at first by the wrenching change in my life to comprehend exactly what *was* happening. But children are extraordinarily resilient, as was confirmed for me later in life in many war-torn countries, and the instinct for survival is strong. It is lucky I had that instinct because, as a city kid, I found that I was fair game for every ambitious youngster anxious to prove rural superiority with his fists. But this was a challenge I could understand and meet joyfully. Inside or outside the school-yard, a half dozen scraps were forced upon me during my first

5

week. The rude coaching under Pawtucketville's gaslights stood me in good stead. Schoolyard enemies later became good friends.

In those days in New England the authority of the schoolteacher was backed up at home. To many of us kids this was automatic and thus unquestioned. Punishment at school meant also a spanking at home. My Uncle John Durant performed his duty in the woodshed, just as my father had back in Pawtucketville, and I did not resent it a bit. Occasionally, when I was not really the guilty party, punishment rankled. Back in Pawtucketville, a bigger boy once jumped me without warning, bloodying my nose; I merely fought back. His father came complaining to my father next day. While my father spanked me without spirit I heard him say: "Didn't like the father; didn't like the boy." Too bad that Dad didn't live long enough for us to have become better acquainted.

I adapted quickly to life on the farm, and acquired an affection for Vermont, for its mountains and lush summer valleys, for its winters and crisp clean air; it was an affection that followed me half across the world on military adventures, and eventually brought me home again for a second career. At fourteen I could manage and care for stock as well as Uncle John Durant, handle a team in a deep forest snow, and bed down animals in a steamy, redolent, ammoniac barn when a blizzard was on the way. Our recreations were limited. There was, of course, no radio, no television, and most of us had never seen a movie. I hunted deer in deer season, and woodchucks any time between chores. In the winter youngsters sledded and skated, and in warmer weather Thursday night prayer meetings were an accredited meeting place. There the boys and girls socialized and made sly eyes while their elders wrestled with the Lord and a few of the more ruffianly types like Wellman Tuxbury and I wrestled each other in sheer high spirits on the churchyard turf. Wellman was my age and has been a lifelong friend. One of his sisters, Leona, was to become my wife.

6

My own horizons began to broaden when our country district opened a new one-room schoolhouse at the foot of Rogers Hill, only a quarter of a mile from home. I became not only a student but also the janitor and caretaker. I shoveled the snow and kept the fires for fifty cents a week. Once a year I went to the woods, and cut five cords of rock maple logs and piled them neatly in the woodshed. For this I was paid fifty cents a cord. Thus, for the first time, I earned money on my own.

Two women exerted great influence on my life at this point: my Aunt Minnie and Mrs. Julia Rollins, teacher of the Rogers Hill school. Both of them seemed to think I had talents of which I certainly was unaware, a native ability which might qualify me to be something other than a laborer in a mill town or a small farmer in the hills. Looking back, I am sure I was then something of a jackass. I learned easily at Rogers Hill and that gave me plenty of time to act the clown and bother the other students. One afternoon Mrs. Rollins kept me after school, ignored me while she graded papers, and finally approached with a big, fat tug-strap in her hand. I was already apprehensive.

"Ernie," she said, "we've come to the parting of the ways. You have to decide this evening whether you are going to behave yourself, or whether I use this strap. If you decide to behave yourself, we can continue to be friends."

Mrs. Rollins was a big woman and I was then small for my age. Prudence got the better of valor, and I elected to behave. But the story doesn't end there. Julia Rollins sat down at the school desk next to mine and began to talk about learning, and the need for learning, and the challenge of the great world outside our hills and hollows. Then she promised to give me my first-year high school studies right there in our little schoolhouse. And that's exactly what she did.

The result was that I was able to enter Bradford Academy as a sophomore. Bradford was four miles from the Durant farm, and, in the beginning, I walked it both ways. Later I was

7

able to ride with Willy Putnam, a neighbor, in a little two-wheel gig. Most of our neighbors' kids had ended their schooling with the eighth grade, and Uncle John grew increasingly restive. Aunt Minnie believed in higher education; he did not. When I was about to enter the junior year of high school, Uncle John was at the end of his patience and we had an altercation which pained everybody. I must leave school or leave home, he said. I left home. With Aunt Minnie's help I found a job in Bradford working a small farm for a widow named McDuffy. I ran this farm, completely by myself, the last two years I was at the Academy.

Other people who started with few advantages have acknowledged their debt to teachers and schoolmasters. To their witness I add mine. Dr. Speare, a Dartmouth graduate, was principal of Bradford and he understood my situation. Whenever I needed a day off to plow or to put in crops, he gave it to me, and I was thus able to earn $1.50 a day. This money enabled me to clothe and feed myself and to graduate.

I worked hard but I also managed to have a hell of a good time. I played on the baseball team, was a guard on the basketball team, and served as captain of an almost nonexistent track team. In an interscholastic meet I ran the 100 yard dash, the 220, the 440, the half-mile, and the mile races in a single afternoon. I also entered myself in the broad jump, but that came late in the day and by that time I could not have jumped over a barnyard puddle. My faithful associate during this trial of strength was the Bradford town drunk, an ardent sports fan. After each event he massaged my legs with medicinal alcohol and never drank a drop. With his example of loyalty and self-sacrifice, I felt I had no choice but to carry on.

For winning the highest number of points in the track meet I was awarded a box of 500 shotgun shells; this was certainly more satisfactory and useful to me than a medal. Whether or not 500 shotgun shells makes you a professional I never found out, because I told nobody about it when I participated as an amateur in the Olympics some years later.

8

I was graduated from Bradford Academy in 1912 and was salutatorian of my class. I wanted to go to Dartmouth because Dr. Speare came from there but it was obvious that I could not afford it. I worked hard that summer and entered Norwich University with seventy dollars in my pocket and an extremely modest scholarship from the State of Vermont. I had elected the civil engineering course and four more years of study.

Norwich, located in Northfield, Vermont, is a military college with an ancient and honorable history. Captain Alden Partridge, the founder, had the idea of preparing young Americans for the twofold function of the citizen-soldier. In times of peace they would serve as engineers and surveyors, businessmen and teachers. In times of war, they were prepared to serve their country as soldiers in the function of command. And so they did serve—in the Mexican War, in the Civil War, and in every war since. General Grenville Dodge, the engineer who built the first transcontinental railroad, was a Norwich alumnus. Admiral Dewey, a hero of Manila Bay in the Spanish-American War, was a student there.

Needless to say, I was quite ignorant of these traditions when I took up residence. It quickly became evident that my $70 would not last very long, and I set out to find work. Northfield was a small town with few opportunities for a youngster with no special skills, but persistence won out. I found a job milking cows for Professor Ethan Allen Shaw, who taught mathematics and also ran a small milk route on the side. My payment was board at his very pleasant family table.

A little later I was invited to join a fraternity, and worked for my board there. I rose at 4:30 each morning, built the fires, shoveled the snow, swept the house once a day, mopped the floors once a week and waited tables three meals a day. I enjoyed the happy brotherhood but, lamentably, was to prove a Benedict Arnold to the fraternity system much later in my life.

Fraternity affiliation did not end my association with Profes-

9

sor Shaw's cows. Good hired help has always been at a premium in Vermont's dairy industry, and this time Professor Shaw came to me: if I would continue to engineer the udders he would pay me $3.50 in cash money and provide me with occasional day work at other agricultural pursuits. This income and a small free-lance business as a pants presser enabled me to buy my books and keep a hop, skip, and jump ahead of expenses. My charges to fellow cadets for the ministrations of the hot iron now seem reasonable enough: 15 cents for a blouse and ten cents for trousers.

In the main I was as contented with my lot as a man of my temperament can be (which means, of course, that I have never been contented at all). I missed participation in athletics, but because of the battle of the books and the pressure of outside work there simply wasn't time. I knew I was doing reasonably well scholastically; upperclassmen were democratically kind, and faculty members helped me in every way possible.

Yet at times I was completely despairing. In those days Norwich played its opening football game each season against Dartmouth, and it was the custom for the entire corps of cadets to charter a special train to transport them to the Hanover campus. Half boy and half man, it seemed to me on one particular opening day that everybody was going to the game except me. I didn't have the carfare and I needed money so badly I had engaged myself to cut corn for Professor Shaw.

The professor's cornfield was right next to the railroad track. The special train with its flamboyant banners, its tooting whistle, and cheering kids at the windows passed right by on that carnival day. Everybody waved at me. I didn't wave back. To hide my tears and hide my face, I bent over and cut corn, cut corn. It was a discouraging day and I immersed myself in self-pity. It was the kind of disappointment, I know now, that all of us must rise above many times in maturity. But the recollection still stings.

My undergraduate days at Norwich were to be limited. I

10

took to military life as some of my Maine ancestors must have taken to salt water. Militarily, Norwich was of the cavalry persuasion, and horses were something I knew about. Colonel Frank Tompkins, on assignment from the War Department, was then commandant of cadets at Norwich. For some reason he seemed to think I had the makings of a professional soldier and he suggested I apply for appointment to West Point. He also talked persuasively to our local congressman, Frank Plumley, who conveniently lived in Northfield. I got the appointment. Then, as later, I was willing to take a reasoned gamble; I dropped my college studies to devote all my remaining time, less than a month, to preparing myself for the West Point entrance examinations.

Then, as now, there were special schools which prepped aspirants for the West Point and Annapolis examinations. I did not know about them, and, if I had known, I could not have afforded their tutoring fees. In fact, I could not afford the trip to Boston where the regional examinations were held.

This led to my first confrontation with bankers and the banker mentality: I was to learn more when, in the far and unsuspected future, I became a college president. I went timidly to the Northfield Savings Bank to ask for a fifty-dollar loan. Henry Orser, the cashier, listened patiently to my story, told me I was a poor credit risk for the bank, and refused the loan. Then, as I was about to retreat in confusion, he told me he would accept personal responsibility for my indebtedness and would co-sign my note. So I paid my carfare to Boston, took the examinations, and, after a long and anxious wait, found that I had passed and been accepted for West Point.

I was still broke, so I went back to the bank once more. I needed money for my carfare to the military academy and to meet the initial expense of buying my uniforms. I am pleased to say that I paid back Henry Orser and the bank four years later when I was graduated.

There is nothing very exciting to report about my career at West Point. Relieved of financial stress (Uncle Sam was now

11

paying for my education), I floated along scholastically in the middle of my class. I was still too much of a country boy to shine at the tea-dance social game, but I was happy to compete in athletics once more. I managed to win the middleweight boxing championship, played hockey, and ran on the track team. But my big ambition was to win my letter in football, and no one ever worked harder or with more fanaticism. I had to work because I weighed about 155 pounds wringing wet. My appraisal of my own abilities was modest and I was understandably overawed by the stars on the varsity (one of them was the great Elmer Q. Oliphant, a genius in the backfield but something less in the classroom), and by the redoubtable Charlie Daley, who was then our coach. Daley had been an all-American quarterback at Harvard and then, after transferring to the Academy, an all-American once again. And Pot Graves, our line coach, had the reputation of being the most merciless slave driver on the public scene since Simon Legree turned in his whip.

There is a story about my timidity which I have told many times in the past. I am not quite sure what the story proves, except the power of psychology in dealing with men, or, as in this case, boys.

It was early in the season and we had played only two games. Washington and Lee University was coming up from Virginia with blood in its eye and three victories under its belt. Then through the underground (or however such news travels) came word that the team's supporters were bringing along $2,000 to wager on the game. In those days cadets were not allowed to carry currency; our meager monthly spending money was issued to us in "boodler's checks" which were honored at the school canteen. Be that as it may, half of that Confederate money—which, in this case, was very real— somehow managed to get covered by the Cadet Corps and the other half by the Officers' Club.

After dressing in the gymnasium, the football squad assembled in what was known as the West Academic Building for

12

final instructions from the coach. On a blackboard appeared the names of the starting players and the expected substitutes for each position. I was not particularly concerned; I was sure my name would not be there. But it was: I was to start the game! By storybook tradition I should have been greatly exhilarated; instead I was acutely distressed. I retired to a distant corner and sat down on the floor. Other players came in, read the blackboard, and gave incredulous whistles when they saw my name. I was in total agreement with their spontaneous judgment; I believed I was, at best, a third-string halfback and too new and inexperienced to start an important game.

When Charlie Daley arrived I was still lurking in my corner with my head in my hands. He came over and asked what ailed me. I told him, and then he started talking.

"Washington and Lee," he said, "has a back named Young. He is the team's fastest man and greatest ground gainer; if we stop Young we can win. Now you are the fastest man on our squad, and your job all afternoon is to catch Mr. Young. That and nothing more. On every play you will line up back of the end, sweep into their backfield, and mess up Young. If you are caught for holding, that's okay; but you are to see to it that he doesn't get that ball beyond the line of scrimmage. Now that sounds simple enough, doesn't it?"

It did—while he was talking. Anyway, my blue funk had lifted when I lined up for the kickoff. Well, we won the game 12 to 0, and Mr. Young didn't star. Neither did I, but I did have a giddy and breathless shot at glory. It was late in the game and we took the ball away from Washington and Lee on our five yard line. My quarterback sent me five yards into the end zone where I was to fake a punt. The fact that I hadn't carried the ball during the whole contest probably made the deception work.

Anyway John McCuen, Army's all-American center, arched the football beautifully into my hands and I was off and running like a scared rabbit—an accurate description of my

13

frame of mind, if not of my running style. Soon I was past midfield with nothing except daylight between me and a touchdown. I had visions of my name in the record book as the hero of a 105-yard sprint. Unfortunately, the fates looked down and snickered. In a maneuver to elude the opposition's safety man, my feet had become inextricably entangled and I fell flat on my face with the football in my belly. Before I could arise, the whole Washington and Lee football team was upon me and I am surprised that even the football survived. I didn't. I was carried off the field.

I was one of the many members of my West Point class to serve in combat overseas during World War I. Congress declared war on Germany in April of 1917 and my class was hurriedly graduated later that month. Instead of having to wait until June, I immediately became a second lieutenant of cavalry and was assigned the Second U.S. Cavalry at Fort Ethan Allen, Vermont. This was convenient for a matrimonial project I had in mind. While superior officers wrestled with tactical problems, I pursued Miss M. Leona Tuxbury in my spare time and ultimately convinced the young lady that it would be easier for her to marry me than to keep up the fight. We exchanged vows in August of 1917, and fifty-odd years of marriage have proved that our romance was something more than a passing fancy.

Those were busy months at Fort Ethan Allen. The United States had entered the war singularly unprepared, and this was nowhere more evident than in the Cavalry Branch. Cavalry horses must go through long and intensive training before they are qualified for their specialized job, and at Fort Ethan Allen, as at other cavalry posts, they were in painfully short supply. Men we had in abundance; they were expendable. Horses were precious and had to be hoarded like a miser's gold.

Our recruits were willing and tractable but most of them hadn't even rudimentary equestrian skills, and I should have

14

known it. Fresh out of West Point, proud of the single brass bar on my shoulder, completely at home in the saddle, I let my own exuberance carry me away on one regretted occasion and earned my first official bawling out. I was giving riding instruction at the time. I had learned at the Military Academy that the monotony of drill should be broken up at intervals, so after thirty dull minutes of going round and round the bull ring I decided to take the recruits with me on a ride across country. They were innocently delighted at the prospect of a cross-country jaunt.

There was a little bridle path through the woods with which I was familiar and it didn't seem very hazardous to me. We were all riding bareback; I led the procession and we took off in a cloud of dust. Unhappily, there was a double curve in the bridle path at one point and my neophyte riders didn't lean very well while going in and out among the trees. Result? Seven men hurt: broken arms and broken collar bones. We took them to the hospital and I was summoned by the "Old Man."

Our commander was Colonel Joseph T. Dickman, who later became a major general and a corps commander with the American Expeditionary Forces in France. I stood before him and, in a considerable sweat, told my story. I feel reasonably sure that if any of our horses had been hurt I might have been court-martialed. Because they had more sense than their riders, all the horses came through without injury. When I had finished, Colonel Dickman pushed his spectacles down his nose and looked me straight in the eye.

"Young man," he said, "I admire your spirit, but your judgment was God-damned poor. That will be all."

Of course he was right, and that lesson stayed with me. Spirit is a prime essential for combat commanders, but spirit without judgment can result in disaster as complete as that of Custer at Little Big Horn. I was to be known in a later war as a bold and bullheaded general, but the several men who served me as chiefs of staff have testified that I never entered

15

a battle without clear and careful planning, or without a careful balancing of possible casualties against the importance of an objective to be attained—and that I was (however flamboyant my military image) a conservator of the lives of the troops who served under me. I can also say truthfully that I never sent a platoon, a squad, or a regiment any place where I was unwilling to go myself. And I think my troops knew it.

16

*1917 - West Point gradua-
tion picture.*

*1918 - Captain E. N. Har-
mon on Juniper, Le Val-
dalion, France.*

*1918 - F Troop of the 2nd U.S. Cavalry moving up to the St. Mihiel battle.
Captain Harmon, commander, rides at the head of the column.*

1919 - Captain Harmon upon his return from France.

1941 - Major Harmon conducting a training exercise with "combat cars" of the 1st Mechanized Cavalry Regiment of the 7th Mechanized Brigade.

1942 - Lt. Colonel and Mrs. E. N. Harmon on the twenty-fifth anniversary of their marriage celebrated at Ft. Knox, August 15.

1942 - Brigadier General Harmon in field uniform during 2nd Armored Division's maneuvers in South Carolina.

1942 - Generals Harmon, Devers and Crittenberger discuss training during South Carolina maneuvers.

TWO
★ ★
France

EXACTLY WHAT MISSION the high command envisaged for the Second Cavalry regiment in Europe never became quite clear to me during my confusing combat experience in World War I. To question the mission never occurred to me in mid-March of 1918 when I awoke in the North Atlantic and knew we were on our way. The regiment had shipped down from Fort Ethan Allen to Hoboken, New Jersey, and, after a wild night on the town in New York, put its gear aboard a former passenger liner called the *Martha Washington*.

Our morning problem was not only hangover (we had amply earned that), but an inability to locate any spot where we could lie down, sit down, or comfortably stand up. Landlubbers all, we found ourselves the captives of wild, mountainous seas which were not to give us peace for many days. There were four transports in our convoy and we were led by a single battleship about a mile out in front. Weather was so bad we seldom saw the battleship. The once-glistening *Martha Washington* was now like a ghetto tenement: badly overcrowded. In addition to our cavalry regiment there was also aboard a battalion of Negro troops—about a thousand in all—who were to do engineer duty overseas, serving as stevedores on the military docks, builders of bridges, and repairers of roads.

Because of the overcrowding, because of the danger of fire,

because of the omnipresent danger of German submarine attack, it was necessary to set up an elaborate system to police the troops and ship; we took over duties which once would have been the responsibility of the ship's crew. We cleaned up after the seasick, enforced the rules against smoking, kept order at impassioned crap games, and shared the twenty-four hour vigil against submarines; from every angle of the deck a pair of eyes or more watched from dawn until dark for telltale periscopes. As a freshly promoted captain I had command of a section of the deck watchers; before daybreak every day I led troops to the lifeboats for what the Negro soldiers, with considerable realism, called "drownin' drill." When we were two days out an incident occurred which still creates skepticism when I describe it to Navy friends. It did happen. I know because I was there.

The *Martha Washington* and the *George Washington* originally had been German-owned vessels which, under those venerable American names, did a profitable peacetime business between Hoboken and Hamburg. They happened to be in American ports at the outbreak of war, were seized and repaired after crew sabotage. The *Martha* had a tall foremast with crow's-nest atop it which provided a perfect spot for periscope sighting. Now word came to my superiors that three Negro soldiers had been in the crow's-nest since the voyage's beginning and had not been heard from.

Were they sick, were they dead, or were they afraid to come down the narrow iron ladder because of the rolling of the ship? I was asked to climb the foremast to find out. No assignment could have been more unpleasant to me. Since boyhood I had had a fear of heights which I had rather successfully concealed; and I could not expose my weakness at this late date.* The climb was a real horror, every gasping step

---

*A year or so ago, reading Captain Eddie Rickenbacker's autobiography, I was comforted by finding I shared this phobia with one of America's most intrepid men. Like him, I don't experience this fear of heights in an airplane.

a triumph of will over panic. I could feel the foremast bend with the wind, and when, two-thirds of the way to the summit, I looked down, I could see that the rolling of the ship had left me hanging out over the sea. Or so I thought. Paralysis set in. I could not move up, I could not move down. Somehow, with one last effort, I reached the top of the ladder and beat on the trap door. The soldiers in the crow's-nest opened it. They gave me no bodily help, but desperation drove one elbow after another and I pulled myself up and in.

I got only grunts from the three soldiers, who lay at the bottom of the crow's-nest in their own vomit, so seasick they hoped death would catch up with them. I was pretty discouraged myself and ill to the gills, but a faint spark of duty-sense was left in me, so I stumbled to the edge of the crow's-nest and took three observations of the seascape. All I could see were mountainous waves and a black and white horizon like a chiaroscuro drawing. Then I became hopelessly seasick and slipped to the floor with the others.

Over the years I have never been able to puzzle out this incident and I was able to get no information at the time. Who sent those three men, totally unfamiliar with all ship's usages, aloft and left them two days without rations? Could it have been sailor pranksters who, the good Lord knows, played plenty of tricks on the deck-bound troops? Confusion on overcrowded transports was normal, of course, but this situation was something else again. Navy friends advise me that officially soldiers would never be ordered to a crow's-nest; for the safety of the ship and for the safety of all aboard, only the sharpest-eyed sailors would be assigned to such a key spot. Maybe, but there I was.

When my own heavings lessened, I began an effort to rally my fellow prisoners. I had some difficulty in understanding their Deep South dialect, but soon found they were good fellows and cheered by my arrival. I pointed out that we all had come up the ladder, so all could go down. I finally persuaded one man to try it and promised we would watch him all the way. What help this would be to him I don't know, but the promise gave him courage. So we opened the trap door, saw him reach deck, and the other two quickly followed. I stayed up there another twenty-four hours until someone came to relieve me.

About three days away from France, on a foggy morning, we were joined by eight destroyers who circled round and round the ship to protect us from all angles against the German subs we understood lay off the Bay of Biscay. Orders were given that clothes and life preservers were to be worn both day and night. I remember our only underwater attack with a curious combination of excitement, humor, and humiliation. When the sirens sounded, men came running to the appointed lifeboat stations, bells rang all over the ship, and we could hear the barking of the destroyers' guns. It was a grand spectacle to see the destroyers wheel and turn to the rear, where they dropped their antisubmarine charges (ashcans) and continued to fire from their decks. The sinking of one German sub was claimed.

The ludicrous often has its part in war. As troops came boiling up from the bowels of the vessel, many of them had to pass the officers' galley. Cooks had just completed baking a number of pumpkin pies for the next meal and had laid them out on counters to cool. The noses of American doughboys are infallible. They paused in their mad flight to raid the galley and I saw them on deck, nonchalantly stuffing pumpkin pie into bulging cheeks while the destroyers fought to save our lives.

The humiliation was mine. I occupied a stateroom with three other junior officers. I had had night watch and, against orders, had removed both my clothes and my life preserver before crawling into my bunk. Roused by the bells and the general hell-raising, I woke up in total bewilderment. I couldn't find my clothes or my life preserver. So I threw a raincoat over my naked body and ran up on deck where I belonged. At least I was at my post of duty, and with any luck

20

might have got away with the whole situation. But, before release from quarters was sounded, my troop was inspected and discovery of my state of undress became inevitable. When Colonel Arthur Thayer concluded a public indictment of my dereliction and analysis of my character, I was thoroughly convinced of the gravity of my crime and went morosely to the stateroom. There I found my uniform kicked carelessly into a corner and also solved the mystery of the missing life preserver: an excited fellow officer was wearing two.

Two days later we landed at the little port of Poullaic at the mouth of the Gironde River; we were told Lafayette had sailed from there when he joined the American Revolution long years before. My outfit promptly went ashore to get the sea-kinks out of our legs and briskly marched from the port to Poullaic village. To our surprise, this late in the war, we were greeted with great enthusiasm by the townspeople who appeared from houses and shops and bistros with bottles of wine and cognac as welcoming gifts. When we returned to ship a good many of the youngsters in the regiment were feeling no pain and ready for anything.

We embarked almost immediately for rail disbursement to scattered depots in France and there was considerable laughter about the small French trains which were to transport us. The enlisted men traveled in boxcars marked for "forty men and eight horses," the officers and noncommissioned officers in rude, wooden-benched, third-class carriages. Passengers were housed on three decks, and I remember there were four NCOs—sergeants major and color sergeants—on the top deck of my carriage. I sat with the colonel directly below them.

Colonel Thayer, commander of the Second, was a graying scholarly gentleman then approaching his sixties who had spent a lifetime in military service. He was quiet, philosophical, and ordinarily imperturbable. That day he regarded the high spirits of his troops with indulgence. After the long boredom of a sea voyage, he told me, they had earned the right to celebrate—so long as their celebration was kept within

21

bounds. But a moment later Colonel Thayer was not imperturbable at all. We heard our first gunfire in France and it came from our own people. The cognac-primed sergeants on the upper deck were shooting .45 pistols through the floor and they narrowly missed Thayer's feet. The colonel in a cold fury at once stopped the train, ordered the sergeants to assemble beside the railroad track. There they were stripped of their chevrons and placed under arrest. The high jinks came to an end, and we proceeded into Bordeaux without further noisy interludes.

This chapter tells the personal story of a junior officer who, of course, was not privy to the strategic and tactical decisions of American commanders on an elevated level. During the ensuing months my troop and I were to be buffeted across the French countryside; to a god's-eye our course might have seemed as aimless as a cork in a freshet. Not so. There were always orders from mysterious headquarters to send us wherever we went. In later years I made a technical study of the activities of the Provisional Squadron of the Second Cavalry Regiment in the St. Mihiel and Meuse-Argonne campaigns. Some people were astonished by my recollection of place names, rivers, roads, and side roads. There was nothing magical about this. I have been a map-maker all my life; I taught map-making at West Point, and place names stick in my memory. But in my personal memory of the campaigning place names are really meaningless; we traveled endlessly, it seemed to me then, in rain and mud and misery over landscapes as unfamiliar as the moon and hardly more hospitable.

Even a junior officer's story needs some explanation of what American commanders hoped to accomplish with cavalry in the prolonged attrition of Europe's trench warfare. Four cavalry regiments went overseas, my own Second Regiment, the Third, Sixth, and Fifteenth. Because of the congestion of shipping we came without horses. It was expected that we would be mounted by the French. It can be assumed (because

22

there is little firm information on the subject) that commanders believed our own mounted troops could be highly useful
in many ways to the American infantry divisions already
committed to the front lines: for intelligence sorties into
enemy positions, for communications between our own forces,
and, perhaps not an impossible dream, for all-out pursuit of
the Germans in case of a breakthrough.

At Bordeaux our regiment was fragmented and the several
units sent to different posts. My own troop and another troop
were promptly ordered to a quiet sector of the front near
Belfort where we were attached to the 42nd Infantry (Rainbow) Division. I can report one incident of youthful folly
there. Another officer and I went to a front-line trench to
reconnoiter. We stood up on a parapet of a dugout just as the
Germans were sending over their 6 o'clock message of four
shells. I was blown down the dugout steps and suffered a
concussion from which I quickly recovered. There was a rumor
at this time that our two troops would be sent into the line to
relieve infantry units. This wispy dream of glory was soon
dissipated. Instead we were dispatched to La Valdahon, a
huge remount station where we literally became nursemaids to
a herd of sick and wounded French horses. Our job was to get
them ready to serve an American artillery brigade still on the
high seas.

This was dull and unglamorous duty which lasted for
several months. I found some relief from boredom in long
rides on a horse of the hunter type which had somehow ended
up at La Valdahon along with the halt and the maimed. I
could pick a church steeple on the horizon, head him straight
for it and jump everything in between: fences, stone walls,
lusty brooks. The horse became celebrated at the depot, and
when we were about to depart the newly arrived artillery
commander asked that I transfer the horse to him. This was
formally done, but the animal disappeared. The mystery was
later solved. A daffy second lieutenant, determined to possess
the hunter and to thwart the general, had given it a coat of

paint and changed the army numbers on its hoof. The lieutenant was court-martialed. Thwarting generals is a risky avocation.

My Troop F arrived at Gievres, located almost in the center of France, on July 13, 1918. There the real story of the Provisional Squadron of the Second Cavalry began. Small as it was, this was to be the largest American cavalry force—14 officers and 404 men—to engage in combat action in France. But that was still in the future. At Gievres our immediate job was the construction of a remount depot of 6,000-horse capacity. Of course, this was really work for engineering detachments, but we undertook it cheerfully. Later Troops B, D, and H joined us. Saddles and bridles and weapons were stored and the men were equipped with shovels, axes, hammers and saws. Ditches were dug and stables and other frame buildings soon began to take shape at the compound.

Six weeks later we received orders which charted the next move. Our four troops of cavalrymen were to proceed to Neufchâteau and there await instructions of the American First Army, then in the line. Shortly before, horses had arrived from three veterinary hospitals to mount us for the expedition. They were a sorry lot. Most of them were just recovering from wounds, gas, and battle fatigue. They were poor in flesh, showing lean high withers; some were lame and ill; none had ever been trained for cavalry and 42 were snow white! White horses were never used by cavalry and for an obvious reason: they were too conspicuous for even night sorties.

The squadron left Gievres August 22nd by train and after two days of travel arrived at Neufchâteau. From there we marched overland 32 miles to a new destination, Toul. The roads were macadam and hard on the horses' feet, so we did the trek in two stages. At Toul we were quartered in a first-rate French cavalry installation where we had barracks for the men, water for the horses, and plenty of room to drill and maneuver. God knows we needed that drill! All the officers were young and inexperienced; for the most part, the enlisted personnel had seen only one year's service. And because so far in France we had served virtually as a labor battalion, some of the men had almost forgotten their cavalry training.

Major General Dickman, former commander of the regiment who now commanded the IV Army Corps, came to Toul to take a look at the squadron. In a traditional cavalry review, troops pass the reviewing stand three times: once at a walk, once at a trot, and the third time at a gallop. I suggested to the general that the gallop be eliminated. Otherwise, and I was only half humorous, the horses might run away and the squadron disappear. The general smiled and agreed. I must say we looked deceptively military at a walk and a trot, but he knew the score.

A good deal was accomplished during the ten days. We worked out small combat problems with ball ammunition. Hand grenades were procured and all noncommissioned officers were taught how to use them. The 42 snow-white horses were exchanged for less vulnerable mounts. Four of the new and scientifically advanced automatic rifles were issued to the squadron to determine their practicability for cavalry use. They were not only practical, they were wonderful; but in combat, we soon learned, four to the squadron were not enough. On the eve of the St. Mihiel battle the Provisional Squadron was a group of eager amateurs under the command of a captain (myself) who had been a commissioned officer for eighteen months. We had no staff and (woeful absence) no accompanying demolition outfit.

At about this time Lieutenant Colonel O. P. M. Hazard joined the squadron and took over command. He was an older Regular Army officer who had served with distinction in the Philippines and had taken part in a daring expedition which had resulted in the capture of Emilio Aguinaldo, who led the Philippine Insurrection against the United States around the turn of the century. Colonel Hazard was an ambitious officer, but the recurrent bouts with amoebic dysentery which were his battle scars from the Philippines, made it necessary for him to spend more time at the division headquarters to which we were attached than in the field with us. This put me in a position I did not welcome; I knew how green I was and I longed for the security of taking orders from someone wiser and better informed. Anyway, the job of marching the squadron, putting it into position on the battlefield, commanding it on those rare occasions when we acted as a unit, devolved upon me.

On September 2 orders came for the squadron to proceed by night to a wooded location about eight miles behind the front-line trenches. Night marching was not fatiguing for the horses but it was fatiguing for the men. The NCOs did a really sharp job in keeping troopers awake; sleeping and slouching in the saddle produces saddle sores. Anyway, there were sights to see and things to hear: railroad trains carrying ammunition and men to the front, star shells which illuminated the whole landscape in silver and perilous glory. Twice we heard German airplanes overhead. I began to have a sense of personal loneliness I had never known before. Was I competent to command this column? Did the men have confidence in me? Self-doubts filled my mind. My orderly was a gnarled old-time cavalryman named Murphy. "Murphy," I said, "ride up along side me; I want to ask a few questions. Do the men in the column have confidence in me? Do they think I will do all right in the coming battle?"

Murphy was understanding. "Captain, my boy," he said, "you will be all right if you listen to me. The men trust everything about you except your personal courage. Now don't get me wrong: they mean too much courage, not too little. Such as being too rash at the beginning of their first battle. Otherwise, they have complete confidence in you. You know, Captain, people are odd. These boys seem to have a personal prejudice against being killed in the first five minutes."

This I could understand, and I had plenty of time that night to mull over Murphy's advice. At 2 A.M. rain began to come down in torrents. Wet horses and wet men reached our camp at 4 A.M.; we were about a mile and a half behind the front

26

lines. Between flashes of lightning we strung lariats from tree
to tree and tied our horses, unloaded our equipment, dropped
down on the wet ground and slept. Our wagons and kitchens
had lost their way, but at 8 in the morning they reached camp
and, miraculously, came up with a hot breakfast for the sad
and sodden. At a certain age, maybe at any age, a hot
breakfast can do more than philosophy to exorcise fears which
have spooked you through the night.

Anyway, we felt pretty lively in our carefully combed
French grove. We had orders to remain there in concealment
and the smoke of our kitchens was well screened from aerial
observation. Many of the horses had lost shoes during the
stumbling darkness and there was the cheerful ring of blacksmiths' hammers and the charcoal smell of their portable
forges. Captain Lambert and I rode to division headquarters
to get instructions from Colonel Hazard. Lambert and I were
already good friends; a quarterback at Wabash College, he
was the first small college football player to be selected for one
of Walter Camp's all-American teams. Lambert and I were to
fight together a couple of decades later in another war against
the Germans.

Colonel Hazard sent us forward to reconnoiter our next
objective. This was an open field about three miles away and
perhaps a thousand yards behind the trenches. The reason for
the daylight investigation quickly became evident. There were
many crossroads and the concealing woods were literally
crammed with American troops waiting to make the St. Mihiel
attack; if we had not seen the terrain by daylight we would
have never found our way. At 8 P.M. the squadron moved out
and I led the column. At 10 the rain began again, and
progress seemed impossible. Congestion on the narrow main
road was indescribable: artillery, wagons, ammunition trucks,
infantry struggled forward in the dark. Even our mounted
troops could not skirt the road jams: there were swamps on
either side. But the process of inch-ahead and wait, inch-
ahead and wait, finally got us to our destination.

Big guns were all around us. At 1 A.M. bombardment began.

27

In youthful moments of meaningless cussing I had often used the phrase "All hell broke loose." I never knew what it really meant until that moment in a distant French field. And it went on and on with the sky ablaze. Yet I found out something about both men and horses: fatigue is more compelling than fright. Despite the thunderous din, horses drowsed on their feet; the men tied the horses' reins to their own legs and fell into a heavy sleep on the ground.

At daybreak we watered the horses in nearby mudholes, saddled and made ready for duty. At 5 A.M. a rolling barrage was laid down, and after that, we knew, the infantry was scheduled to go over the top. We stood at the ready until 11:30 when we finally received orders to proceed to Seichprey, a village which long before had been battered to rubble. There was every evidence that American infantry had made its advance: we passed long files of German prisoners proceeding to the rear and long lines of ambulances full of American wounded. From Seichprey we went on to Nonsard (which the First Infantry Division had taken from the Germans by noon), and then proceeded toward Vigneulles where our assigned mission was the blowing up of a railroad line. This was an assignment for which we were ill-chosen (we had no demolition equipment and only a few hand grenades), but we continued to move. The fought-over trenches, the ditches and the barbed-wire entangled fields provided cruel going for our horses. In some places a few of the primitive tanks of that era had plowed their way through the barbed wire, but they were not mechanically up to the job, and most loomed like small islands immobilized in the field of battle, stalled, useless, abandoned.

The road to Vigneulles wound through a dense wood which was also dense with German supply troops, stables, horses and piles of hay. At one point, my trumpeter and I turned down a side road to find out why a flank patrol had halted. Suddenly a German on his horse broke out of the brush. I fired with my pistol at twenty-five feet, but missed him. Then he slid from his horse and I had my first prisoner. I sent him to the rear and interviewed him that night. He was an 18-year-old kid with a little bit of down on his upper lip and I was glad for the moment that I had been such an excited and inferior marksman.

I was now convinced—mistakenly, as it turned out—that the Germans were in wholesale retreat and returned to find my formation at a complete standstill. I was informed that Colonel Hazard had ordered us to halt until further notice. While I tried to determine the authenticity of what seemed to be a very doubtful order (actually no such order had been given), part of the squadron took off on its own, and both Lambert and I agreed this was a dangerous mixup. The two of us climbed the crest of a hill and looked down the opposite slope. There we saw on a side road a continuous stream of German troops, artillery, wagon trains and mounted men. Our first thought was to bring up two automatic rifles, and that is what we did. Lambert and I lay down in the middle of our road and opened fire on the German column. We inflicted casualties and the Germans quickly deployed into convenient timber. At this precise moment our squadron was fired on from the front and the left and the right. Three horses went down with their riders. Because of thick bushes and trees we could not see the enemy, but I later learned we were surrounded on three sides. I gave orders for return to a crossroads in the rear where a stand could be made. Men and horses behaved very well until machine guns on our left opened up. Our untrained horses bolted, and a gallop is as catching among horses as rock throwing in a riot. Pistol fire at a gallop promises little marksmanship, but luck or Providence was with us. Pistols silenced the machine gun nests and six dead Germans were subsequently found there. I managed to rally the men and to get them into orderly formation again.

It was now almost dark and Colonel Hazard rode up with the information that the First Division would continue the attack at 7 P.M. We fell back to Nonsard and made camp,

29

fortunately, just outside the town. The Germans bombarded Nonsard that night but we had no casualties. I got little sleep that night, as I tried to figure out what had gone wrong during the day. Our casualties were: one dead, one missing, three wounded and five horses killed or wounded. That there had been a lack of discipline and liaison under unexpected fire was not surprising. But I believed then and believe now that I was partly at fault. Where a leader should position himself in battle is always a difficult decision and there is no ready-made rule. When Lambert and I lay in the road and opened fire with automatic rifles on the Germans, we were not acting as commanders of troops, we were engaging in boyish heroics. In short, we were too far out front to be in control of our men. It was a lesson which could be learned only in the field.

We were up at 3 A.M. and in the saddle by 5. The town of Vignuelles had been captured at midnight by the 16th Infantry Regiment. When we were a few hundred yards east of the town we divided our column, with one section heading west to look for German troops in a wooded area which also had high hills and steep ravines. They did very well and met French cavalry, at least a day behind us, at Heudicourt. Troop F was ordered to proceed north along a railroad line running toward Metz. Our assignment was to maintain contact with a retreating enemy, locate his new line of resistance, and send back information. This was ideal country for cavalry, almost an open plain. Our advance led through a half-dozen towns already ablaze—left burning by the Germans. We did not halt our advance when fired on; occasionally a small group was detached to overcome a German point of resistance. Prisoners were escorted to the rear.

We came upon our most solid information in the town of St. Maurice where I interviewed the former mayor of Joinville. (I was happy to find my college French adequate for the purpose.) A German officer, the ex-mayor said, had told him where the next German defensive stand was to be made: on a line formed by the villages of Champion, Doncourt, Joinville

30

and Chamblay. I sent the report back, for what it was worth, and then dispatched patrols for a personal check. The information proved to be accurate.

Our patrols found the enemy entrenched at precisely the points the mayor had mentioned. This forewarning was extremely useful to our infantry next day. We had a number of small skirmishes during our sortie into enemy territory. At Woel a patrol was fired upon from a church. In order to reconnoiter Joinville it was necessary to clear the enemy from Woel, and this was our last skirmish of the day. We proceeded up a dry creek bottom, tethered our horses, worked dismounted up the village main street, surrounded the church where the Germans had taken shelter. We took five prisoners; a few others escaped.

It was now 7 P.M. and dark approached. It had been a hard day, and both men and horses were tired. We were comforted when an American airplane, dispatched to find out where we were, waggled its wings and went home. As we proceeded to the rear, we met our infantry coming up to hold the ground at St. Maurice. They had already plundered German stores, and they gave each of our troopers a sack of German hard tack and three bottles of beer. This assuaged hunger pangs until we reached Vignuelles two hours later. Somehow or other, under Sergeant Rock, our mess sergeants had snaked their wagon trains through the jam of traffic, and had hot rations ready. We took care of our horses, ate, and made ready for a hard march on the following morning.

THREE

★★
The Decisive Battle

IT WAS THE destiny of the Provisional Squadron, a microscopic unit in a land war which involved millions of men, to participate in both the St. Mihiel attack and the decisive breakthrough on the Meuse-Argonne front. Today historians tell us that both were vital to the defeat of the German Reich. By September of 1918 Allied forces were ready for an advance along the whole bloody, wasted, long-fought-over Western Front. General Pershing, the American commander-in-chief, now had forty-three combat divisions in France (almost all of them untried), along with American engineer troops, auxiliaries, and supply lines. Ten days before the St. Mihiel battle there was a council of Allied commanders. Marshal Foch, Allied Supreme Commander, proposed that American divisions be assigned to the French II and IV Armies. Pershing had earlier announced his intention of fighting the main body of American troops as an integral American force, and he could not be moved. It was finally agreed that immediately after the St. Mihiel operation, the American First Army would attack the Meuse-Argonne salient.

Actually the vital portion of the German front was astride the Meuse river because there, in the words of Pershing, the enemy's main supply artery—the Carignan-Sedan-Mézières route traversing the difficult Ardennes Forest—was closest to

32

the battle line. Withdrawals could be accepted by the German high command on all fronts except the Meuse-Argonne. As one general thinking about another general's decision, I can only say that this operation was a very hard mouthful to chew. After four years of occupation of that particular stretch of French soil, the Germans had created in a zone some twenty miles in depth an unsurpassed defense complex which included numerous strong points and interlocking machine gun emplacements. And because of historic geographical considerations (battles had been fought there for three hundred years and were to be fought there again), everyone on both sides knew it was an ideal position for German defense. The French high command hardly expected the reduction of the fortified zone before the spring of 1919.

"A possibility of ending the war in 1918 and full confidence in the fighting quality of his troops," General Pershing wrote later, "prompted the American commander-in-chief to risk his partially trained army in this difficult operation. In two weeks, this army was to reduce the St. Mihiel salient, change to a front about one hundred kilometers distant and attack the fortified Meuse-Argonne zone, a task without parallel in the World War."

The Germans were expecting a further advance at St. Mihiel, so Allied forces were able to accomplish a full-scale movement of troops, apparently without their knowledge. This was accomplished principally by night movements on all major and minor roads in that embattled territory. Pershing estimated that, including French forces who were to come under his command, not less than a million men engaged in this operation. On September 22 the American First Army, General Pershing commanding, took over control of an area (including the Argonne Forest), where a concentrated attack west of the Meuse was to be made three days later.

But on the morning of September 16 we of the Provisional Squadron knew only that the St. Mihiel attack was over. Infantry was coming up in strength to dig in and hold, and we had orders to move south to Ménil-la-Tour, a distance of about twenty-four miles. Even as we left Vigneulles German artillery began to dog our footsteps. Our column stopped at a stone watering trough on an exposed road and D troop was allowing its horses to drink when a salvo of four high explosive (HE) shells came over, landing seventy-five yards short of the trough. Then came a salvo which hit about seventy-five yards over. Even a greenhorn could recognize this as a bracket in artillery ranging. Troop D left the area at a gallop and Captain Lambert and I went to the rear and brought our wagon train through safely. On the third salvo one HE shell made a direct hit on the watering trough. There was a hidden German battery about two thousand yards beyond Vigneulles. An infantry company discovered and captured the guns a little while after they began firing.

Our progress was painfully slow but we reached Ménil-la-Tour about 8 P.M. and made camp in open field where our German prisoners were under guard. The exhaustion of our horses made a two-day stay there mandatory, which heartened the men. There were facilities for bathing and for the exchange of filthy clothing for clean clothing. Clean garments and clean bodies add up to a powerful psychological restorative for weary combat soldiers, as I was to find out in two wars. We were to need all possible fortitude for the experiences of the days immediately ahead.

We left Ménil-la-Tour on September 17 and made an uneventful night march to the Rangerval Forest. The next night we went on to Boncourt and somewhere along the road B Troop—which had been doing messenger duty for the First, 42nd, and 89th Divisions—rejoined the squadron and shared with us the discomfort of bedding down in a pouring rain. It rained again on the night of the 18th as we headed for Pierrefitte; the night was exceptionally cold and the men had no overcoats. They were beginning to show their weariness by falling asleep in the saddle. It was steep up-and-down country, and, of course, strange country to us all. It was there I learned how to prevent the straying of army units in darkness. At crossroads I ordered each troop to drop off men to guide following units safely on the proper route. I was to utilize this technique many years later in the Battle of the Bulge when I took a whole armored division one hundred kilometers across country to intercept German panzers at their farthest point of advance.

Through no fault of his own, we saw little of Colonel Hazard. He was engaged in a tussle with his old microbic enemy, tropical dysentery. He caught up with us at the Rangerval Forest but was almost immediately put to bed in a nearby engineering camp. He promised to come up by automobile in a couple of days and he did. On September 19 Hazard once more took command and we began our fourth successive night march. His discomfort on horseback was obvious and his determination to "stick it out" obscured his judgment. At one point we marched three hours without a halt: horses had no breathing spell and cavalrymen no chance to empty their bladders. When we reached our destination, Colonel Hazard found a billet and went to bed at once. I relate this without rancor. Colonel Hazard had earlier proved himself as a professional soldier, but there is no proper place in combat leadership for officers—however willing—who are not physically fit to meet its rigors. Their own very real miseries may lead them to forget the welfare of those under their command.

On September 23 the Provisional Squadron arrived at Rarécourt-en-Argonne and camped in a thick wood above the town. We knew now we would move forward soon and would be attached to the 35th Infantry Division. For us the Meuse-Argonne attack began three days later. At 2 A.M. we saddled and moved toward Aubréville. The American artillery bombardment had already begun. The noise was deafening and the fireworks resembled a hundred Fourth of July celebrations combined in one. At times the sky had the unearthly aspect of a great electrical storm: complete darkness split apart a moment later by such an immense illumination I could see the tense faces of my troopers and the quivering nostrils of the horses.

Again we shared a road with a pushing, pressing conglomeration of troops, artillery and wagon trains but we arrived in Aubréville before sunup. An hour later, and on schedule, advance elements of the 35th Division went over the top to be engaged immediately in desperate fighting. We were having our own small difficulties in Aubréville which was being shelled. The Germans were aiming at heavy Allied naval guns on railroad tracks behind us and we were in the direct line of fire. Then came shrapnel. Bursts were too high in the air for real effectiveness, although two enlisted men were wounded. We now made contact with the 35th's reserve infantry brigade and moved forward with them. Following out orders, we were a thousand yards in their rear.

It was rough passage all the way. Our objective was *Cote 290* (rough translation: Hill 290) and, of course, the only way to get there was directly across now abandoned German trenches. Shrapnel fire had ceased, which indicated the Germans were moving their light artillery to the rear, and there was only an occasional long-range shell. Yet our progress was painfully slow. The Germans, always masters in defense, had left behind indescribably complex wire entanglements. The trenches themselves were pits of the devil for cavalry. Sometimes we jumped our horses into the trenches and jumped them out. At other times soft mud made this impossible. Then we dismounted (we had no trenching tools) and scooped earth with our helmets until we had filled a wide trench sufficiently so that horses could cross in single column. Eventually we reached our destination, camouflaged ourselves in a bit of timber, and were so gratified by a respite that we did not mind the fact that American long-range artillery was firing all around us.

Late in the afternoon, when most of the troopers had caught their breath (but had not yet caught up with their sleep), we

36

witnessed the destruction of three American captive balloons. The value of balloons for reconnaissance was obvious; now we had dramatic evidence of their vulnerability. There were eight balloons in line. Suddenly a single German plane arrived on the scene, so high at first glance that it seemed no larger than a bee. It went into a deep dive and rammed home its sting. A balloon went up in flames. Now the sky was full of white puffs of smoke as our antiaircraft went into action. The daring pilot circled away and, a moment later, another balloon was ablaze. During that interval five balloons were hauled down to safety, but he made embers of a third target before scooting home.

Late in the afternoon Colonel Hazard returned and gave orders for us to move forward to Cheppy, the advance command post of the 35th Division. Again we wormed our way through entanglements, and my young men from Fort Ethan Allen saw enough to cure them of romantic ideas about war. This area had been fought over. At a crossroad a few hundred yards below Cheppy lay the bodies of eight American soldiers.; a corporal and his squad had been hit by a well-directed shell. Now the Germans began cannonading again and I took the squadron to the reverse side of a steep slope just south of town. Atop the slope was a German pillbox, with dead Germans within and around it and nine dead Americans who had been part of a unit which earlier captured the ridge.

We made camp and dusk was upon us when several of the enlisted men came to me with reports of a suspicious light in a German-made dugout down a series of steps in the hill. I could have sent a squad to investigate, but I didn't. We had been almost too thoroughly briefed about German ingenuity in booby-trapping abandoned areas and it was obvious my youngsters were nervous. So was I, but it seemed this was a time to prove myself for the benefit of troop morale. Making light of the whole matter, I started down toward the pit, expecting at each step to be blown sky high. Nothing happened. At the bottom I found an abandoned machine gun and a deserted artillery observation post. When they departed the

Germans had left a single candle alight; wick and tallow were about to gutter when I arrived. Perhaps I swaggered a bit when I climbed the hill again. On such flimsy evidence a commander sometimes achieves a reputation for calmness and courage.

Now the squadron began its ordeal of night patroling the front lines. Our job was to get reliable information for division headquarters in the midst of the confusion of battle. Where, exactly, *was* the front line as it changed from hour to hour? What units were actually up there and what units were lost, strayed, or destroyed? Because of the exact technical information sought, it was necessary in most cases for a commissioned officer to lead each rotating eight-man patrol. The customary practice at night was for the patrol to approach to within two hundred yards of the supposed front line and then, in darkness, dismount and proceed the rest of the way on foot or, often, on a knee crawl. The job was perilous and fatiguing.

We were living then, for want of better lodging, in filthy German dugouts infested with brown fleas which made morning, afternoon, or night sleep intolerable. At 3 A.M. on September 28 we received a battle order for an attack at 5:30 A.M. This order should have been—and perhaps was, for all I know—saved for a military museum as an example of incompetent intelligence work. It began with the statement that the main body of the enemy had retreated, and that all that lay in front of the 35th Division was artillery and machine guns. This directly contradicted reports from our own patrolling, which had convinced us that the Germans were massed in force ready to throw our forces back. They did just that; the 35th advanced five hundred yards but suffered such heavy losses that it had to be relieved by another division.

Planners of the attack made every effort to use the squadron sensibly. One troop of cavalry was to cover the left flank of the division (resting on the Aire River) and to maintain contact with the 28th Division, which was also in the line and on the left side of the river. Other elements of the squadron were to maintain communications between American units. All this, as I have said, was based on unreliable information that the enemy was in retreat. Actually the Germans drew back a few hundred yards in the morning and in the late afternoon hit hard. Their airplanes hovered over all targets, and our troops were driven back almost to their jumping-off points. For our tiny unit of cavalry, it was an experience in complete frustration. The German defenses of barbed wire were high and low: too high for horses to jump and—ten inches above the ground—low enough to trip them at the fetlocks.

In the first place, we were too visible. Our horse patrols were spotted instantly by enemy glasses as we followed out our flanking assignment. Result? Enemy fire on our infantry, which left to itself would have been easily able to find concealment. September 29th in the Argonne was a hard day for everyone involved. It was dark and foggy as we started up a valley. A gas alarm was given (the Germans had thrown gas shells into the valley all night), and automatically gas masks went on. A few minutes later I removed mine and smelled the mustard gas; it was in weak concentration and masks were ordered removed. As usual our extremely visible patrols were seen by the enemy, drawing fire on both us and the infantry reserve. From ridges and hills the German artillery opened up. To proceed up the valley was to invite annihilation; to return over the ridge was almost an equally desperate option. It seemed to me that the only feasible course was to cross the Aire toward the high ground rising from the river.

Our only hope was a narrow bridge two hundred yards to the rear. I gave the signal and we headed for it. A German observation balloon in plain view was directing artillery fire, but my troop got across the bridge safely. Once there, I realized that the appearance of a conglomerate force of horsemen would ruin any possibility of the mission's success. To continue our reconnoitering assignment I chose 15 men and moved toward the enemy in the valley. I left instructions with Lieutenant Burbank to lead the rest of the troop back across

39

the bridge in twos and threes during the lulls of artillery fire and then to report back to our camp at Cheppy. This was accomplished safely, but it took all morning because there were few lulls.

My patrol and I rode to within five hundred yards of Apremont and met machine gun fire there. The 28th Division was attacking the German-held town, and we got ourselves in a good place for observation. We were able to send back steady messages on the progress of the 28th, and, looking across the river valley, we could see the attacking lines of the 35th on the plateau. Those brave men ran forward in waves about three hundred yards apart. A line of small tanks— arrayed at wide intervals—came along with the attacking waves. Enemy artillery was pounding at the plateau and the air was filled with smoke of bursting shrapnel. All the while you could hear the tac-tac-tac of machine guns.

I am sure the information we sent back served a useful purpose, but, in the main, I believe cavalry was out of place in a battle where the enemy had the high ground and the Allied line moved forward only a thousand yards a day. I moved back from Apremont and recrossed the river. Almost immediately the patrol was a target of the balloon-directed artillery; we lost two horses and had three men badly wounded. And some of the shells aimed at us landed on the well-hidden infantry reserve. This did not make friends for us among the foot soldiers.

By nightfall all patrols had drawn back to Cheppy, exhausted and unhappy; we were extremely conscious of the fact that our very *visibility* made us a Jonah to the infantry on attack. Many horses had been killed during the day and many wounded. Many of those only slightly wounded by the German shells developed raging—and often fatal—infections within a few hours.

As always in combat, there were miraculous escapes from death which involved both officers and men that had to be chewed over in bivouac. I did not discuss my own close escape,

40

but it was real enough. Going over the ridge, my horse entangled his feet in low German wire and was thrown heavily. He fell across my legs, pinning my body under his. My trumpeter (a bugler who, by cavalry tradition, gave the signals for advance or retreat) jumped off his horse and began the tough job of cutting the wire which entangled both horse and me. I suspect the balloon had spotted us; anyway we were being shelled closely. At that moment, with a 1000-pound horse on top of me and fireworks going on all around, the future looked dismal. I urged the trumpeter to get out of there and save his own skin. He refused and, ignoring the shelling, cut me and the horse free and saved my life at the risk of his own. People are odd. This is the same man who, after the war was over, got into my trunk locker, stole $150, and blew it on a visit to Paris. I should have court-martialed him, but I didn't. I really hate a thief, but how can you send to prison a valorous man who has saved your life? (Perhaps my leniency was well placed—he eventually paid the money back.)

On the morning of September 30 the general attack was renewed without satisfactory results. I led another small patrol up the valley. I had significant information to report to advanced headquarters: American artillery was firing too short and hitting our own people on the flank. This time the patrol stopped short of headquarters and a sergeant and I went forward on foot to deliver our message. When Sergeant Lamond and I returned we found our own horses still tethered, but the rest of the patrol gone. They had been fired upon by snipers and had sought safety in flight. The same snipers opened up on us but the sergeant and I managed to make our escape.

The 35th Division had fought valiantly to achieve a breakthrough against the finest and most experienced German troops. They were also trying to penetrate defense lines designed by gifted siege engineers; battle-wise French and British troops had not been able to get through. Patroling a line that evening I knew the 35th was in great trouble. Very few of the line officers had survived, and whole companies were commanded by noncoms. An engineer regiment was called forward and put into the line as combat infantry. There was a great confusion of orders, and many of the soldiers who, under ordinary circumstances, might have been called stragglers had been properly ordered to assemble in the rear because of reports the division would be relieved that night. The reports were true.

About midnight I was moving down the valley with my trumpeter to rejoin the squadron at Cheppy. All of a sudden out of the darkness we saw or felt or heard a mysterious group of men moving toward us. We knew the fluid condition at the front: what outfit was this? Friend or foe? The trumpeter and I turned off the road into a wood. As they went by, rank after rank, all closed up, I knew this was the relieving infantry division. I called out in the darkness: "What outfit is this?" A voice called back: "This is the First Division, you son of a bitch. How far up are the Germans?" Well, I knew how far up the Germans were and that this cocky division would have to fight for its life as had the 35th. But somehow this response from a sawed-off soldier dragging behind him an entrenching shovel gave me heart. I felt the front was secure, and the Germans would not be able to counterattack down the valley that night.

Under First Infantry Division command the squadron's duties were less onerous. We sent up small liaison patrols to maintain contact with divisions on the right and left and to bring in reports of locations of front-line units. This made sense because our horses were decimated; those alive were in lamentable condition: they had been ridden day and night. We had blacksmiths to shoe them but no veterinarians to treat their ailments. There was no opportunity for grazing and our rations were skimpy. The horses were poor in flesh, the weather was as cold and rainy as before, and we were under nerve-racking shell fire. Stomach ailments and dysentery were endemic among the men, but I suspect that our shabby diet was less responsible than was that sense of imminent death which sobers even congenital optimists when a great battle is under way.

Events continued grim for the next few days. The First Division fought desperately to advance and took punishing casualties. The squadron's liaison assignment was, admittedly, a miniscule part of the battle, but the cavalrymen now carried out their daily missions without murmur and with the traditional discipline of the old Regular Army. Lieutenant Burbank had been wounded, but insisted on returning to the outfit as soon as the medics had performed their repairs. Artillery fire never ceased; we often experienced heavy bombardment with no cover available. To give an example of the routine of patroling, the search for information which goes on in battle, I chronicle a day of my own in the Meuse-Argonne when the First Division was attacking.

The assignment of my small patrol was to reconnoiter the front line from Fléville and Sommerance. These were the rumors I had to check: (1) that a battalion of the 28th Infantry Division had crossed the Aire River and taken over a sector which belonged to a battalion of the First Division; (2) that there was a gap in our line and a lack of liaison between First Division's own units. What we found out after hours of toil and trouble was that there was no encroachment from the 28th Division, no gap in the line, and that liaison had been fully restored. In the course of this mission our patrol passed through the front lines into Sommerance, which was held by the enemy. As we passed through in a hurry we located three machine gun positions—or perhaps they located us. We were fired upon but managed to make it home and report their locations. The machine gun nests were eliminated.

By mid-October it was evident to most of us that our usefulness was at an end. We were reduced by casualties to 150 horses, and, accordingly, to 150 riders. The First Infantry Division had fought its heart out in the Meuse-Argonne sector and was replaced by the Rainbow Division. I reported to

43

Brigadier General Douglas MacArthur; this was my first meeting with the man under whom I was to serve a few years later at the United States Military Academy. The Provisional Squadron of the Second Cavalry I still hold in deep affection. We were in the Argonne from September 26 until October 16 and were constantly under fire. On October 17th we reported to the commander of the Second Cavalry Regiment at Camp Mallory near Rarécourt and, because of the impossibility of getting remounts, the squadron was disbanded as an entity. Individual patrols were assigned various duties, and Lieutenant Burbank and fifteen men were within 3,000 yards of Sedan just before the Armistice. F Troop, still under my command, was attached to the Second Infantry Division, fighting toward Grandpré; we were bivouacked at Sommerance when the announcement of the end of the war came on November 11, 1918.

The Squadron received four official citations for distinguished conduct. Oddly enough, two of them were concerned with the St. Mihiel engagement when we were just finding our way. The third was from the 35th Division with which we had fought in the Meuse-Argonne. The citation from the First Division gave us kudos "for conspicuous and tireless devotion to duty in harassing the enemy and procuring valuable information during the advance of September 12-13, 1918." The other general order reached us when morale was low:

HEADQUARTERS FOURTH ARMY CORPS
25 September 1918

Subject: Commanding General, IVth Corps.
From: Commanding Officer, 2d Cavalry.
To: Service of the 2d Cavalry in the Operations of September 12-13th, 1918, in the Woovre.

1. The Squadron of the 2nd U.S. Cavalry, Troops B, D,

F, H, with new and untrained horses not well adapted to cavalry purposes, and with the greater part of its personnel of comparatively short service, nevertheless exhibited a devotion to duty and spirit of action worthy of the best traditions of the regiment and the American Cavalry.

2. Held back several hours longer than appeared necessary the squadron passed through the forests of La Belle Oziere, Nonsard and Vigneulles, scouted the open country as far as Heudicourt, Creue and Vigneulles, eventually advancing to St. Maurice, Woel and Jonville, pursuing the enemy, fighting his rearguard, capturing numerous prisoners, forcing deployment and delaying his retreat, in fact, doing everything that so small a force could accomplish.

3. It is requested that you convey to the officers and men in a regimental order the expression of appreciation and thanks of their former Colonel for their excellent service rendered under such difficult conditions.

J. T. DICKMAN,
Major General, U.S.A.

FOUR
★ ★
Back Home

WHEN WARS END I always seem to get home later than anyone else. My regiment and I arrived in New York in July of 1919, and I was met by my wife, Aunt Minnie Durant, and a baby daughter I had never seen. She was Barbara Ruth Harmon, born November 14, three days after the end of the war, and for a father long separated from any family contacts she was a delight to see and a pretty bundle to handle. Because it demands so many separations, military service is often the assassin of family relationships.

My regiment was sent to Fort Riley, Kansas, and my small family came along. After normal regimental duty there, I entered the troop officers' course at the Cavalry School, and had an interesting and successful year. There I met a Captain Ben Lear whom I instantly disliked; I told friends that when the Army and Providence made Lear an officer they spoiled a good first sergeant. He later became a lieutenant general, and in World War II a trainer of vast numbers of troops. When I served under him in the Louisiana maneuvers of 1942 I discovered my opinion had not changed.

Some people will recall him as the commander who disciplined his troops because they "yoo-hooed" at girls either off or on the army reservation—I don't quite remember the geography. Troops in training live lives so ordered and so dull

46

it is surprising that they do not burn down their own camps. The celibacy of intensive training is very real and "yoo-hoos" at pretty girls seem to me a rather innocent affirmation of the fact that young men like young women. I have always despised moralists, real or pretended. To this day I do not know whether or not Ben Lear thought he was doing a politically expedient thing.

After completing the Cavalry School courses, I was directed to report to the Military Academy in a teaching capacity. I was to be an instructor in drawing (including map-making), riding drill, a teacher in the tactical department, and assistant football coach. So far as the coaching was concerned, I rested easy because the head coach was Captain John McCuen, the all-American center of my undergraduate days. These were happy years between 1921 and 1925, because I was still enough of a kid at heart to enjoy all sports.

General Douglas MacArthur, a sports enthusiast himself, was then Superintendent at West Point. After coaching football and varsity lacrosse, I rather ambitiously decided to try out for the Olympic Games which were to be held in Paris in 1924. The competition I chose for myself was the modern military pentathlon. This is a five-event affair which required competitors to swim 300 meters free-style, fence with dueling swords, shoot a pistol rapid fire, ride a horse 10,000 meters over jumps, and run 4,000 meters cross-country.

I took a cool and analytical look at my talents and deficiencies. I had never had much chance to swim as a youngster, and that was my weakest point. I could ride, I could shoot, and with chest and lungs like a blacksmith's bellows, I knew I could outlast most competitors on a distance run. But at fencing I wasn't worth a damn. West Point experts told me my only chance was to be so aggressive at the start of a match that cautious and more skillful opponents might be caught off guard.

This worked so well in the national tryouts that the American candidates were cut down to a team of four, of which I

47

was captain. We went over to Paris and I finished sixth among forty international contestants. I did well in riding, shooting, and running—and have medals to show for it. I was a bust as a swimmer, and my aggressiveness didn't fool European fencers very long; they waited awhile and then coolly dispatched me.

After the West Point assignment I joined the Sixth Cavalry regiment at Fort Oglethorpe, Georgia, where I spent two years. Then, to my delight, I was detailed to my old college as Commandant of Cadets and Professor of Military Science. This brought my wife and me to home country. Norwich then was a small college with an enrollment of about 325 students (all male), and spirit was high. We spent four pleasant years there.

Charles Plumley, son of the congressman who appointed me to West Point, had become president of Norwich, and we got along very well. He was perhaps more a shrewd politician than an educator, but he ably protected Norwich's interests before the state legislature, and I enjoyed his company. Both of us had a passion for the outdoors. We took many fishing trips to Lake Champlain, and those trips inspired in me a love of the Lake Champlain country which is still warm and viable. Ten years ago my wife and I bought a place on South Hero Island which is now our home in retirement.

One of my fishing companions was Sheriff Charles Tudhope. I think he was the greatest fisherman I ever knew. He was also a perfect host. This was the prohibition era, and it was the sheriff's duty to deal with rumrunners who were bringing whiskey in from Canada. Once in a while the sheriff captured a rumrunner, confiscated his illegal import, and invited a few friends to conduct tests to determine whether the import was intoxicating and thus legally actionable. This seemed to several of us a more sensible solution to the problem of contraband than pouring it down the drain.

As Commandant of Cadets I was a firm disciplinarian, but I enjoyed working with young men and tried to understand their problems and to treat them fairly. I was also riding

48

instructor (we had fifty cavalry horses there), and after I departed legends grew up about my equestrian tutoring. One former student told me it was gospel at Norwich that, when it came to jumping, I would flick my whip either on the horse or the cadet—depending upon which needed the most encouragement. Well, we all know about legends, half fact and half more satisfying fiction.

I coached the cadet polo team, and occasionally played with them when we engaged the officers of Fort Ethan Allen and other military installations. My disciplinary attitude, firm but fair, seemed to pay off with the student body, for the graduating class of 1931 dedicated its yearbook to me, and the university awarded me an honorary master's degree in military science. The citation read: "He neither spared the rod nor spoiled the child."

My next assignment was a great honor. I was ordered to report as a student to the Command and General Staff College at Fort Leavenworth, Kansas. A military historian recently asked me how the United States, indifferent and even contemptuous of the military in peacetime, had been able to produce a group of generals proficient enough to lead armies successfully against German might. He said a British friend had decided the only rational explanation of Allied victory in the Second World War was the intervention of Divine Providence. I did not quarrel with the British gentleman's opinion, but it did occur to me that Hitler's decision to invade Russia and thus fight a war on two fronts might have been a more significant factor in his defeat.

The historian's question, however, set me thinking. It is true that the nation was blessed with some immensely talented commanders in Europe and in the Pacific. But why? The Navy's record was brilliant but I cannot speak for the Navy. Perhaps I have some credentials to speak for the Army. I am now convinced that the intensive and imaginative training at the Command and General Staff College had a great deal to do with it. The younger group of officers coming up were well

49

aware of our military deficiencies, and, viewing the rise of Hitler and the intransigence of Japan, were impatient with the conservatism of the peacetime War Department. Most of us saw Armageddon as a certainty.

The two years I spent at Leavenworth were the most difficult years of my training. About 250 officers matriculated, and some of us had almost lost the habit of study; we were warned the class would be thinned down to 125 for the second year. I was able to make the second year but only with my wife's encouragement and practical management. There were now five children in a crowded house, five children afflicted with the colics, fevers, and ailments of the very young. I studied upstairs and downstairs, often far past midnight, and my disposition at home became as mean as that of a starving prairie wolf, or—as one of my friends suggested—a cobra without a convenient snake charmer. I was graduated from Leavenworth, but I could not have made it without my Yankee wife's calm acceptance of a difficult situation and her physical and moral support.

There were easier days ahead. Immediately after my graduation from Leavenworth I was informed that I had been ordered to the Army War College in Washington. Only about 10 percent of the top students were chosen for this more generalized postgraduate education, and I was pleased and gratified.

There was a brief assignment before I reported to the War College which gave me considerable satisfaction. I had become so involved with military studies I had virtually lost sight of the economic problems which involved us all. This is one of the dangers of specialization. The Great Depression which hit America early in the 1930s almost wrenched our society apart; the collapse of the stock market in 1929 so undermined our capitalistic system that many people wondered where economic safety lay. Scores of thousands were out of work. In 1933 President Franklin D. Roosevelt and Congress created the Civilian Conservation Corps (CCC) to provide employ-

50

ment for teen-age kids in forests and fields. Without warning I was sent to Fort Des Moines and ordered to develop a CCC camp near Winterset, Iowa.

By training and inclination I am a nonpolitical character, and I must confess I was skeptical of the program. I carried into the Middle West the idea that maybe these kids were not only indigent but laggard and lazy. Much of Iowa is flat, fertile prairie, green to the glorious sunsets. Winterset, however, was in hilly country with a great deal of neglected woodland where conservation practices would be useful. When I got there I found real trouble. A woebegone second lieutenant was in command and he had a full-fledged mutiny on his hands.

Some two hundred CCC boys were sitting in the middle of an open field, *refusing* to work. There were no shelters of any kind on the campsite, and most of the youngsters were poised to take off for home. I called an assembly and spoke to them at once. I said I had been sent from Washington and I was there to listen. If they had legitimate complaints, I wanted to know what they were. Who would speak up? For a couple of minutes there was complete silence, and then a slender, serious young man rose and began to talk—no oratory rhetoric, just a calm recital of what he believed to be the facts in the case. Somebody, somewhere, had erred egregiously in the choice of the campsite. It *was* a desolate landscape, but he made more significant criticisms: (1) there was no available clean well water; (2) the soil did not promise proper drainage for latrines, and (3) they had already killed nineteen rattlesnakes.

Frankly, I was impressed by this presentation and said I would investigate at once. It struck me that teen-age Iowa farm boys might know more about soil content, drainage, and water supply than the unknown political intermediaries who had chosen the site. I went before the Winterset town and county authorities and told them the story. Their cooperation was admirable; almost immediately a new plot of land which met Army requirements was provided, and the two hundred

51

mutinous young men began cheerfully to build the new cantonment. About that time I was recalled to Leavenworth for a week; when I returned, amazing progress had been made and I discovered the CCC cantonment had decided to call itself Camp Harmon. This pleased me, but it pleased me even more that I had learned a valuable lesson: these boys were not lazy or indifferent; they were victims of a depression. Given proper leadership, they would do the job.

There is a postscript to this incident. I had become interested in the young man who stood up and spoke his piece at the time of the work stoppage. His name was Robert Halleck. When I returned East I discovered there was a civilian job as an assistant steward open at the War College. I wrote Halleck and he came on. Later his intelligence and ambition carried him to the top in a great department store chain and he became a wealthy man. When I was president of Norwich, Halleck sent his son Robert there for his college education. The son was graduated with the highest honors in the class of 1964.

Immediately after the Winterset interlude I reported to Washington. My days at the War College there were more or less uneventful. We heard lectures on high strategy, international relations, the various persuasions of economics from John Stuart Mill to Karl Marx to John Maynard Keynes, and were encouraged to participate freely in subsequent discussions. Being a down-to-earth fellow and never glibly articulate, I found myself somewhat at a loss during these intramural talkfests. A West Point classmate decided to give me some advice.

"Look, Ernie," he said, "you must remember you are being weighed and observed here. You have to ask the lecturer questions to show your interest—intelligent questions. Otherwise you'll never make the [War Department] General Staff."

I was both puzzled and amused. I had always considered this particular classmate to be one of the Academy's stupidest cadets. Yet the truth was he asked more intelligent questions

52

than anyone in our particular group. I asked him for his secret formula, and he was generous enough to give it to me. He had discovered that the same lectures were often given year after year, and stenographic reports of the sessions were to be found in the War College library. He simply went to the records and wrote last year's best questions on his cuff. For a moment I was speechless, and then I took a look at his friendly and helpful face. The man, I decided, had a screw loose.

"If this is the way to make the General Staff," I said, "I say to hell with it."

Actually Jack Smith, (which was not his name), *did* have a screw loose and ended up in a mental hospital.

Both Army and Navy officers were attending the War College at the time and I remember a clash between two naval officers at one of our sessions. A supposed expert on naval warfare gave us a talk which shook me down to my shoes. We all thought that war with the muscle-tensing Japanese was inevitable, but we were not prepared for his grim picture. He did not envision the sinking of our ships at Pearl Harbor, but he did predict Japanese triumphs in the early days of the war, the capture of Pacific islands, the ultimate rebuilding of our fleet, and a hard fight back to Japan's mainland.

The Commandant of the War College asked for comment. Captain (USN) Bill Halsey stood up and said he disagreed with every word of his colleague's analysis, and, he added, "word for word." The Commandant then asked Halsey what policy he would recommend if war were declared. Halsey said: "I would weigh anchor and sail right into the homeland waters of Japan."

This was evidence of the aggressive spirit Admiral Halsey was to display throughout the war in the Pacific, but it was to be a long interval before we sailed into the home waters of Japan.

There was time for recreation at the War College and we formed an early-middle-age softball team which did pretty well against younger talent in a just-fun military league. I am

53

afraid few of my colleagues would have achieved stardom in the major leagues, but a good many became celebrities later on in other areas. Colonel Omar N. Bradley was the pitcher, I was the catcher, Bill Halsey played shortstop, Vernon Pritchard, who succeeded me as commander of the First Armored Division in Italy, was at first base, and Lightning Joe Collins, ultimately Army Chief of Staff, was at second. We had some doubts about the athletic skills of Jonathan "Skinny" Wainwright, who was to command our troops at the last stand on the Bataan Peninsula and spend the rest of World War II in a Japanese prison camp. We appointed Wainwright our official umpire with the spoofing agreement he would give our team a hairline advantage on all close decisions.

At the end of the War College course, I was sent to Fort Bliss, Texas, home of the First Cavalry Division. Here I was assigned to command the First Squadron of the Eighth Cavalry regiment, which in turn was commanded by Colonel Arthur H. Wilson. Colonel Wilson was beloved in the service and was a living legend. He had won the Congressional Medal of Honor as a young lieutenant for incredible bravery while fighting the fanatical Moros in the Philippines, and a scar like a ragged collar around his neck was truthful evidence that he had been almost decapitated by a bolo knife. In peacetime he became a ten-goal polo player, one of the best the Army ever produced, and at Fort Bliss he coached the Eighth Regiment polo team on which I played; we managed to win the First Cavalry Division championship. The Colonel and I were casual friends first, and then good friends. I think he knew I admired him. He was a kindly man who was nearing retirement age. Looking back, I suspect he was somewhat bored with the Army itself and the struggle of ambitious men for advancement.

We had a number of fledgling bachelor lieutenants at Fort Bliss, and it was their custom on occasional weekends to cross over the Rio Grande into Mexico for a good time. Few senior officers objected; the youngsters were prisoners of the strictest

54

discipline the rest of the week. But one puritanical squadron commander complained often to Colonel Wilson about his juniors' antics, and as is inevitable in a close-knit community, the word got around.

At permanent military installations in those days there were houses and lawns for married officers, and signs at the edge of the lawns to identify the resident officer. On a sweltering Texas Saturday night, the commander of the Second Squadron was sitting on his porch in a bathrobe when he saw his identity sign come sailing over his head. He immediately sprinted out and got the names of the tequila-happy jubilants. Within a few hours he preferred court-martial charges against them and sent his report to headquarters.

Next day I came in from drill (I was a major now) and found Colonel Wilson with his spurs dug deep into his desk. He was reading the charges. He turned to me and said: "Ernie, what is this all about? Have you heard anything about the fracas?" Well, of course I had; the career sergeants and NCOs were buzzing about it. The performance of the young lieutenants was, according to Army tradition, inexcusable, but their vandalism consisted only of giving a drop-kick treatment to a few posted signs. Certainly I thought a court-martial was excessive for a bit of horseplay.

"What would you do?"

"I would bring the culprits in, bawl hell out of them, confine them to Post for a week—and tear up the charges."

That's exactly what Colonel Wilson did. A court-martial for those young officers would have gone permanently into their career records, prevented future advancement, and ruined their usefulness. I recall the names of four of the young men. Two of them died for their country: Major Joseph A. Cleary on Bataan Peninsula in the Philippines in 1942; Lieutenant Colonel Jess Hawkins, serving with the Second Armored Division in 1944, at Péronne, France. Johnny Pugh was Skinny Wainwright's aide in those last desperate days at Bataan, spent several years in a Japanese prison camp, and eventually

55

became a major general. James Polk, now a four-star general, recently commanded American forces in Germany.

When Hitler came to unchallenged power in Germany, many of us in the military were convinced that war was inevitable; we also suspected that the United States was ill-prepared for military involvement. In 1935 I was ordered to the General Staff in Washington and found that our unpreparedness was, indeed, a fact. I was assigned to the G-4 section which dealt with all Army supply services including what was then called the Air Corps. For four years I was to be leashed to a desk and I often strained at the leash. Yet it was an important assignment and it made me both friends and enemies among my colleagues.

During those years Congress seemed indifferent to the explosive international situation and gave only niggardly financial support to defense measures. Nevertheless, we were able to plan and create many of the new weapons which helped to win World War II. My particular job was concerned with research and development, so I have personal knowledge of our progress. Conceived and developed during that period were such weapons as the Garand rifle, the 105 howitzer, the B-17 bomber, and the blessed C-47 workhorse transport plane which, sturdily and mysteriously, continued to function under the adverse conditions which made other planes conk out. Last but not least was the jeep—that springless little gasoline buggy which went anywhere and everywhere in a hundred battle areas. I share the affectionate regard of a friend of mine who called the lowly jeep the "Magnificent Louse."

I had a problem of my own during this interval. I had been in the cavalry since the beginning of my military service. I liked horses, I liked to be in the saddle, and I liked polo. But long before my service on the General Staff I had become convinced that, in modern war, horse cavalry was as obsolescent as the arrow and the spear. Part of my judgment, of course, was based on my own experience in World War I;

56

more important, I had been following German, French, and British military reports on the development of the tank. It seemed to me, as it did to many other officers, that mechanized units could and should take over the traditional battle functions of cavalry—reconnaissance and pursuit. Any residual doubts vanished when, in 1939, German armor swept across the plains of Poland in jig time and effortlessly destroyed Poland's plumed cavalry and the valiant, if foolish, feudal noblemen who charged their fine horses against machines.

The General Staff had tried to spur tank development in the United States but always ran into the stubborn opposition of the Ordnance Department of the Army which, before a wartime reorganization, had traditional control of weaponry. Tradition is one of a combat unit's greatest assets, but tradition, widened to a section of the service such as Ordnance or the Cavalry, may play havoc with progress. The General Staff had been able to bypass the traditionalists sufficiently to set up an experimental Seventh Mechanized Cavalry Brigade: two cavalry regiments had been equipped with tanks and armored cars and ordered to learn the problems of mechanized warfare.

At the end of my service with the General Staff I was called in by General John Herr, then Chief of Cavalry, who generously asked me where I would like to be assigned. This was a painful meeting for both of us. General Herr, who had always been kind to me, still believed the horse had an important part to play on the battlefield. I did not. It hurt me as much as it hurt him when I said I wanted to go to tanks to learn about the new kind of combat. General Herr told me I could expect no more friendship from the office of the Chief of Cavalry. I did not resent his anger and distress, but it seemed to me that more than personal loyalty was involved.

A short time after my meeting with General Herr, I was assigned to the First Mechanized Cavalry regiment at Fort Knox, Kentucky. There, and on maneuvers with infantry in New York State, I became acquainted with General Adna R.

Chaffee, who had managed to persuade the General Staff to create a new branch of service called the Armored Force. He asked me to join him as a staff officer in charge of supply and equipment, and I did. Because I knew my way around the War Department I believe I was able to be particularly useful during those pioneering days when the Armored Force was, like a child, taking its first tottering steps. If Adna Chaffee, thin, dark, and soldierly, had lived, I am sure he would have become one of the outstanding commanders of World War II. Unhappily, he died of quickly progressive cancer just before we entered the war. There can be no tangible record now of his brilliance, but there were to be times in Africa, Italy, and Germany when the Allied Command could have well utilized his judgment and shrewd intelligence.

By the late spring of 1941 America's preparations for war, so long somnolent and lacking in public support, had taken on a feverish tempo. France and the Netherlands and Norway and Denmark had fallen, and Britain stood valiantly alone, braving the flame and death and destruction of Hitler's first air blitz. I was ordered back from Fort Knox to serve with the War Plans Division of the General Staff. The assignment did not please me because, for a second time, I saw myself isolated at a desk when I thought my mission was to command troops. But it did have one very satisfactory result: my reintroduction to my family.

We were now seven. Barbara Ruth Harmon, the eldest child, was graduated from the George Washington University while I was on the General Staff. Then, in order of age, there came Halsey, Robert, Ernie, Jr., and Jeanne Leona. My wife and I arrived in an already crowded Washington seeking to rent a house which an Army officer dependent upon his salary could afford. Eventually, distraught, we searched in the country, decided to buy a small place in Vienna, Virginia, and put down the first payment. This was to be a base for the family during the long years when I was wafted around the map by Army orders. The younger children rounded out their high school education in that healthy, middle-class community, and it was *home* for a group of Army brats who, after all, had never really known one.

Along about this time the Army Ground Forces, under the command of Major General Lesley J. McNair, was given the overall mission of organizing, equipping, and training our troops for combat, and I was transferred from War Plans to be General McNair's G-4. President Roosevelt had already antic-ipated our entrance into the war by a series of diplomatic agreements which permitted us to establish bases in Iceland, Trinidad and other places. My first job was to get our soldiers there and to make arrangements to feed and supply them. My next assignment was much more sweeping. Maneuvers had been set up in Louisiana where large numbers of infantry, artillery and armored units would work together for the first time. Mark Wayne Clark was McNair's operations officer (G-3) and I handled transportation of troops to Louisiana, their support in the field, and the training of our green supply contingents. It was about this time that Wayne Clark, a classmate at West Point, and I had our first disagreement.

General Clark, who later commanded the American Fifth Army in Italy and was to be my superior there, was an extremely handsome soldier. He stood two or three inches above six feet, his Roman nose in a bony face had real distinction. Bright, resourceful, and diplomatic, he was to serve General Eisenhower well on a secret mission to North Africa which helped to bring dissident French commanders into the war on our side. Our disagreement had to do with prepara-tions for war which seem deadly dull now but were important to the both of us then.

Battles may seem to the layman haphazard, and sometimes are. But overall planning before actual combat is a first necessity; the military must assess the dimensions of the problem which confronts a nation. All of us knew there was a possibility, even a probability, of hostilities in two hemi-spheres. The General Staff asked General McNair to draw up

59

a grand blueprint of the manpower necessary to fight such a two-front war, and McNair assigned Clark to do the preliminary study.

Clark told me he was recommending one hundred infantry divisions and five armored divisions. I protested at once that this was unrealistic in view of the German armored strength, which already had subdued Poland and swept across France for a blitz victory. I maintained that a more sensible proportionate organization would be one armored division to every five infantry divisions; thus, if he envisioned one hundred infantry divisions for the future there should be twenty armored divisions. Clark said I was wrong, and that McNair was in agreement with him. I then said I would get an audience with McNair to present my point of view.

"Over my dead body," said Clark.

"Over your dead body or your live body, I will get in to see him."

And I did. General McNair listened to my presentation and recommended to the General Staff that twenty armored divisions be organized. Because of technical problems, this recommendation was never entirely realized. But by the end of the war the United States had sixteen armored divisions equipped and ready to fight.

General McNair was a brusque realist who sought to break through the nonsense of outdated military thinking to prepare the ground forces to meet an excellently trained German foe. Fortunately, he had the complete confidence of General George C. Marshall who was to direct our destinies throughout World War II, and he was able to establish the toughest kind of training for our troops—including training under live ammunition, which probably saved thousands of lives when the real heat was on. It seems to me that McNair's imprint on the troops who fought the war has never been sufficiently recognized or acknowledged. At the time I knew him, the general was deeply distressed about his increasing deafness which he feared would prevent him from serving overseas. At

60

congressional hearings he was sometimes considered an over-cautious witness because he consulted his staff frequently before answering involved questions. Actually he was so hard of hearing that he needed the service of better ears before he could make an adequate reply. McNair did get overseas in 1944 but only in the role of a training observer. He insisted on going to the front in Normandy and was killed there as the result of an accidental bombing by our own airplanes.

I am quite conscious of the antiwar attitudes of many of today's young people: I spent fifteen years as president of Norwich University, and I still keep in touch with the academic situation. But on occasion there rises in me an almost unquenchable resentment against public indifference to the sacrifices professional military men and their families have made for their country. Mrs. Lesley J. McNair, a charming and intelligent woman, lost not only her husband but also her only son in the war. I doubt very much that General McNair left much in the way of an estate except his army insurance. This would have been my family's exact position if I had been killed in action in North Africa, Italy, Belgium or Germany.

While I served with General McNair I was advanced to colonel with the promise of the one star of a brigadier general in the near future. In the autumn of 1941 General Jacob L. Devers, new commander of the Armored Force, came to Washington and asked me to return to Fort Knox as his chief of staff. Together we went in to see General McNair, who agreed to let me go if a commitment was made for my promised promotion. Jakie Devers, for whom I had the highest regard, readily agreed, and I stayed with him for more than a year. Then I requested and was given field duty with one of the neophyte armored divisions I had helped to organize. I was at last with troops again.

FIVE

★ ★

Forgotten Invasion

THE FATEFUL AND decisive bombs were dropped at Pearl Harbor and a once-divided America closed ranks. War was upon us and we could not turn back. The spring of 1942 found me on the old familiar grounds at Fort Riley serving as a brigadier general with the newly formed Ninth Armored. Then in August I was abruptly summoned east to command the Second Armored which was taking part in maneuvers in the Carolinas. This was one of the most celebrated outfits in the new army, and I felt honored indeed that I had been selected to lead it into battle.

The division had had three distinguished commanders before me, Major General Charles Scott, Major General George S. Patton, and Major General Willis Crittenberger. Scott gave it excellent tactical training, Patton gave it dash and vigor, and Crittenberger added the spit and polish which impressed foreign dignitaries and our own high brass in Washington.

Frankly, I was troubled about the division as I flew east. It had been highly publicized, but I wondered just how good it was. What were its *real* as opposed to its potential capabilities? I made a firm promise to myself that I would find out, that I would prepare it for the tough field service which was inevitable overseas. Spit and polish and the elegance of demonstration troops were fine, but it was up to me to make sure the self-propelled artillery knew how to shoot accurately and fast, the tankers how to support one another in desperate fields, the armored infantry how to advance in concord with the clanking tanks which function both as transport and protection.

The Second Armored had just completed the first phase of the maneuvers and was to have a day or so of rest before beginning the final phase. This recess promised time for the ceremonial transfer of command from General Crittenberger to me. I arrived at maneuvers camp about five o'clock in the morning, tired and dusty after a long jeep ride from the airfield at Greensboro, North Carolina. I was wearing coveralls and a combat helmet liner and had a bandanna handkerchief around my neck. I grinned at the young officers who met me, looked at myself, and decided I was, at the moment, anything but a spit-and-polish general.

General Crittenberger, who had just been promoted to corps command, had arranged a rather elaborate pageant for his farewell to the division. A platoon of tanks, with motorcycle outriders, escorted us to lunch and a distinguished guest was Justice Frank Murphy of the U.S. Supreme Court, who was also a colonel in the Reserve Corps. A platform had been erected for public speaking, and a good part of the division had been assembled to listen. By two in the afternoon I was entirely presentable; I had a clean blouse, a pair of ice-cream britches, and brightly polished boots. General Crittenberger made a brief but inspirational speech; he was generous to me, he praised the troops, and he remarked at the end that the President of the United States had said the Second Armored was one of the finest combat divisions. After introducing me, he and Justice Murphy vanished in a cloud of dust and the command of the Second Armored was mine.

It was now my turn and I stood up among my soldiers to speak for the first time. I did not attempt eloquence. I said I felt honored and proud to take command, but the training

63

period was almost at an end and we would be faced shortly with the grim realities of war.

"General Crittenberger has just remarked that the President of the United States considers you one of the finest combat divisions in the Army." I paused a moment and looked over the assembled GIs. "That may very well be true. But let's ask ourselves another question before we swell with pride. What in hell does the President of the United States know about the Second Armored? How does he know—way up there in Washington—whether you are good or not? You and I are now working together. We will find out."

I found out a little right there, because when I bowed off the stage I got quite an ovation. Rude I may have been, but the troops seemed to appreciate my down-to-earth talk. Now I met my officers. Colonel Maurice Rose was my chief of staff and Lieutenant Colonel Lawrence R. Dewey was my G-3. Rose was a cool, able soldier, distant and removed in temperament, and no one could know him well; he was killed leading an armored division in Germany. Dewey accompanied me to North Africa and stayed with me as chief of staff during my part in the Italian campaign. My indebtedness to Dewey, now a major general in retirement, is registered here. The success of a general, I have had occasion to reflect, depends less on his talent in tactics than upon the choice of a brilliant and resilient chief of staff. The man I chose was Dewey.

The names of other officers upon whom I learned to depend belong in the record. Lieutenant Colonel Oscar Koch was divisional intelligence officer (G-2) and later served in the same staff position for Patton's Third Army. Koch was succeeded in Africa by Lieutenant Colonel E. A. Trahan. Lieutenant Colonel Ralph Butchers was my G-4 and ended up as Provost General of the Army after the war. Commanders of the two tank brigades were Brigadier General Hugh J. Gaffey (Combat Command B) and Brigadier General Allen F. Kingman (Combat Command A). Colonel Isaac D. White commanded the 67th Armored regiment, Colonel John H. Collier the 66th, and Colonel Sidney R. Hinds the 41st. The chief of artillery was Colonel Thomas A. Roberts, and chief of engineers was Lieutenant Colonel Henry W. Hurley. Colonel Hurley was killed by a mine in Sicily and "Tory" Roberts died during the hedgerow fighting in Normandy.

I thought we did very well in the marshes of the Carolinas and the bridging of the Pee Dee River. Almost immediately the division was ordered to proceed to Fort Bragg to go into training for a secret mission. Just about this time I was promoted to major general but I had so much trouble on my hands that promotion seemed unimportant. The campsite selected for the Second Armored—15,000 officers and men— had been earlier occupied by another military outfit apparently indifferent to sanitation and properly covered latrines. The hours I had expected to spend in training were occupied by cleaning up the rotten, unsanitary conditions which shamed the troops who had been there before us. We had come out of unhealthy marshes healthy and were now decimated by an epidemic of dysentery and other illnesses. Doctors and nurses came down from Washington and worked with us twenty-four hours a day until the epidemic was under control. Few laymen perhaps realize that flies feeding on human wastes can cause more casualties to a close-living Army division than mortar fire. In the old wars dysentery caused more deaths than musketry.

A lighter incident in those times of strain and stress gave me considerable amusement along with one American soldier's uninhibited opinion of his commanding officers from platoon to regiment. I had dinner with the Fort Bragg post commander and was returning fifteen miles to my headquarters one night in a driving rain. The red clay road was both a mess and a morass and the headlights of my car picked up a man who was making very hard going of it. He had a bottle in one hand and was weaving from side to side. I told my sergeant-driver to pull over, pick him up, and put him in the front seat. The driver objected. He said the soldier was drunk, dirty, and

65

probably disorderly. I said he was obviously one of our own and should be helped to get home. We picked him up. He was a friendly fellow, oblivious of his surroundings, alcoholically loquacious, and anxious to share his bottle, which, to my astonishment, was French champagne. From the back seat I thanked him (he never turned around), but refused.

He identified himself as a member of L Company of the 41st Armored Regiment, and then began his critique of his superiors. Some of them he liked, some of them he didn't like, and he told us why. Finally he rose in rank to me, and paused.

"Well," he said, "he is a general and, I suppose, more or less of a son of a bitch. But, in all fairness, he hasn't been here long enough for me to come to a decision."

I felt that, even in champagne, he had been judicious. We were now in camp where guidons had been placed at the end of each company street. When we approached the proper guidon, we let the soldier out. When the door was opened, lights automatically popped on and fully illuminated the back seat; the soldier suddenly saw me or my two stars. He stood up straight and said, "Jesus Christ!" I said: "No, only your Division Commander." I liked that man but I never saw him again.

After establishing the division at Fort Bragg I was ordered to Washington for a secret conference. There I went into a closely guarded suite of rooms and met General Patton and General Marshall, Army Chief of Staff; they were studying a map of North Africa. General Patton said: "Ernie, do you want to go to war?" I said, "Sure, when do we start?"

Thereupon the secret plan for the invasion of North Africa was disclosed to me. The plan had the code name TORCH and three separate expeditions were contemplated. One, called the Eastern Task Force, was to come through the Straits of Gibraltar and land at Algiers; troops and materiel would be transported from England in English ships and protected by the English Navy. The Central Task Force had Oran, also a Mediterranean port, as its objective. The Western Task Force

66

was to come directly from the United States. Casablanca, an ancient and important city on the west coast of Morocco, was our objective.

The Western Task Force, under General Patton's command, was itself to be divided into three parts. In the north a sally against Port Lyautey was expected to overpower an important French air base; the main force would land at Fedala and secure the port of Casablanca. The southern section of the attack, under my command (with the code name BLACK-STONE), was to capture Safi, the only deep water harbor south of Casablanca. The Western Task Force had already done a great deal of planning, and I left Washington loaded down with charts and intelligence reports, and other information calculated to enable me to make my detailed plan for the Safi operation. I returned to camp near Mott Lake at Fort Bragg and took my chief of staff, Colonel Rose, and my operations officer, Colonel Dewey, into a small room and told them the story. They were sworn to secrecy and we three, until our troops were on the high seas, were the only ones in the division who knew where the exigencies of war would lead us.

The entire expedition was limited by the number of ships available. Only a small part of the Second Armored was to go overseas immediately—a supply of armored vehicles deemed sufficient for the job ahead and about 1500 selected personnel. The 47th Infantry regiment of the Ninth Infantry Division were also included in Task Force Blackstone, bringing our numbers to about 4,000 men. The general plan of the attack was to secure the port of Safi; then to leave Safi in the hands of the infantry while an armored column rolled north along the coast for some 140 miles to assist in the capture of Casablanca.

There were a thousand things to be done and, as always, too little time to do them. Every night we held maneuvers in the dark, crossing little Mott Lake in improvised rafts, establishing an imaginary beachhead on the other side, digging trenches, getting ready to move inland. Repeatedly the staff hammered into the skulls of the men that these practices were not for show; they were practices for real warfare, and exercises which might save the soldiers' lives. On one occasion I came across an artillery battery which had come ashore and, literally, gone to sleep. They had made no effort to put their guns in position or to obtain firing data; they hadn't even removed their gun covers. I promptly relieved the officers and sent them to a supply battalion—for keeps. New officers put new life in that battery.

It was said then, and it was said later in Africa, that I was hard on my officers and easy on my enlisted men. This, of course, was an exaggerated statement, but there was some recognizable truth in it. I took seriously the responsibilities of command and expected all officers, even junior officers, to accept full responsibility for the well-being of troops under *their* command—and I would not settle for less. Slack officers can be found in most military outfits but I wanted as few as possible in mine. A soldier who wears bars, an oak leaf, or an eagle on his shoulders has special privileges which the man in ranks does not have; he also earns more money and, as a rule, has a more substantial educational background. If I was "hard" on my officers it was because I expected more of them; the GI had enough troubles of his own. Status always has its price; in the Army it is vigor, devotion to duty, and, above all, a sense of concern for the men you may lead—and with whom you may die.

My staff and I were hard-pressed at Fort Bragg. We sent contingents of men and equipment to Newport News almost daily for amphibious training which was supervised by the Navy. Officers were educated as transport quartermasters and were taught how to load big ships. They were also introduced to the mysteries of waterproofing vehicles so they could go through shallow surf without strangling engines with sea water. I commuted between Washington and Fort Bragg and the port. General Patton frequently came down to Newport News to observe the exercises; if I was not present I was sure to hear about his visit later. A unit would return to Bragg late at night with orders to report to me that they were under arrest. Usually the officers were bewildered by their situation; they knew Patton had lost his temper but they did not know why. I developed an easy formula. I told the men I would talk to General Patton; they were released from arrest and sent to quarters.

Usually General Patton, whose sleeping hours were not the same as mine, would wake me along about midnight and ask whether "those bastards" had reported under arrest. When I said they had, Patton's high-pitched voice would soften: "Well, Ernie, release them; they probably did as well as they knew, and we have to manage with them." Patton's quick reaction to his own unfairness was typical of a strange, brilliant, moody, sometimes ill-advised military leader. As a subordinate I had to learn to live with him and I did. Toward the close of our training, Patton came down to address the Second Armored; he told me he was going to "put iron in their souls." The general's swashbuckling pronouncements, his silver-mounted pistols, and his tough-guy attitude in California desert exercises had already made him a hero of the press. Some 15,000 men were assembled as the General and I took the platform. I expected a long Pattonesque harangue. The general, resplendent in riding breeches and shining boots, took over the microphone and after a few opening sentences was so overcome by emotion that he choked up and tears coursed down his face. The two of us then walked off the stage. The Division stood up spontaneously and cheered and cheered again. There was an electrical quality about him which, without even a formal speech, communicated itself to masses of men. I knew, without completely understanding why, that officers and men of the Western Task Force would have confidence in their leaders during the coming invasion.

One of the aims of a personal memoir is, perhaps, an impossible one: a hope of re-creating for a new generation the

69

immediacy, the reality, the heart-thumping excitement of events which youngsters know only by legend or the printed page—or perhaps do not know about at all. I have talked to college freshmen whose information about World War II was so limited they did not know that the first effort of the American and British ground forces to assault Hitler's European empire proceeded by a back door—Africa. Most of them were familiar with the ultimate assault across the English Channel, but few of them had any understanding of the early days of the war when there were numerous pessimists to whom the task of defeating Germany seemed impossible. Not long ago an intelligent young woman put this question to me: "Why did we invade French North Africa? The French were our friends."

Perhaps a little exposition is in order. While the Baldwins and Neville Chamberlains of England and the quickly rotating and ineffective premiers of France gave ground, the militaristic Third Reich with the aid of German science built a land army that no western power could match. French fortifications ended at the Belgian border, and, as in the earlier war, the Germans sliced through Belgium like a cleaver through cheese. The collapse of France was humiliating, and one rather junior brigadier, Charles de Gaulle, took off for England in order to rally, by radio and other means, a resistance movement back home.

French government officials fled south to Vichy,* a spa and resort city like Marienbad where portly or liverish rich men drank the laxative waters seasonally. Hotels, casinos and empty villas provided makeshift office space and shelter for the refugee bureaucrats. There 84-year-old Marshal Pétain, grizzled and enfeebled hero of World War I, became Chief of State with adventurer Pierre Laval as his Vice Premier. They

*For full understanding of the situation in Vichy and North Africa, I recommend the reader to Robert Murphy's book, *Diplomat Among Warriors*. Murphy was President Roosevelt's personal representative and his story of intrigue and counterintrigue will part your hair down the middle.

70

agreed to the armistice which took France out of the war and split the nation territorially. Northern France continued under military occupation. Vichy accepted a position of pseudo-independence; it would rule the southern provinces (about one-third of the nation) and, insofar as it could, the French possessions in North Africa and elsewhere. Two important pledges were made by the Vichy government: (1) the French Navy thereafter would remain neutralized; (2) the French colonial armies would resist British or Allied attack.

In the United States and Britain, professional military men are subject to civilian control. In America there can be no true military hierarchy because of the system of congressional appointments to West Point. General Eisenhower came from a farm family in Kansas, Omar Bradley from a small town in Missouri; I was an almost penniless orphan from Vermont. When we qualified as "officers and gentlemen," it was through the democratic process. The story in France was different. The officer caste came, in the main, from aristocratic families and patriotism was often an abstract ideal. Loyalty to France frequently did not include loyalty to a shabby Third Republic and its shabby political deals: in fact, the military caste's contempt for politics was often so unrealistic as to approach nihilism. These were not to be my problems in North Africa, but they *were* to be the problems of my superiors. They found it difficult to understand a "sense of honor" which obligated French commanders to observe pledges to Germany which had been forced upon a defeated nation by fiat and duress. It was not until much later that I understood the logic of the French position and I shall not pursue it here.

After the armistice there were many pro-British Frenchmen. Their numbers were thinned when the Churchill Government, standing alone in Europe, acted hastily. In the midst of all misfortune, Britain still had command of the sea but it was haunted by the possibility that Hitler would get control of the French fleet. On July 3, 1940, the British Navy took over French warships in British ports and in Egypt; there was only

71

token resistance. But at Mers el Kébir, the port of Oran in western Algeria, French Admiral Marcel Gensoul proved to be a stubborn adversary. After a conference of several hours he refused to take his column to a neutral port. Under orders of the War Cabinet the British fleet then opened fire. Many French warships were destroyed and 2,000 French sailors were killed or wounded.

This was bitter medicine. There was to be other bad news later. Charles de Gaulle, convinced he could persuade French colonial officials to join the resistance movement, undertook with British naval support to capture Dakar on Africa's west coast two months later. (A submarine base at Dakar would have enabled the Germans to play hob with the subsequent Allied invasion and all free movement in the Atlantic; fortunately, they didn't get around to establishing one.) The attack on Dakar was a dismal failure. After a few days of confused fighting it was clear that hope of friendly submission was a fantasy; the assault forces withdrew, and the popularity of Britain—with Frenchmen—reached an all-time low.

The thwarted attack also damaged de Gaulle's international reputation as the spokesman for a Free France. Younger colonial officers retained some of their enthusiasm for his cause, but senior generals like one-legged Pierre Boisson at Dakar and five-starred Auguste Noguès in Morocco, who served as provincial governors and ruled vast territories like haughty viceroys, were definitely embittered. More important, both Prime Minister Churchill and President Roosevelt lost faith in de Gaulle's judgment and discretion. The President never got over this distrust and became convinced that the staff at General de Gaulle's London headquarters could not be entrusted with secret military information. Thus, the future President of France was not informed of Allied plans for the invasion of French North Africa. General de Gaulle, in turn, never forgave what he considered—realistically enough—a public humiliation. This is one of the reasons why French-American relations remain thorny to this day—and a disappointment to men of good will on both sides of the ocean.

General Marshall and Secretary of War Henry L. Stimson agreed that the ultimate defeat of Hitler could be accomplished only by a direct assault across the English Channel into France. But it became obvious by the summer of 1942—whatever the demands of our difficult and hard-pressed Russian ally—that this was physically impossible. Yet there were a limited number of ground forces for which Atlantic transport could be arranged, and it was strongly felt that we must engage the enemy *somewhere*. North Africa seemed the obvious answer. The British, the Australians, the New Zealanders, units from South Africa, operating in the desert along the eastern Mediterranean coastline, had been trading victories and defeats with the Italians and, later, with Rommel's expert Afrika Korps. The British were based on Egypt and supply was a headache and a heartache. From the time of the Napoleonic wars the Mediterranean had been called a "British lake." But no longer. Mussolini's "stab-in-the-back" entrance into the war after the fall of France had changed the picture. All heavy transport from an England already bled white could only reach Egypt by the interminably long sea voyage around the African continent and the Cape of Good Hope. I recall that after an almost disastrous British defeat at Benghazi, an American armored division in advanced training was completely stripped of tanks so they could be sent around the Cape to Egypt. This is evidence of how close the score was at the time.

Then, after what seemed to be an endless calendar of disaster, there came good news. General Sir Bernard Montgomery and his British Eighth Army defeated Rommel at El 'Alamein and sent Rommel into retreat. Now was the time—if there was to be a time—for an Allied invasion of the western shores. If we landed in North Africa without too much resistance from the French, there was the possibility we could push speedily into Tunisia and catch Rommel in a trap. It was a possibility but, in the long, dreary winter and spring, it did not happen. American GIs who expected Africa to be a hot Sahara with occasional cool oases under palm trees—and with

73

an occasional glimpse at harem beauties—were sadly disillusioned. Moving across hundreds of miles by truck or in freight
cars (and here I am quoting Ernie Pyle, my favorite chronicler
of the war), "they damn near froze to death." They could not
know this in November of 1942, but that was just how tough it
was going to be.

1942 - November: A view of the American convoy sailing toward Safi, Morocco.

1942 - October 22: General Harmon and Admiral Lyal Davidson discuss plan to enter Safi harbor.

1942 - November 8: Just before arrival at Safi, chapel services are held aboard the Harris.

1942 - November 8: General Harmon leaves ship enroute to Safi.

1942 - November 8: In the harbor at Safi the Lakehurst *and the* Titanic *are unloaded.*

1942 - General Harmon and the 85-year-old Grand Vizier to the Sultan of Morocco receive salute from Arab guard of honor.

1942 - November: Outdoor conference in Morocco. General Harmon is in the background at left.

1942 - December: General Harmon and French General Nogues at Rabat.

1942 - December: General Harmon and General Truscott are decorated with the Distinguished Service Medal by General Patton.

1942 - At solemn ceremonies in the cathedral at Rabat, French and American war dead are honored by civilian and military leaders.

1943 - January: President Roosevelt and General Harmon inspected the 2nd Armored Division's guard of honor in Rabat, Morocco. General Clarke (face hidden) sits next to General Harmon in the jeep.

1943 - General Harmon, Colonel Rose, Lt. Colonel Dewey and Major Rooney before boarding plane enroute to Tunis to join the 1st Armored Division.

1943 - May: Three German generals, including Lt. General von Borowietz (center) of the 15th Panzer Division surrender to General Harmon.

SIX

★ ★

The Assault

PLANS FOR THE invasion of North Africa were bold in concept and subject to many hazards. Indeed, the very boldness of the Allied operation was a significant factor in its first success. As early as November 4—four days before the projected D-day—the Germans were aware of a threat in the western Mediterranean, but did not fathom Allied purpose. On the night of November 5-6 two convoy sections headed for Algiers went through the Straits of Gibraltar, followed the next afternoon in broad daylight by the slower convoy headed for Oran. Spies immediately reported these movements to Axis intelligence services, but the warnings came too late.

The German Naval High Command believed the Allied convoy would proceed to the embattled island of Malta to reinforce and supply the British garrison there. Hitler was sure (carefully kept German war records reveal) that the Allies intended to land troops at Tripoli or Benghazi (in the eastern Mediterranean) in order to attack Rommel's army from the rear. Mussolini alone—although not celebrated earlier for his military prescience—came up with the proper answer: Allied invasion of French North Africa. As the result of these confusions within the enemy leadership, the Allied convoys were able to reach Algiers and Oran before they could be intercepted by German planes and German and Italian submarines.

But I am ahead of my story. Back home a few weeks earlier those of us who were to lead an amphibious force 2,500 miles across the troublesome North Atlantic were well aware of the expedition's risks. I had studied intelligence reports prepared for the planners of the Western Task Force operation and was aware that, in the beginning, the British opposed an expedition against Casablanca; they were convinced that all Allied strength should be directed toward more Mediterranean landings. Their arguments had force: Atlantic storms often rolled and roared without warning, against the unprotected shores of West Africa; it was quite possible that an amphibious expedition might not be able to land at all. General Marshall had a counterargument. There was always the possibility that, after the original landings at Oran and Algiers, the enemy, with the tacit consent of Axis-leaning Spain, might be able to close the Straits of Gibraltar. Future supply could not come in sufficient quantity from Britain, but must come from burgeoning American industry. Therefore, control of a deep-water port in Atlantic West Africa seemed to him imperative. Put in simpler terms, the capture of Casablanca as a supply port was insurance against disaster in another quarter and could guarantee that our untried troops could and would survive.

The fact that we were on the point of departure proved that Marshall had won his case. It was then that I got together with Rear Admiral Lyal A. Davidson, commander of the naval escort for the Blackstone operation. We met on his flagship. I liked him immediately and I think he liked me. We shared the same problem: untrained personnel, and not enough time for effective education. My low point—and I'm sure his—came during a night training practice in Chesapeake Bay. My troops debarked from his ships and, in small boats manned by his sailors, were supposed to move in orderly fashion toward specified shore points. When darkness came, a friendly lighthouse on shore provided a beacon to assist the novice navigators of the Navy's small boats. Only one boat—

76

oddly enough, the one in which I was a passenger—arrived at
its objective. The rest were scattered up and down Maryland's
coast and it took until noon next day to get the erring lambs
back to the fold. We tried the maneuver again on a second
night but the young sailors and their coxswains were equally
ineffective. I had to ask myself a question: if they can't find an
objective in peaceful Chesapeake Bay, with a lighthouse
beacon to help, how are they going to find an objective in
darkness on a foreign shore and under conditions of war?

There was no opportunity for a third exercise; our time for
training had run out. I was desperately anxious to see my wife,
but there was a problem of distance. My eldest daughter had
married an executive of Pan American Airways and was living
in Buenos Aires; my wife had gone there to be with Barbara
during an appendicitis operation. Without violation of the
secrecy imposed upon the top echelon I was able to send her
an innocuous radiogram which conveyed, or so I hoped, the
news that I was going someplace in a hurry. Leona was able to
read between the lines and, through the magic of Pan Am,
arrived at the Hotel Chamberlain near Hampton Roads, the
morning before my departure. We had dinner together, talked
throughout the evening, and did not sleep at all. I knew, and
she suspected, that I would be gone for a long, long time. It
was three years before we saw each other again. At two
o'clock in the morning I found my way glumly down to the
dock in a pouring rain where a small motorboat with a
hooded lantern waited for me. It took me out to a destroyer
which in turn conveyed me to a rendezvous point in the
Chesapeake where the rest of the vessels in my convoy were
assembled.

We sailed on October 24 at about 8 o'clock in the morning.
What a sight it was as the ships fell into formation when we
left Hampton Roads behind! Control of operations came from
the cruiser *Augusta,* flagship of Admiral Henry K. Hewitt who
was the overall naval commander of the expedition; General
Patton was also on the *Augusta.* On each flank were heavy

77

battleships along with the darting destroyers destined to be the means of intra-fleet communication, since we were under strict orders to maintain radio silence during the long Atlantic voyage. Far out in front two destroyers crossed and recrossed our sea lane with the assignment of dealing with German submarines which might be lying in wait for precious cargo. Destroyers in the rear of the convoy performed similar duty. During daylight hours aircraft from the battleships and cruisers were constantly in the sky searching for the submarine packs which, earlier in the year, had incarnadined coastal waters from Cape Hatteras to Florida and taken murderous toll on American shipping. Because of press censorship, most of the newspaper-reading public in the United States did not know how heavily the Germans had scored in their underwater campaign. Those of us in command knew. One of my staff officers later told me: "I held my breath across a whole ocean."

I have often said that my good luck at the time was based on my association with Admiral Davidson. He was not only an extraordinarily able mariner, but a man whose agile mind was always open to suggestion. At our first meeting on his flag-vessel, the cruiser *Philadelphia,* we found after a few quaffs of excellent bourbon whiskey that we were indifferent to traditional service rivalries and only interested in serving our country as best we could. History has contributed one shining example of combined Army-Navy operations: Wolfe's British expedition down the St. Lawrence River, which culminated in the successful attack on Quebec across the Plains of Abraham. But that took place during the French and Indian War, and the American military, 175 years later, hadn't done much about learning the lesson. Military annals show that Army-Navy cooperation has by no means been the rule in the past; many a well-omened expedition has failed because of jealousies and clashes of personality among the commanders concerned. Somewhere along in the planning I had discovered that the French had laid a boom across the narrow entrance of the artificial harbor at Safi. I had suggested at skull sessions that this hazard should be eliminated, but with no results. When I talked to Admiral Davidson about it, he reacted immediately. I suggested we storm the port of Safi with two destroyers, each carrying a company of infantry, ram the boom, and enter the port without fuss or finesse. On the docks there were huge electric cranes in operable condition, which we would need later on to unload the cargoes we expected to send from the United States. It was important they be taken in a surprise move before they could be destroyed.

The admiral approved of the idea at once, and sent two World War I type destroyers to Bermuda; their stacks and superstructures were removed, and they joined us at sea during the voyage. Davidson utilized his sea experience for a very practical suggestion that would have never occurred to me. He recommended that the infantry companies not board the destroyers until we were about twenty-four hours short of Safi. This would save them from the long days of seasickness almost inevitable among landsmen unused to the pitching and bobbing of the cranky small craft.

The Algiers force consisted of both British and American soldiers from the United Kingdom transported by the British Navy; in hope of more cordial reception from the bitterly divided French, the assault troops were American. Troops on the Oran expedition from the United Kingdom were American but were convoyed by the Royal Navy. Our own expedition from the United States was the largest force. On November 8 synchronized landings were to be made hundreds of miles apart in the hope that far-flung invasion would stun both the French and the Axis.

We had no alternative but to accept many of our cargo loadings on faith. The Western Task Force of one hundred vessels was too large to be dispatched from any one port without attracting undue attention. So the armada as a whole took to sea in bits and pieces from various places and with seemingly different destinations. For instance, our medium

79

tanks were loaded in New York aboard a unique transport which had been adapted for war duty; it was the cavernous seatrain *Lakehurst* which, in times of peace, ferried lines of loaded freight cars between Key West and Cuba. Imagine my feeling of helplessness during the first day of rendezvous when I saw the transport *Calvert,* loaded with light tanks vital to initial success, being towed toward shore by a tug! I was notified the ship's boilers were considered unsafe and that cargo and crew must be reloaded on another vessel which would attempt to join us at sea. I am happy to report that five days offshore the *Titania* faithfully arrived with the *Calvert's* men and cargo. Every effort had been made to equip us before departure with weapons of the latest design. There they were in cartons and crates; men and officers had no chance to try them out. New radios were issued and examined with fasci-nated attention. But we were under radio silence. One weapon in which I was personally interested was the bazooka, which was supposed to be of great value in attacking enemy tanks. I had never seen one and I did not fire one until some weeks after our invasion when I demonstrated American armament ingenuity to a French officer in Rabat, Morocco.

Shortly before our convoy got under way I received a message that Admiral Davidson wanted to see me. The Navy amphibious staff had worked out such complete details for the expedition that the highly secret book of instructions was as thick as a Sears Roebuck catalogue. I tucked it under an arm as I boarded the whaleboat the Admiral had sent, clutched it closely as I climbed the Jacob's ladder over the *Philadelphia's* side. I saluted the flag at the stern and was met immediately by Admiral Davidson, who carried with him exactly the same report.

"Harmon," he said, "have you read this book and do you understand it?"

"No, sir, I haven't read it and I doubt if I will have time before we hit Safi. I don't even know who wrote it."

"Well, let's go to my cabin. You and I are going to run the

Safi show and between us we must arrive at simple understandings which will make it a success."

I stayed with Davidson on the *Philadelphia* for a couple of days. In the beginning we had stubborn differences, but these began to dissolve as, mutually, we worked on basic questions. For example: weather reports for West Africa at that moment were not good. Suppose we arrived ten miles off the coast of Safi, out of range of coast batteries. Who was to determine whether the seas were too rough to make the landing attempt? Davidson said: "That is my decision." The next question: when should the transports move into the harbor? Davidson said: "Harmon, that is your decision. Your job is to go in to silence all batteries and I'll take care of the fort with the guns of the battleship *New York* and the cruiser *Brooklyn*. When the job is accomplished, signal me and I'll send the transports in."

So, one by one, we worked out our problems. When I left Davidson's ship basic agreements were condensed on a single typewritten sheet and I had a complete understanding of what we were going to do.

I was still troubled by the inability of Navy crews to land troops anywhere near objectives in Maryland, and on the voyage over I questioned sailors about it. It seemed to me they had little knowledge of the problems ahead. I suggested to the Navy that I be allowed to give a talk on the invasion plan with a silhouette of the Safi coast and landscape painted on the walls of the wardrooms of each ship. This was readily agreed to, and the men learned by heart where every promontory, estuary and military installation was located. I may as well say right now that the results were almost miraculous. The same crews who had done so poorly in Chesapeake Bay carried us through eight miles of rough Atlantic surf and hit the port of Safi right on the nose. I resolved then that, in future battles, I would brief everyone down to the lowliest private on the divisional plan of battle.

Even before we left port, I was given a strange and embarrassing responsibility. An American officer under military arrest reported to me with secret orders which were to be opened only after we were at sea. When I opened the orders I discovered that he was suspected of being a spy. He had helped in the planning of the expedition, and for that reason must accompany the expedition and then, without leaving ship, be returned to the United States. Actually he had worked with other officers in handling the ammunition which lay at the bottom of the very ship in which we were traveling. This seemed to me extraordinary treatment for an officer whose guilt or innocence had not been judicially established, a situation almost as bizarre as that portrayed in Edward Everett Hale's famous story, *The Man Without a Country*. Later the officer was completely exonerated and made a fine record for himself during the war.

The Navy's handling of the crossing was nothing less than superb. Every effort had been made to deceive submarine wolf packs. The Air Group of Hewitt's command (the fleet carrier *Ranger*, three escort carriers, a light cruiser, and nine destroyers) was ostensibly engaged in maneuvers near Bermuda. When the first section of transports and warships left Hampton Roads on October 23, they headed in that direction. When our section left next day we took a northeasterly course as though bound for the United Kingdom. The so-called Covering Group (seven warships and a tanker) sailed from Casco Bay, Maine, and took its place at the head of the column on October 27. On October 28 the Air Group was sighted and fell in behind the others. The seaplane tender *Bernegat* joined up eight or nine days later after a lonely voyage from Iceland.*

Against all sensible odds, this deception proved to be effective. There were no submarine attacks. But the Navy's guard was always up. We landsmen continually heard the shrill boatswain's whistle over the loudspeaker, and at 5 in the afternoon the cry through the ship, "Close all battle ports!" Then, as the ship settled down to a complete blackout through

*For fuller information, see *Northwest Africa: Seizing the Initiative in the West* by George F. Howe, an official U.S. Army history.

82

the night, came the final order like a bugler blowing taps, "The smoking lamp is out on all weather decks." The armada continually changed course to avoid known shipping routes, and only two vessels were encountered on the voyage. One was Portuguese and the other Spanish; both were boarded and then allowed to proceed.

The ships sailed in columns of lines, with each ship about eight hundred meters from its neighbor on the right and left and an equal distance from ships to its front and rear. Because of the zigzagging course and the blackout at night there was always imminent danger of collision; this put heavy responsibility on every helmsman. On one overcast day the collision sirens blew and we were startled to see the ship to our rear come plunging wildly toward us. Her steering rudder engine had broken down and she was as much on the loose as a steer in a stampede. Our skippers remained completely cool. We sheered to the right, other ships to the left, creating an open passage. After a time, all motors dead, the rampaging vessel came to rest. While we calmly closed ranks again and moved on, that transport sat silent in the ocean like a lonely duck on an Adirondack pond. A destroyer moved back to stand guard until she could be repaired and join us again. Discipline was perfect, but I shivered as we left the duck on the pond behind.

Of course, as on all transports, we were overcrowded. There were only bunks or hammocks enough for one-third of the men. Sleeping had to be on a rotation basis and hammocks were assigned to each man for eight hours a day. There was plenty of activity in the daytime. Rope ladders were rigged forward and aft on the ship and soldiers scrambled up and down like monkeys during certain hours of the day. These were the ladders they would use when they went over the sides of ships to small boats before Safi; it was also excellent exercise for cooped-up young men. A few days away from Africa the whole convoy had to slow to a snail's pace while we were refueled at sea by American oil tankers who had moved without armed protection to the meeting place.

83

November 7 was the day of the armada's dispersal. We separated into three sections. The main assault on Casablanca was to be made at the port of Fedala; a French air base at Port Lyautey was to be overrun; our small force was headed further south. I am sure a good many of the troops shared a forlorn feeling as the rest of the convoy hustled away on a divergent course and disappeared over the horizon. A few hours later, as scheduled, we transferred the assault infantry companies to the two destroyers which were to make the run on the harbor. This was done without incident and, indeed, with considerable light-heartedness. A huge net was extended from the transport to the decks of the destroyers and the men literally rolled down the net and were caught by comrades below. But as we approached our objective, tenseness among officers and men was noticeable. Religious services were held and were well attended. Under Army regulations cleanliness is next to godliness and every man was ordered to take a bath; it could well have been a part of a religious rite. Medical officers believed that a bathed soldier had a better chance of surviving wounds and infections than an unbathed soldier. I still have great faith in baths and bathing, and the pride it restores in men. But I suspect now that internal chemistry has more to do with resistance to infection than external cleanliness. I have seen wounded soldiers encrusted with external dirt survive after days without medical attention while other men died.

We arrived off Safi about 11 P.M. We were eight miles away and a few of us were comforted to find the lighthouse still functioning; it suggested that our approach had not been detected. This comfortable feeling did not last long. At 2 A.M. the light went off; French fishing boats coming home late from their catch discovered the presence of strange ships offshore and notified the harbor master and the garrison. We did not intend to attack until 4 A.M., but in order to avoid the risk of being torpedoed we got our assault force in small boats just before midnight. At precisely midnight the unmistakable voice of President Roosevelt, broadcasting from Washington, came on the air. His message was directed to the people of France and the people of French Africa. He announced the imminent landings by American troops, said we came as friends and liberators, and asked for both military and civilian cooperation against the Nazi oppressor. Every American who took part in the landings had a small United States flag sewed to his sleeve for easy identification, and sometime after the President's broadcast one of our destroyers by prearrangement fired off a rocket which, on burst, scattered across the night sky a fireworks semblance of the Stars and Stripes. I never found out whether it was seen ashore.

These preliminaries were undoubtedly wise and necessary from the point of view of diplomancy, but those of us before Safi had our own worries. We were under the firmest of orders not to fire until fired upon. Who knew what the French garrison would do? We expected to find no more than 1,000 men there (actually the number turned out to be somewhat smaller), but there was also artillery ashore, at a key position called Pointe de la Tour four 130-mm coastal guns with a possible range of 19,000 yards. Admiral Davidson and I had discovered from submarine reconnaisance that there was now no boom across the narrow entrance to Safi harbor, but we still thought it best to go ahead with the surprise raid by the two destroyers, the *Bernadou* and the *Cole,* which had been refurbished in Bermuda. My troops were already aboard. Shortly after 2 A.M. a scout boat from the transport *Harris,* where I had my headquarters, started in toward the harbor with orders for the *Bernadou* and the *Cole* to execute the attack plan. The scout boat was commanded by Ensign John J. Bell, who was to distinguish himself for his creative and impromptu assistance to the assault forces.

A few hours earlier the U.S. submarine *Barb* had disembarked Army scouts from the 47th Infantry who rowed ashore in a rubber boat; their job was to find the harbor entrance and to guide in the *Bernadou* and the *Cole* by infrared signals. Unfortunately, they lost their own way in the darkness,

85

entered the harbor itself, and took shelter ashore when they were fired upon by sentries. The submarine maintained its position, continued to send signals, but, as Ensign Bell soon discovered, these signals could not be seen by the *Bernadou* and the *Cole*. He told the skippers of the destroyers that he would proceed to the tip of the harbor jetty and assist their approach. This he did with great intelligence and a singular devotion to duty. At one point Bell, from his scout boat, saw the *Cole* was on a course that seemed certain to pile her up on the rocks. By flashlight and by voice radio (our silence had been lifted), he gave the warning that saved the destroyer thirty yards short of calamity.

As the *Bernadou* passed the north end of the jetty to enter the harbor we quickly learned the decision of the Safi commanders; they would resist. There was fire from a 75-mm battery at Fronte de Mer, from machine gun emplacements along the bluffs, from rifles on the wharves. A little later the 130-mm battery on Pointe de la Tour began to bombard our transports. There was an agreed-upon code signal if the French fired on us: "Batter Up." This came at 4:28 A.M. At 4:38 Admiral Davidson gave the companion signal to the battleship *New York* and the cruiser *Philadelphia*: "Play Ball." The *New York* with its long-distance guns chose Pointe de la Tour as its target, smashed the fire-control tower with its second salvo of 14-inch shells, and killed fifty-five French soldiers. The *Philadelphia* shelled the supposed site of a battery somewhat to the south. It was all very noisy.

Meantime, offshore, troops had been climbing down or rolling down the nets from the transports to the landing craft with celerity and agreeable orderliness. The unloading of tanks and other vehicles was something else again. This did not surprise or dismay me: the hurried and disorganized processes of loading in the United States had made this partial snafu inevitable. My hope and my prayer (and my gamble) was that the surprise attack on the harbor would guarantee victory before the tank and artillery lighters even shoved off from their host transports. Also I could look from the bridge of the *Harris* as H-hour arrived and thank a kindly Providence: the sea was remarkably calm. We had chosen one of the twelve days at that time of the year when a calm sea off West Africa was even remotely possible.

Now, as I paced the bridge on the *Harris,* my job was to wait. First news from the beaches was discouraging. The communication stated the destroyers had gone aground and the crews were lost. But I had learned in World War I not to take too seriously early messages from the battlefront; often they were colored by hysteria and, too often, they were wrong. My job was still to wait. Fifteen minutes later another message arrived. This announced, to my great joy, that the destroyers were safely in harbor, the troops ashore, and the port in our hands without serious damage to installations.

There were several small beaches outside Safi Harbor with rather inadequate access to the mainland. There was also, seven or eight miles to the south of Safi, another beach which offered an alternative approach if our original operations were not successful. In my planning I had set considerable store on this plot of land, which we called Yellow Beach. Colonel Edwin H. Randle, a gallant officer who later became a brigadier general, led the infantry assault columns and, by my instructions, sent another group in landing craft to lie off Yellow Beach until the results of the primary attack could be determined. Because of the difficulty of land communication I stayed aboard ship and awaited bulletins before making my decision. The news from Safi continued to be good, and about two hours after the fighting started, I became convinced that we should concentrate our main strength there. Accordingly I directed Colonel Dewey to go to Yellow Beach and call off that operation. Immediately after his departure Captain Tom Rooney, my personal aide, and I boarded a small boat so I could make a personal inspection of the situation at Safi.

When I went ashore I found soldiers lying so close to the water that wavelets were beating against the soles of their shoes. There was some sniper fire and bullets were raking and puffing the sand here and there. I remember that Captain Rooney ducked to the ground and then got up with a wry grin on his face. I grinned right back. He had never been under fire before and his reactions were entirely normal. Next I spoke to the young officer commanding the troops. I asked why his men were lying so near the water that their feet were awash. He said they were lying there because they were under fire.

"Yes," I said, "I realize you are. But how many people are shooting at you?"

"About six," he said, and then *he* grinned.

It was easy to isolate the building where the snipers were located. I directed him to attack the house with a squad of twelve men and to get going with the rest of his company to reach his planned objective. This he did with promptness and dispatch. Actually, although they didn't know it, these men would have been in less danger if they had actively advanced; prone there at the shore, they were easy targets for the sharpshooters. They were good troops and brave troops, but they were suffering from the stagefright of their first deadly encounter.

I conferred at length with Colonel Randle and assured myself that the attack was being pushed aggressively. It was important that we establish a defensive line some 10,000 meters inland to prevent hostile artillery fire from endangering the unloading of our cargo ships. I told Randle to push on; the remaining resistance at the port would be contained by waves of troops not yet put ashore. Communication between ship and land was still so imperfect that I had to return to the *Harris* where I could maintain contact with Admiral Davidson. There were still important joint decisions to be made in this first day of invasion. One of them came up almost at once.

We received information from secret intelligence sources ashore that seventy trucks filled with French soldiers were coming from Marrakech, ninety miles away, to reinforce Safi. I immediately asked the Navy to send dive-bombers from their carriers to intercept the caravan. At once there was admirable cooperation; thirty-five of the trucks were set on fire; the troops scattered and took cover. It had been a long night before, (no commanders slept), and it had been a long day. Yet we were not satisfied. All cannon defending the port had been put out of action except a battery of French 155-mm guns no one seemed to be able to locate. Once more I appealed for Navy air support and got it. The fliers found the battery and put it out of action.

Earlier we had sneaked seven or eight light tanks ashore on small lighters, but at 2 P.M. I was able to tell Davidson that the *Lakehurst,* loaded with medium tanks, and the *Titania,* loaded with light tanks, could be accommodated in the harbor. My staff and I went ashore and set up a command post in a little house near the wharf where we could supervise the unloading of the tanks and direct land operations.

I guess we must have slept then, but we woke up to headaches in the morning. The crane on the *Lakehurst* had lifted a medium tank out of the hold and over the side when gremlins took charge; engineers couldn't get the tank either up or down. It took nearly five hours to solve the problem. A hoist on the *Titania* had a light tank six inches off the floor when the cable snapped. It took seven hours to find another cable. In the meantime Brigadier General Hugh J. Gaffey of the Second Armored, commander at the front, was appealing for tanks to help stop the French who were coming in from the east. Actually, the situation was not at all perilous; the French commanders had preserved their honor by resisting, and were about to seek surrender terms, although we did not know this at the time. When the crane on the *Lakehurst* was restored to action I was there in person to direct every tank toward the front with instructions to start fighting even before they joined Gaffey.

During this period of insufferable mechanical delay we were being sniped at by enemies hidden in the cliffs around the harbor. Most of the fire seemed to come from one particular small dwelling. Twice I sent a squad of soldiers up the hill to investigate, and each time I got the report that only a harmless man and woman were in residence. After the soldiers' return, gunfire would open up again, and we had several casualties. Anger now possessed me, and I sent a tank up the slope with orders to go within ten feet of the house and to blow it off the map. This was done, the "harmless man and woman" were killed. There was a trap door under the living-room rug, and a French officer and thirty men were hidden in the cellar. They had been doing the firing. We took them prisoner.

90

SEVEN

★ ★

Toward Casablanca and Beyond

IT WAS EVIDENT that everything was going our way. One by
one the reports came in. (1) The 47th Infantry Regiment had
reached its objective 10,000 meters from the port and was
digging in defensively against French reinforcements. (2)
General Gaffey had led forward the few tanks we were able to
pry off the transports, met the broken French column from
Marrakech, and sent it into the hills. (3) In the center of town
a unit of the French Foreign Legion occupied a small barracks
and refused to surrender; we placed three or four tanks and a
mobile gun within seventy-five yards of the barracks, and
white flags from the garrison ended that episode without
needless casualties.

The port was now completely busy as the transports moved
close and began to unload cargo in small boats. The artificial
harbor was too small to accommodate anything except the two
large vessels unloading tanks and the two destroyers that had
led the assault. The destroyers were beached in the sand
alongside the dock, their sides riddled by small arms fire, but
otherwise intact. The skippers of the *Bernadou* and the *Cole*,
who led the assault, later got the Navy Cross; they deserved it.*

An earlier report that dock installations had been captured

*The *Bernadou* was commanded by Lt. Comdr. R. E. Braddy. The *Cole*
was commanded by Comdr. G. G. Palmer.

91

intact was incorrect. Those treasured electric cranes had been put out of action temporarily by the French, but Navy technicians quickly got them in shape for the heavy jobs ahead of them. Many of our French prisoners opposed the Vichy regime and helped with the unloading of ships. My orders were clear: I was to treat the French military with all courtesy. Despite the complexities of politics, we hoped that we might fight together as allies in French North Africa and, eventually, liberate France itself.

As soon as resistance ended in Safi, I sent Colonel "Steamer" Nason as my representative to hold a conference with the French civil authorities. Colonel Nason spoke French fluently and was a man of tact and compassion. He explained that the Americans were not there for conquest but to defeat a world-disturber—Hitler—and to restore a once-peaceful world to peace again. This could only be done by battle and bloodshed and we were sending our own young men across a wide ocean to pursue a crusade. Would they join us? I discovered later that this conference had been most fruitful; it established a firm foundation there for future cooperative relations.

I had spent the night after our landing aboard the *Titania,* which was unloading light tanks and gasoline at a pier. The docks were piled high with gasoline cans and cases of ammunition. During the small hours I was awakened by a message from Navy radio: a French air attack was expected at dawn. When I stepped ashore the docks looked like a city park on a stifling evening—officers and men alike were stretched out asleep at the precise spots where they had fallen from exhaustion after the first day's hard fighting. We roused everyone, manned the antiaircraft guns, cleared for action as best we could. When dawn came one lonely French plane darted down through the overcast, a brave pilot on a forlorn mission. He was almost immediately shot down in flames, but the bomb he dropped killed or wounded several men. Had the bomb dropped among our combustibles, the damage might have been critical. When the electric cranes were repaired next day we soon cleared the docks, vastly assisted by a captured narrow gauge railroad train.

On the second night after the landing I jeeped out to a crossroads five miles east of the port where General Gaffey had the armored units assembled. The progress of the rest of Patton's Western Task Force was almost unknown to us. We had sent word of our safe landing and our plan to march forward immediately but, of course, we did not know whether our messages had been received. All we knew about the Casablanca situation was that there had been a stiff sea battle off the coast.

My orders from General Patton were to proceed to the north as fast as I could. After consulting with Colonel Randle, and taking a good look around the town, I decided that the 47th Infantry, with the help of some light tanks, could well hold the beachhead. Randle still had the artillery power of the warships behind him, and, frankly, I suspected that the ill-equipped French at Safi had no stomach for further combat.

By prearranged battle plan our next objective was Mazagan (now known as El-Jadida), ninety miles away. The harbor there was shallow, about sixteen feet deep, but it could be negotiated by destroyers. We were traveling light; there were no trucks in our column and we had to carry our men and supplies on our combat vehicles. We then had no idea what our opposition might be. The Navy had agreed to send one destroyer with three hundred tons of ammunition and another destroyer loaded with gasoline—lifeblood of the tanks—into Mazagan harbor.

So Combat Command B of the Second Armored turned its back on Safi and started north. The night again was pitch black. The road was narrow and high crowned, and it was easy to slip into a ditch on either side. Occasionally this happened. Everybody tried to keep up. Our troops had no apprehensions about the French, but somewhere along the line they had heard exaggerated tales of wandering Arab bands who stripped the wounded on the battlefield, tortured and emasculated prisoners. We had no stragglers.

It was a troubled night. Every time the column halted, Dewey and I went forward to find out why and to get the advance going again. On one occasion the answer was innocent; the leading vehicle had stopped, the men had fallen asleep and had not got the word to move up. At 2 A.M. there was a long halt and I went forward. I found a circle of soldiers around something in the road. All I could distinguish at a distance was a light, but I pressed on. What I found was an elderly Frenchman with an enormous Wild West mustache, who was standing beside an enormous rock in the middle of the road, holding up the column. On his shirtfront were combat ribbons and bravery ribbons from earlier wars, and on the rock was a placard proclaiming "Egalité-Fraternité-Republique Française."

Our troops had offered him no violence; they could not understand a word of his flowery rhetoric, and they were both amused and puzzled. He was holding a lantern in his hand when I came up. I asked him in French why he was there. He told me he had been ordered to put up a barricade which would slow our advance. He said it was a *barricade symbolique,* as, indeed, it was; we could push around the rock or roll it away. Somehow his position seemed to me to be an exemplification of the ambivalence of the French military in regard to our invasion. When I asked him why he stood there with a lantern, he replied—with candor and simplicity—that he wanted to provide enough light so my young Americans wouldn't injure themselves!

This odd meeting in the darkness had dramatic impact for me. It was plain that this single barricadist was a superannuated soldier of France who had been granted homestead rights in Morocco for his long service. (Perhaps we had fought a few miles apart in the Meuse-Argonne.) A dim lamp winked in the window of his little villa; undoubtedly I would have seen by daylight a small vineyard neatly kept, a few domestic animals, a flock of geese, a checkered tablecloth in a sunny farm kitchen. He was a friend of the United States, yet the obligations of duty had required him to give witness of his patriotism by a completely unrealistic maneuver. He had, of course, risked his life; it was the sheerest luck he had not been shot down. I shook his hand, told him he had done well by his country, but that he could not hope to stop a column of armor. Then I sent him back to his wife and, I hope, to the tranquility he well deserved. The lantern disappeared over a rise, the troops got back in their vehicles, and men and machines moved on.

Our forces halted at the edge of Mazagan and I gave orders for investment of the town at 6:30 A.M. Now followed a sequence of disturbing and quickly changing events. Soon after our halt we received a radio message from General Patton, our first communication from him. I was greatly concerned. Although the message was marked "urgent," it had been sent the day before. It directed me to be prepared to attack the southern exits of the city of Casablanca at 11 A.M. This called for immediate action and a perhaps impossible timetable. We were still forty or fifty miles short of Casablanca; we had a river to cross and a town and a port to capture. Even if this capture proved easy, we would still have to refuel from the gasoline supplies we hoped to find at Mazagan harbor.

The dilemma was resolved fortuitously. A few minutes after the first Patton message, another arrived. The French in Casablanca were going to surrender! All attacks were to be stopped at once.

Our tanks were already climbing a gentle slope in the dawn to proceed against Mazagan. The staff and I piled into jeeps and other vehicles and whizzed off in several directions in a frantic effort to halt the forward movement before anyone was killed. At this moment our radio went dead, a not infrequent occurrence in those days. In the sky above, American airplanes already circled lazily, waiting for the appointed moment to

95

drop their bombs. How to reach them? In an emergency one uses the tools at hand. The pilots aloft were treated to the surprising spectacle of a hundred officers and men maniacally waving towels at them. ("It was a grand day for laundry," one of the pilots told me later.) In the end the squadron leader decided something was wrong and returned his group to their mother-ships at sea, the carrier *Santee* and the *Philadelphia*. Unbeknownst to us, Admiral Davidson had come north to Mazagan to give us Navy firepower, if firepower were needed.

When all our tanks had been successfully corralled, my staff and I proceeded to the center of town where I received the formal surrender of military and civilian authorities. I learned that the garrison, which consisted of a battalion of Moroccan soldiers under French officers, was located across the Oum er Rbia River where they expected us to attack across a heavy stone bridge at Azemmour, twelve miles northeast of Mazagan. We had been told that the bridge was strongly guarded by artillery and antitank guns, which probably had been sent along with the infantry to reinforce Casablanca, for we found only barricades which would have proved no obstacle to our tanks. Colonels Nason and Dewey and I jeeped to Azemmour, where we walked across the bridge to meet the French commander. His battalion stood in military formation with stacked arms. He saluted and inquired what my plans were for disposition of his troops.

I replied that he and his battalion would be permitted to march back to barracks under arms and with the French colors flying. Every useful purpose would be served by mutual observance of the terms of the armistice: (1) there would be no firing by American soldiers, and (2) all orders for his troops would come from me. He thanked me for my military courtesy. To break up the stiffness of the ceremony, and with perhaps a thirsty eye, I asked the French colonel what kind of liquid he carried in the canteen at his belt. He smiled broadly and said "Wine."

Thereupon we drank a toast to the future friendship of France and the United States and to success in fighting our

96

common enemy. At the stone bridge there was a colorful tableau; his Moroccans in their vivid uniforms on their way back to town met our column of tanks. The flags of both countries snapped in the breeze and the young Americans standing in their tank turrets and watching with fascinated interest showed that, like so many other Americans, they were sightseers at heart. Let them get a few hours away from bullets and they would invariably be buying picture postcards.

After the confusion of early morning hours in which we underwent the almost comic change of face from grim ravagers to preservers of the peace, Combat Command B could relax. There was now a supply base at our rear; the *Bernadou* and the *Cole* had, indeed, arrived with food, ammunition and gasoline, and refueling was in progress. I directed General Gaffey to go into bivouac, and took off for the city of Casablanca along the coastal highway. With me in a half-track vehicle were Dewey, Nason, Rooney, and a civilian interpreter. We were tired but happy, and flew our flag at the head of the half-track. On the way we met many refugees and advised them to turn back because the war in Morocco was over.

We found the American headquarters in Casablanca and were advised that we would find General Patton near Fedala to the north. As a result, we were the first Americans to cross the whole of the handsome city. There were great crowds in the streets and hysterical disorder. Angry party leaders of many persuasions were seeking the opportunity to release political prisoners (we were to learn much about the complexity of the political scene during the next few weeks), but, in general, the crowds were friendly enough to us. As we approached Fedala we came upon an American outpost and were led to Patton's headquarters at the beautiful Miramar Hotel. We had hardly shaken the dust out of our beards before Patton emerged from the hotel and greeted us. His greeting to me was typical: "Where in hell have you been all this time?"

For a moment I did not take this in good part. I thought we

97

had done a remarkably quick job at Safi, and certainly we had not wasted a moment in our push to reinforce him. Perhaps the small boy still under my skin expected a slap on the shoulder, a gesture which meant "well done." Then I saw the slightly sardonic twinkle in his eye and the smile and realized once again that this was Patton's way.

The general told me that he was expecting Admiral François Michelier of the French Navy in a few moments to discuss surrender terms. After I had briefly advised him of the situation at Mazagan and Safi, he directed me to return with my staff next day to discuss future plans for Second Armored. On the way back through Casablanca our light-hearted party stopped for lunch and had our first civilized meal in many days. American soldiers were enough of a curiosity in the hotel dining room to excite considerable interest among the civilians who sat at adjoining tables. But their interest in us was not reciprocated; I like to think that we paid our modest tribute to our Ally by the undivided attention we gave to delicious French cooking.

Everything was in good order when we returned to the bivouac. True enough, Sub-Task Force Blackstone's principal mission had ended "without commitment to battle in the vicinity of Casablanca" (the quotation is from the official U.S. Army history), but I don't think a single enlisted man cared about that: stretched out exhausted on the hillside, they were catching up on sleep. Looking at them there in the late afternoon, I suddenly wished I could think of some splendid gesture to show my appreciation of their uncomplaining conduct in Safi and on a long, forced night march. But, as usual in such moments, nothing—not a damn thing—came to mind.

By evening I was ravenously hungry again. Someone directed me and a few companions to a small restaurant near the sea. There, raising the eyebrows of an incredulous waiter, I ordered and devoured an omelet made of a dozen eggs. Over coffee, the idea hit me—fresh country eggs for breakfast for my whole command, which at that moment consisted of about

1,500 men. I called the French owner of the restaurant into consultation and asked him if 5,000 eggs could be delivered at camp next morning. He said cautiously that this was unprecedented in his memory—as I am sure it was—and he would need to consult with some sort of group or guild of Arab merchants. He put on his hat and went out. The credit of the U.S. Army was never questioned, and after about a quarter of an hour the cafe owner returned with a promise that the order would be delivered.

When I awoke next morning the quiet bivouac was full of Arabs—Arab profanity, Arab donkeys, Arab carts—and crate after crate of eggs. The first sergeants and the cooks took charge and a memorable breakfast was had by all. I stayed out of sight.

The next day we reported to General Patton and got our orders. We were to proceed to a location just east of Rabat, the capital of Morocco, and set up camp in the cork forest of Mamora to await the arrival of the rest of the Second Armored from the United States. One of our assignments was to stand guard over a narrow section of North Africa which belonged to Spain and which might imperil Allied forces from the rear as they struck east toward Tunisia. There was never even a crackle of hostilities during our time there, but the area was always highly suspect and later in the campaign Hitler's advisers pressed him to authorize just such a sortie through Spanish Morocco. Pressures from the Soviet front were so severe that Hitler felt he could not spare troops for a chancy adventure which might even be resisted by Spain itself.

Our tank column headed on for the Mamora Forest, content to rest and train in the Rabat country, where oranges and tangerines grew on convenient trees and chickens and eggs, bought by the individual soldier, offered a welcome change from dull Army chow. Romantically inclined GIs, however, were to find Arab women disappointing.

During this period I was frequently in Casablanca and was filled in by staff officers on details of the Casablanca, Oran, and Algiers invasions. The landings at Algiers met almost no opposition, and General Eisenhower later credited this to the prior operations of Robert Murphy and his secret connections with such pro-American French commanders as General Mast, and "the sympathy, even if cloaked in official antagonism, of General Alphonse Pierre Juin." Oran was harder. French forces in that section, particularly naval elements, resisted bitterly. The American attack was undertaken by the First Infantry Division and elements of the First Armored Division. Both had been stationed in the United Kingdom for some time. Their commanders were Major General Terry Allen and Major General Orlando R. Ward. Task Force commander at Oran was Major General Lloyd R. Fredendall, a veteran soldier who had achieved a reputation among his superiors at home as an efficient trainer of troops.

The fight for Casablanca proved to be the most punishing. The port itself was so strongly defended that, in the planning, any idea of frontal assault was quickly abandoned. There were coastal defense guns and powerful warships in the harbor; the partially completed dreadnaught *Jean Bart* (dreamboat of the French Navy before capitulation to the Germans) floated at dock with modern radar equipment and a battery of 15-inch guns. Destroyers and submarines were present which ultimately issued into the open sea to harass our convoy. Reports on French first-line aircraft indicated a force in Morocco of 74 fighters, 81 bombers, and 13 reconnaissance planes.

Probably more important than military strength was the temperament of the high level Army and Navy commanders who controlled Morocco. Under Marshal Pétain's agreement with Hitler, they still ruled a population of 6,500,000 Arabs and Berbers, and to them the dream of French Empire was not yet a mirage. The nominal ruler and Moslem religious leader was the Sultan of Morocco who had his palace at Rabat. The actual ruler was Auguste Paul Noguès, French Resident General, who also had his headquarters at Rabat. Admiral Michelier was the Navy commander, and General

100

Georges Lascroux commanded the troops. These men were belligerent, surprisingly ill-informed, and quite willing to fight.

It was eventually decided that American troops would land in the Bay of Fedala and move overland to attack Casablanca from the rear. There would also be an independent attack on Mehdia, a good many miles away. The objective there was the capture of Port Lyautey. This was an excellent modern airfield with concrete runways which we would need in the future for land-based American planes. Elements of the Second Armored—armored infantry and light tanks—supported both the Fedala and Mehdia attacks, but in the Casablanca surf—we had no lighters—there was no way to get medium tanks ashore. And that, of course, was the primary reason for the Safi expedition 140 miles away.

Many things went wrong at Casablanca and, because I had been a partner in the tactical planning, I made it my business to learn as much about the operations as I could. We were certainly there in strength; Army forces totaled about 19,500 officers and men. But from the first, ill luck haunted the landings. Running through intermittent rain squalls, naval people discovered that an unexpected sea current had carried the convoy beyond its destination. An emergency turn-around caused more trouble; radar revealed that some transports were 10,000 yards from their designated places. Delays became unavoidable, and in the end transports began to send their landing craft ashore at Fedala independently and without regard to battle plan. I quote from the official Army history:

"Faulty navigation, attributable to either compass deviations, inexperienced crews, or other causes, brought boatloads of troops to shore sometimes miles from the designated points, and onto rocky obstructions or reefs rather than at sandy beaches. The consequences were serious even when the boats were able to retract from these landings, with such major ill effects as the scattering of troop units, the loss of control over ensuing deployment, and the separation of weapons and equipment from units expecting to operate with them. But the

101

boats too often could not retract and met destruction under circumstances which drowned some of the passengers and left survivors cut and battered and deprived of weapons or radio sets needed in the assault."

Actually, about one-third of the landing craft were lost in the Casablanca operation—not because of enemy action but because of Navy and transport crews who were as much johnnies-come-lately at war as our soldiers. What did they know about the heavy surf at Mehdia or the problems in dealing with it? I could not help but look back at Admiral Davidson's horror and mine at the practice performances in Chesapeake Bay. Yet after education aboard ship about targets ashore, crews like these had carried troops eight miles through surf at Safi and landed them almost precisely at the beaches where they were supposed to disembark. I thought then that the Army and the Navy had a great deal to learn about amphibious operations and the cooperation between the services which would make them effective. History shows that the United States *did* learn the lesson. The island-hopping campaign in the Pacific under Generals MacArthur, Eichelberger, and Krueger was transported and supported by the Navy and shared by the Marines; Eichelberger's Eighth Army alone made 103 amphibious landings among the islands of the Philippines in sixty days. There had been nothing like it before; it was a brilliant and unique example of service cooperation.

The mysterious problems of radio transmission created a problem for all hands in the Moroccan expedition. I have said earlier that Admiral Davidson and I could get no firm news of the Casablanca operation. General Eisenhower, vexed by his dank, underground headquarters at Gibraltar, fared no better than we did. Oran and Algiers were in American hands, but on November 9 Ike still had no substantive information about the Patton-Hewitt operation. Radio gave his technicians only unintelligible signals. Now I quote from his book, *Crusade in Europe:*

102

"Thereupon we tried sending light bomber craft to Casablanca to gain contact, but after French fighters had shot down several of them,* we knew this method was futile. In desperation I asked Admiral Cunningham [British naval commander] if he had a fast ship in port. By good fortune, one of the speediest afloat was then at Gibraltar. . . . The Admiral offered her to me for the necessary time to make contact with the Western Task Force. I chose Rear Admiral Bernhard H. Bieri of the United States Navy to head a staff group, and they took off within the hour."

Within this same hour the sub-task force under Major General Lucian K. Truscott, Jr., was undergoing singular difficulties. The unpredictable day of calm ended and winds sprang up at sunset; by daylight wave crests reached fifteen feet in height. The chosen beaches in the neighborhood of Mehdia were angry with surf, and men and boats were lost and stranded in scattered landings. As Truscott drove toward the prized airfield at Port Lyautey, the French and their native troops fought back desperately and bravely.

This small engagement was not to be settled by arms, but it should be said at once that the capture of Port Lyautey, at the cost of seventy-nine soldiers killed, won for the Allies a vital airfield, and a seaplane base, from which to engage in the still un-won and critical battle for superiority on the Atlantic.

In the late afternoon of November 8 General Noguès received indirect information that Admiral Jean François Darlan in Algiers had issued orders in the name of Marshal Pétain for the cessation of fighting. About 9 P.M. the exact text of Darlan's order was telephoned to Noguès and passed on by him to Admiral Michelier and General Lascroux. They were instructed to arrange for a meeting between Noguès and General Patton next day.

The French submission came the next day, just a short time before the Americans were prepared to launch a coordinated

---

*Actually one British aircraft on the same mission was shot down by American planes.

attack on Casablanca itself. Formal negotiations between American and French leaders took place at Patton's headquarters at the Hotel Miramar on November 11, twenty-four years to a day since the end of World War I.

Our casualties in three days of combat in the Casablanca area were 337 killed, 637 wounded, 122 missing and 71 captured. French losses were much heavier. And, except for stubbornness and lack of vision on the part of a few men in French high Army and Navy command, there would have been no battle. It needn't have happened.

EIGHT
★★
Trouble in Tunisia

WITH THE COMING of peace to Morocco the time arrived to mesh the Second Armored into a single fighting force again. The 4500 men of the division assigned to the Moroccan invasion had been broken up into three specially selected task forces numbering about 1500 apiece, one for each of the three landings. I was happy to welcome the three groups to our rendezvous point in the remarkable cork forest of Mamora east of Rabat, an area some of the troops subsequently renamed "Boring Acres." The rest of the division—about 11,000 men—arrived from the United States and joined us at Christmas time.

While I sympathized with those who found our stay in the cork forest tedious—the troops had returned to spending their days in intensive training and there were few diversions to while away the long evening hours—I found our surroundings anything but boring. The forest, which covered perhaps 100 to 150 acres, was the property of the Sultan of Morocco. The trees, rising 90 to 150 feet from the ground, provided an excellent shield from the blistering tropical sun for our men, who lived in pup tents arrayed beneath them. There was no underbrush, and one could look down long corridors between ancient pillars that seemed impervious to time. Sections of cork bark had been harvested from the trunks of these trees for hundreds of years; a single tree, I was told, is ready for harvest about once every fifteen years. Synthesizers have now devised a plastic stopper, but every reputable vintner still demands cork to close his bottles.

In those still early months of American participation in the war, there were no USO shows or Red Cross movies to help fill my men's leisure hours. There was, however, the Souk-el-Harmon, Arabic for "Harmon's Market," a fixed-price trading post I ordered set up opposite our camp so the men could buy eggs, chickens, oranges, tangerines, and other provisions from Arab traders without being gouged. By night the darkness under the cork trees was broken by the lights of little fires, round which the men sat and talked as they cooked up eggs and chicken. The men made these fires by filling number 10 cans with sand, dousing the sand with gasoline, and then igniting it. These makeshift cookstoves were consuming about five hundred gallons of gasoline a week.

Soon this mysterious consumption of gasoline caught General Patton's eye as he went over the manifests; he knew we were moving our trucks and armor very little. One day my telephone rang and Patton was on the other end, asking where all that gasoline was going. I told him and added that the campfires were a good morale booster. As was his custom when presented with a new piece of information, "Uncle George" cussed a few moments over the wire while he thought about it, and then he said brusquely, "Okay, let's continue it. I guess it's a good idea."

When the last of the division arrived, those men who had taken part in the Moroccan campaign had a fine time solemnly warning the newcomers about the savage atrocities they could expect to suffer if they ever became separated from their buddies and fell into the hands of the Arabs. What nonsense! The mass of the Moroccan people of that day were desperately impoverished; modern ideas had as yet touched them little, and a common sight was that of a woman yoked with a horse or a cow, drawing a wooden plow through the fields while her

106

husband guided it along the furrows. Yet, for all the hardness of their way of life, they were among the most inoffensive, harmless people I have ever met.

Since we were in somebody else's country, incidents between our men and the local inhabitants were to be expected and the usual number occurred. I soon learned that the practical solution (whether or not it was socially desirable in the long run) was a liberal application of money. One day an imprudent battalion commander called a rest stop for his men immediately beside an orange grove that belonged to the sultan. When the Battalion moved on, the oranges moved on with them. I no longer recall what that grocery bill came to, but I'm sure it would have been cheaper to have filled the order at the Souk-el-Harmon.

I have never understood the fatal fascination civilians find in live ammunition, but we saw the phenomenon in full flower in Morocco. Despite repeated warnings, scavengers persisted in combing through the division's target areas, with the usual disastrous consequences. Sometimes a child, playing with a dud he took home to the family tent, would inadvertently detonate the lethal mechanism and kill the entire family. These dreadful occurrences also had their price. A dead camel cost 25,000 francs ($500), and from there the indemnities ranged downward: a boy, 15,000 francs; a donkey, 10,000 francs; a woman, 5,000 or 6,000 francs; a girl, 500 francs. The Arabs put little value on the distaff side of their households.

The political confusion in Morocco that followed the French surrender posed problems of a diplomatic sort that I gladly would have traded for the questions of the battlefield.

Despite their theoretical turnabout from enemies to allies, many of the French officers maintained a private loyalty or at least a deep affection for Marshal Pétain, the leader of Vichy France. Even those officers now thoroughly committed to the Allied cause were divided: some were loyal to General Henri Giraud, who had been selected by the Allied Command to head the French forces after Admiral Darlan was assassinated; others were attracted to the striking figure of General Charles de Gaulle. Civilian French officials all seemed deep in one political intrigue or another, and many U.S. generals—including me—were secretly approached by agents of the underground Arab independence movement who saw no reason why their defeated colonial masters should be returned to power. Every dinner party was, for guests of my temperament, an exasperating exercise in avoiding political missteps and entanglements.

Political tensions at that time were heightened by uncertainty about the intentions of the Spaniards who controlled Spanish Morocco. The boundary between the two territories was one of those arbitrary lines drawn at a nineteenth-century European negotiating table. We heard repeated reports that the Spanish were planning to exploit the French defeat as an opportunity to push their boundary south to the Sebou River. Because the United States was pledged under the surrender terms to maintain inviolate France's African territories, American forces were obliged to resist any such attempt. General Patton conceived the idea of inviting Lieutenant General Luis Orgaz Yoldi, the Spanish commander, to pay a visit to Rabat and review the Second Armored Division. I thought this invitation was risky, since a review would show General Orgaz exactly what we had, but Patton proved shrewder than I. The Spaniards lacked the equipment to compete with the armament of the Second Armored, and after Orgaz's visit we heard no more of a possible advance to the Sebou.

In January I was invited to Casablanca, as were all the top Allied commanders in Morocco, for the closing of the Allied strategy conference. Heading the guest list at the elegant Miramar Hotel were President Roosevelt and Prime Minister Winston Churchill of Great Britain. My role at the conference was minor, a mere divisional commander amidst the top civilian and military brass of Washington and London, but I got a small-boy pleasure out of seeing names from the newspapers take form as men right there in the same room

108

with me. During the cocktail hour, I watched delightedly as the rotund, ebullient Churchill smoked one cigar after another and enjoyed numerous helpings of his characteristic brandy and soda.

At that cocktail party I had my first opportunity to take the measure of General de Gaulle. I reflected, as I shook his hand, that the experience was like grasping a flounder. There was no warmth in his grip. It was clear that he viewed both Americans and British with contempt. Roosevelt and Churchill, I observed, gave de Gaulle as little notice as possible. General de Gaulle apparently was quite bitter that the Allies had put General Giraud, who was also present, in command of the French forces. In my opinion there was every military reason—experience, age, rank—for the choice. Furthermore, I saw no reason the French should receive overmuch consideration. They had fought against us; their devotion to "honor" had unnecessarily cost many of our men their lives.

One night during the conference Churchill dined with Patton at the Villa Maas. As was his custom, he stayed up very late with the dinner company telling stories. Finally, at about 3 A.M., he decided to return to his quarters near the Anfa Hotel. He insisted on walking alone. As he approached the wire enclosure round his hotel, the American sentry, a farm boy from North Carolina, challenged him. Churchill's identification of himself failed to satisfy the sentry.

"Corporal of the Guard," he called, "I have a feller down here who claims he is the Prime Minister of Great Britain. I think he is a goddamn liar." Fortunately, the Corporal of the Guard was more familiar with the likenesses of world statesmen. He permitted Churchill to enter his quarters. I am told that Churchill was delighted with this incident and told the story of it frequently.

The following day, as the conference concluded and the world first learned that Roosevelt and Churchill had journeyed secretly to Casablanca, the President came out to see the troops. He arrived by car at the reception point outside

109

Casablanca on the road to Salé. Troops of the Second Armored had formed a cordon three hundred meters back from the road on either side—no one was going to get into those bushes to snipe at our President—and the division's tanks and infantry were lined up solid along the shoulders. Further up the road was that part of the Third Infantry Division that was not guarding the President's temporary residence in Casablanca. As the presidential car stopped, large screens were put in place around it so the troops could not see the paralyzed Chief Executive transferred from his automobile to an open jeep.

When the operation was completed and the screens removed, General Mark Clark and I joined the President in the jeep for the inspection. Later Roosevelt had lunch with us in the field and I had a chance to exchange a word or two with him. He was most affable and interested in what we were doing. After lunch he ceremoniously placed the Congressional Medal of Honor around the neck of Colonel William H. Wilbur, who had been recommended to receive the decoration in recognition of his valor at the invasion of Casablanca. I never saw President Roosevelt again.

In Morocco in those early weeks of 1943 the fighting war seemed far away, but half a continent away to the east—in Tunisia and Libya—the stage was being set for events that would profoundly affect my future military career. As Lieutenant General Sir Bernard L. Montgomery's British Eighth Army slowly pushed the German and Italian forces of Field Marshal Erwin Rommel westward through the Libyan desert, Allied forces—British, American, and French—commanded by Lieutenant General Sir Kenneth A. N. Anderson had raced from the landings in Algeria eastward. There seemed every reason to expect a speedy capture of Tunisia. Shortly before the turn of the year, optimists had thought the war in North Africa was almost over, that all that remained was to drive scattered Axis forces in Tunisia into the sea and then calmly squeeze the celebrated Rommel from west and east until he submitted.

110

That, however, was not to be. Even as good luck had contributed to the speedy successes of our campaigns in Morocco and Algeria, bad luck—and bad weather—made impossible Allied hopes to seize the remainder of Africa quickly and cheaply. By the end of January, we later learned Axis forces in Tunisia under the command of Generaloberst Jürgen von Arnim had grown to more than 100,000 men, and Rommel's 70,000 men, harried though they were by Montgomery, were on their way to join them. What was in fact taking shape was Rommel's audacious thrust through southern Tunusia toward Algeria that culminated in the bitter American defeat at Kasserine Pass on February 20. Heavy casualties were suffered on that and preceding days by the First Armored Division, the principal U.S. force at the scene; but the division was not so much beaten as simply misused by a corps commander who didn't understand time and space and logistics.

Sketchy reports of the deteriorating situation in Tunisia had already reached us in Rabat when on February 20 I received a telegram ordering me to report immediately to General Eisenhower's headquarters in Algiers for "limited field duty." What this meant I did not know, but I hoped it did not mean a permanent separation from the Second Armored. Next morning my aide, Captain Rooney, and I boarded a plane for Algiers and that afternoon I was seated in Eisenhower's office.

Ike's encouraging and magnetic grin was not much in evidence. Word had arrived that our forces had been overrun at Kasserine Pass, and Ike was concerned that Rommel would continue his advance and strike at Tebéssa, a vital Allied strongpoint in Algeria just over the border from Tunisia. He was even more perturbed by reports of dissension among American commanders on the battle front. General Fredendall, commander of the II Corps, he said, had reported unfavorably on General Ward's handling of the First Armored and had requested his immediate replacement. At the same time Ike had heard that General Fredendall was losing the

111

confidence of the men under his command by his tactical handling of the battle situation.

As Ike unfolded his worries, the mission he had in mind for me was at first unclear. Then he explained I was to take over command either of the II Corps from Fredendall or of the First Armored from Ward, whichever I thought necessary.

In my astonishment I blurted out, "Well, make up your mind, Ike, I can't do both."

"That's right," he replied, "but right now I don't know what is to be done down there. I'm going to send you as deputy corps commander. Your first job is to do the best you can to help Fredendall restore the situation. Then you will report direct to me whether you should relieve Ward or Fredendall."

I went to bed that night with a heavy heart. I knew nothing about the alignment of our troops, the positions of the British and the French, and yet I was to help fight a battle. I was staying at the Alletti Hotel; Ike had told me he would call for me there at 2 o'clock in the morning and could ferry me as far as his advance command post at Constantine, some three hundred bumpy miles away. On the way he would fill me in on the sketchy reports he had received. They were, as I soon found out, sketchy indeed.

I tossed around in bed and finally lost consciousness. A light in the room soon woke me from my brief and profitless sleep. I was completely disoriented, did not know where I was. And this is a moment I treasure. The Allied Commander and his Naval aide, Captain Harry C. Butcher, helped me to get dressed. I have enjoyed telling my grandchildren that a future President of the United States once laced up their groggy grandfather's combat boots.

As we were about to leave the hotel, German planes were sighted, air raid sirens sounded, and we went into a shelter. Finally, at about 3 A.M., we set out for Constantine. At the wheel of the car was Captain Kay Summersby, Ike's WAC driver; she was pretty, she was English, she was fearless, and she handled an automobile better over a bad highway than any man in my whole division. Rooney sat with Miss Sum-

112

mersby. Ike, Butcher and I were in the back seat. There was still some gunfire and the blackout was complete. Ike at once began to describe the Kasserine position and I, I am sorry to say, fell sound asleep while the Allied Commander talked. After the battle was over, he wrote me a nice letter in which he complimented me for my calmness on the way to the front. I wasn't calm, I was just plain tired out.

We drove through much of the day. I remember passing a truck train stopped at the side of the road. The men were all out urinating against the tires of the trucks. I speculated briefly on Miss Summersby's reaction, but then she volunteered that she wasn't bothered in the slightest. She was used to seeing that sort of thing, she said.

Late in the afternoon we arrived at Constantine, a walled and ancient city on a plateau some 2100 feet above sea level. From times as distant as those of Julius Caesar it had always been a prize sought in war. The city was cut off from the surrounding country—save on the west—by a beautiful limestone ravine through which the River Rummel finds its way. We went immediately to the headquarters where General Truscott was Ike's representative.

With just an hour of daylight left, Rooney and I—now on our own—set out for Tebéssa, one hundred miles to the southeast. I have never forgotten that harrowing drive: it was the first—and only—time I ever saw an American army in rout.

Jeeps, trucks, wheeled vehicles of every imaginable sort streamed up the road toward us, sometimes jammed two and even three abreast. It was obvious there was only one thing in the minds of the panic-stricken drivers—to get away from the front, to escape to some place where there was no shooting. Two or three times Rooney and I were forced off the road into the ditch, and I began to worry that he and I might be wrecked, possibly killed. Eventually I suggested it might be wiser for us to pull off the road and wait for daylight. I praise my aide; his reply was, "No, we must keep on, we must keep on."

We kept on, and finally arrived in Tebéssa around 2 A.M.

113

The town seemed virtually deserted. My recollection is there was only one sentry on duty to challenge us. We identified ourselves and asked directions to the II Corps Headquarters. The solitary sentry couldn't direct us to headquarters but he pointed to a nearby building where he thought we might locate a corps staff officer. There we found the G-4 of the corps at work. He traced out on a map the route that led us to General Fredendall. This curious headquarters, dug into the walls of a ravine outside Tebéssa, was accessible only by a single precipitous road built by Army engineers. Eisenhower, who had visited it ten days or so before my arrival, noted tartly in his memoirs that his trip to Fredendall's headquarters was "the only time, during the war, that I ever saw a divisional or higher headquarters so concerned over its own safety that it dug itself underground shelters." Aside from the matter of the shelters, I can add my own opinion that such a command post belongs near a road and should be close enough to the front so that frequent visits to combat troops are possible.

Rooney and I found General Fredendall sitting in a chair near a stove in this dugout working with his operations officer Colonel Robert A. Hewitt. Fredendall's first words to me came as a shock, for I still felt terribly ignorant about the state of the battle. "We have been waiting for you to arrive," said he. "Shall we move the command post?"

I had journeyed out there in the dark; at that point I didn't even know where the command post was, much less where the front was. I decided on the spot I would operate decisively, counting on intuition to fill in where I had no knowledge.

"No, sir," I replied in my firmest tones. "We will let it stay right here."

"That settles it," said Fredendall, turning to his operations officer. "We'll keep the command post right here." Fredendall then handed me a typewritten sheet: I was to take battlefield command of the U.S. First Armored Division and the British Sixth Armoured Division. Finally I got a chance to inquire

114

about the battlefield situation. Fredendall summed it up in his customary colorful manner. The Germans, he said, were through the pass, the Sixth Armoured was holding the line on a road outside Thala, the First Armored was blocking the road leading to Tebéssa, and he was expecting the Germans to give their "Sunday punch" at daylight. It was then about three in the morning.

The telephone rang. Fredendall answered and immediately began arguing with his caller about moving the Sherman tanks. He made a gesture of disgust in my direction and I asked what the trouble was. Fredendall explained that 33 of the new diesel tanks had just been delivered in Tebéssa and he wanted a provisional unit formed from men of the First Armored to move them up to Thala at once to join the British. The caller, Lieutenant Colonel Hamilton H. Howze, the First Armored's operations officer, was doubtful about the order's wisdom since the crews had come out of light tanks and were unfamiliar with the Shermans. They had never fired the guns.

"If I am in command, I'll handle this," I said. So I got on the phone and ordered Howze to get the tanks to Thala by dawn. The tanks would do nobody any good if the Germans got to Thala, I told him. Howze again protested that he considered the order a mistake, but he promised to carry it out.

With that matter disposed of, Fredendall went to bed and I went off in a radio-equipped half-track to see the divisional commanders. Fredendall had assigned a driver, a signal officer and a young staff officer, Lieutenant Colonel Hamlett, to function as my staff. We made our way first to the headquarters of the First Armored at Haidra, a village some 20 miles northeast of Tebéssa that was originally established as a Roman military post in the first century B.C. By now it was getting on toward dawn. I found General Ward there asleep in a slit trench. He got up and I showed him the paper General Fredendall had given me. I knew General Ward well. But since I was junior to him in time of service, I found it

115

embarrassing to inform him that he had been put under my command.

"Ward," I said, "I'm about one thousand files behind you"—meaning my name was that far behind his on the rolls of the Regular Army—"but these are my orders and that's how it is."

He immediately assured me that he understood the circumstances and would cooperate fully.

By now I was fairly sure what needed to be done about the battle. My decision may seem a bit simple-minded. It was this: We were confronted with a situation in which our troops were running away. First those in authority must order the men to stop running and turn around. Then we must try to win back the ground that had been lost. I adopted a little motto for the day: "We are going to hold today and counterattack tomorrow. Nobody goes back from here."

General Ward promptly issued an order to his subordinate commands that summarized the tactic perfectly: "All units will be alerted at dawn for movement in any direction except to the rear."

I set out for Thala and my first confrontation with the British. As I rode along I reflected on my rather peculiar position in the command structure and came to the conclusion I had been handed a real no-glory assignment. If the battle was won, I would get no credit for it, but if it was lost, I surely would get the blame. So I decided to do just as I damned pleased all day long. Each time we came to a detachment on the road, I stopped to advise its commander of the new battle "plan"—hold today, counterattack tomorrow.

The Germans were shelling Thala when I arrived and I made my way with difficulty through alleys and between houses to the cellar headquarters of Brigadier Cameron G. C. Nicholson, commander of the Sixth Armoured. I was dirty and unshaven from my trip through the night; I had had no sleep and no breakfast, and I was a little apprehensive about presenting myself in the midst of British spit and polish.

116

Nicholson, predictably, was freshly shaven and crisply uniformed. I identified myself and told him my orders. I asked him what his situation was.

"We gave them a bloody nose yesterday and we are damned ready to give them another one this morning," he replied.

I knew that he and I were going to get along together just fine. I told him about the contingent of tanks scheduled to arrive from Tebéssa and repeated my decision to hold today and counterattack tomorrow.

There was a commotion outside at this point and Brigadier General S. LeRoy Irwin, whom I knew from West Point days, came bursting into the room. Irwin and I greeted each other and then Irwin reported excitedly that he had just received an order from General Anderson (the British commander of Allied troops in the Tunisian theater) to move his artillery brigade from Thala to Le Kef, a village about fifty miles to the north.

"Oh my God, you can't do that," Nicholson exclaimed. "If my men see your brigade pulling out of here, it will be a terrible blow to their morale."

"Indeed it will," I broke in. "Irwin, you stay right here."

With these words I countermanded an order of the commander of the Tunisian campaign. I figured that if I won the battle I would be forgiven. If I lost, the hell with it anyway.

Irwin broke into a broad smile. "That's just what I wanted to hear," he said.

I went out and got in the half-track again. We headed back toward Haidra and Tebéssa, where I took another look at the First Armored's front and had a quick breakfast. I made a brief report to General Fredendall, telling him that all seemed secure along the line and that I planned a counterattack for the next day. Looking back at the ease with which I moved about that day, I am reminded anew of the virtues of a small staff. Often as a staff swells in size, the commander finds he and his aides are spending as much time figuring out who

117

does what job as they do in carrying out their mission. I am convinced that the five of us in the half-track—the driver, the second lieutenant signal officer, Lieutenant Colonel Hamlett, my aide Rooney, and myself—ran the battle was well as if we had been fifty men, probably better.

At dawn the Germans launched their customary artillery barrage all along the line, but it seemed rather weak to me and was broken off quickly. I sensed that they had decided against an all-out attack that day—the artillery preparation wasn't strong enough. It wasn't until months later that we learned the German advance had already ended. Rommel had concluded that if he was unable to capture Tebéssa and the Allied supplies stockpiled there within two or three days, he would have to withdraw in order to prepare to meet Montgomery, whose British Eighth Army was moving steadily westward across the top of Africa toward Tunisia. The battle was over, but those of us in command of the Allied forces west of Kasserine Pass had no way of knowing this.

We got back to Thala just before Lieutenant Colonel Louis V. Hightower arrived with the tanks that had been the subject of such vigorous debate in the early hours of the morning. Virtually the first thing that Hightower said was that his men had never fired the tanks' guns, hadn't even had a chance to bore-sight them.

"Put the tanks up on that hillside, Hightower," I said to him. Then I got up on top of the tank with him and added, "And I want you to stay right there. You can bore-sight to beat hell. There's nothing in front of you but Germans to shoot at."

With that I went off to General Ward's headquarters to work out the plan for the counterattack to regain Kasserine Pass. It was a simple but effective scheme we laid out. Allied infantry were assigned to seize two promontories overlooking the Pass while artillery pounded the Pass itself. Then, after the infantry had won control of the heights, we would run forward with the tanks and drive the Germans through the Pass. We set the action to begin at midnight.

118

During the night the Germans began their withdrawal and by morning most of them were out of the Pass and in full retreat back toward the Tunisian coast. They had mined the Pass and the roads leading to it with considerable thoroughness and we had to lift all these mines before we could proceed. As a consequence the enemy made a clean getaway. I have been criticized for not making a faster pursuit, but it must be remembered that when I took command twenty-four hours earlier, the Allied troops were running away. In one day they were turned around and on the attack.

As soon as it became clear that the Germans had withdrawn and the battle for Kasserine Pass was over, I returned to General Fredendall's headquarters to report the news. But the news had preceded me. I found the general in bed, showing some effects of several helpings of whiskey he had taken in celebration of the occasion.

General Fredendall called General Anderson, the British commander, on the telephone and said a few unsavory things to him. Then he turned to me and asked if I intended to relieve General Ward. I replied that as far as I could see Ward was doing all right.

"If you will let General Ward command the division and you command the division through Ward, I think you'll find he will give you good cooperation," I said.

Fredendall thought about this a bit and then said brusquely, "If you're not going to relieve Ward, you might as well go back home."

I looked at him for a long minute. "Fine, that's just what I would like to do," I said then. "I'll go back to Morocco and take command of the Second Armored Division."

I went outside and collected Rooney, and we set off for Algiers.

General Eisenhower's headquarters was full of jubilation when we arrived there and, for that brief moment, I was held in high regard. Unfortunately military favor tends to be fleeting and my "moment of glory" for what I accomplished at Kasserine Pass was no exception.

Ike was particularly interested in my assessment of Generals Fredendall and Ward, and I spoke to him bluntly about what I had found. Ward, I said, was doing well, but had been badly handled by Fredendall. I told Ike that Fredendall had by-passed Ward and given orders directly to Combat Command B, one of the two fighting units into which the First Armored was divided.

"Well, what do you think of Fredendall?" Ike asked.

"He's no damned good," I answered. "You ought to get rid of him."

"Do you want to take command of the II Corps?" Ike asked.

I hesitated a moment, for it was a temptation. But then I said, "No, ethically I can't do that. I have reported to you that my superior is no good. It would look like I had sold him down the river to better my own assignment. My recommendation would be to bring Patton here from Morocco—let him take command of the II Corps. Let me go back to my Second Armored. That's the best way out of this mess."

That was in fact the way things worked out. Eisenhower relieved Fredendall in favor of Patton; Fredendall was promoted to lieutenant general and returned to the United States to train troops. He received a hero's welcome upon his return, I later learned, and few suspected that his performance at Kasserine had been less than adequate.

After one night in Algiers, Rooney and I caught a plane for Morocco. We arrived just about noon at the cork forest, while the men of the Second Armored were having lunch. Rooney had made it his business to get the word out through the division about what their commander had accomplished in Tunisia. The men all came running down through the forest to the road to welcome us. Some were in fatigues, some in their underwear, depending on how the time caught them. They lined the road for five solid miles, waving and cheering, as I was driven by in a sort of procession of state. It was a fine welcome and one of the most rewarding commendations I got for my labors at Kasserine Pass.

120

That commendation lingers in memory only. Another, of the more permanent variety, still hangs (a little yellowed now) on the wall of my den:

12 March, 1943
Dear Harmon:

I hope you know how much I appreciate the effective manner in which you functioned as a Deputy to the Second Corps Commander, when I recently sent you to the battlefront for emergency duty. I was impressed not only by the cheerfulness and promptness of your response to an order that plunged you into a most difficult and delicate situation, but by the calmness, courage, and leadership that you displayed during the final stages of the German advance and the beginning of his retirement. Without detracting in any way from the great value of the services rendered by other officers on the field, I think it only just to say that you definitely enhanced your already high reputation as a soldier and demonstrated that kind of leadership that we need in the prosecution of this war. I am truly grateful to you.

With cordial personal regard,

Sincerely,
Dwight D. Eisenhower
General, U.S. Army
Commander-in-Chief

NINE

★★

Victory in North Africa

MY RETURN TO command of the Second Armored Division was brief. On the morning of April 5 I found myself again in Tebéssa—or rather over Tebéssa, peering out the window of a C-47 transport plane at a dogfight in progress between several German Messerschmitts and the American fighters escorting us. Our transport plane was circling lazily in an attempt to take evasive action and simultaneously stay safely inside the ring of trouble. Those of us aboard had considerable personal interest in the outcome of the fight. If the Messerschmitts triumphed, they would turn and shoot our lumbering, defenseless craft out of the sky like an overripe grapefruit. Happily our Air Corps boys drove off the German fighters; we landed safely at the Tebéssa airfield.

In my pocket were orders from General Eisenhower to report to the II Corps headquarters, now under Patton's command, for assignment as commander of the First Armored Division. In a conversation held in Algiers before I flew to Tebéssa, Ike told me that Patton had decided he could not work with General Ward and had asked that I be brought in to relieve him.

Three men accompanied me in the move from Morocco to serve as my staff in the new assignment. They were Colonel Rose, my chief of staff, Lieutenant Colonel Dewey, my operations officer, and Captain Rooney, my faithful aide.

122

At the Tebéssa airstrip we picked up a jeep and set out on the hundred-mile drive to Gafsa, where Patton had established his II Corps headquarters. The front was now well to the east of its position during my previous brief stint as battle commander for the II Corps. Not long after we set out on the drive, we heard the sound of a plane coming in from behind us, low and fast. It was a Messerschmitt. The four of us dove out of the jeep into the ditch without pausing long enough to put the brakes on; the jeep rolled on down the road and smacked into a big stone. The Messerschmitt swept past, its machine guns chattering, and we got up and dusted ourselves off. No one was injured and even the jeep had only a minor dent or two. We drove on.

Patton was just awakening from a midday nap when we arrived and I was shown into his room. He was seated on the edge of his bed, lacing up his boots. His dog Jimmy, who sported a black patch over one eye, was there panting and scratching: the air in the room was hot and fetid, and Patton was in a bad humor.

He grunted that he was glad to see me, and told me to go at once to Maknassy, forty miles to the east, and relieve General Ward.

"Fine," I replied. "Do you want me to attack or defend?"

Patton's always short fuse was even shorter that day. "What have you come here for, asking me a lot of goddamned stupid questions?" he roared.

"I didn't think it was stupid," I answered. "I simply asked a very fundamental question, whether I am to attack or defend."

"Get the hell out of here and get on with what I told you to do, or I'll send you back to Morocco," Patton bellowed at me.

With that, I left the room, closing the door very gently behind me, and went off in search of General Gaffey, Patton's chief of staff.

Gaffey explained that Patton's ill temper was partly fired by his annoyance with General Ward, and Ward's cautious style in dealing with the Germans. The First Armored, he said, was holding a critical pass; regularly every morning Ward reported

123

that the enemy was attacking, withdrew a few thousand feet, and then, counterattacking, regained the lost ground by nightfall.

This explanation made things clearer to me. The four of us from Morocco got into our jeep and continued on to Maknassy, a most unpleasant drive. The day was stiflingly hot and the dust from the road rose in choking clouds. General Ward was standing at the roadside as we drew up just about dusk. He had his bedding roll, his aide was at his side, and it was obvious he planned to depart at once. As soon as my feet touched the ground, he saluted and said, "The party is all yours, Harmon."

"I'm sorry, Ward. I had nothing to do with your relief," I said. "Can't you stay here tonight and show me the situation? General Patton didn't tell me anything."

"No," he replied. "I'm not allowed to do it. I was ordered to take off and get out the minute you arrived."

We discussed the matter a moment and then Ward said he would be glad to stay until morning if Patton okayed the delay. I telephoned Patton, and he roared that he didn't give a damn what happened to Ward so long as I understood I was in charge. I edited Uncle George's assent in transmitting it: "The General said he would be very happy for you to stay if you care to," I told Ward.

We climbed into a half-track sealed with blackout curtains, and Ward introduced me to the staff. I asked the operations officer to brief me on the situation. A British officer stood up and started to speak.

"Are you the operations officer?" I asked.

"No, I'm the liaison officer," he replied.

I thereupon issued my first order as commander of the First Armored: No liaison officer was to come to my headquarters unless I invited him and he was not to offer his opinion on any subject unless I solicited it. I found out later that uncertainty about the role of the liaison officers was one of the problems that had been unsettling the command structure of the First

Armored. Both the British and French liaison officers were of the opinion that their responsibility was not limited to keeping their respective armies informed and that they had a real part to play in the division's operations. I put an end to that misapprehension.

Lieutenant Colonel Howze, the bona fide operations officer, then was given the floor and he briefed me skillfully on the situation. After he explained the daily pattern that had been so unsettling to Patton—defend and give ground in the morning, counterattack and win it back in the afternoon—I set a new strategy.

"What's been going on apparently bothers the people down there at Gafsa, so we will do just the opposite. From now on I want us to make a limited attack every morning, from five hundred to one thousand yards. If we meet the Germans on the way up, we'll fight it out. And we will inform the Corps each morning that we are attacking."

We put this policy into effect the next morning, and Patton soon reacted.

"What in hell are you doing out there?" he roared at me over the telephone.

"Nothing," I replied innocently. "We are just attacking here."

"I told you to stay on defense," he shouted.

"You didn't tell me a damned thing. You just told me to get the hell out," I said. Then I explained that the attacks were limited, designed simply to keep the Germans off balance. Patton approved the new tactic and hung up.

While Patton's relentless, driving determination to maintain constant pressure on the enemy was a powerful restorative to sagging American morale, it sometimes led him to wreak cruel and unjustified vengeance on his subordinates. I saw an illustration of this not long after I took command of the First Armored.

The Germans were falling back northward and events returned the First Armored to the vicinity of Faïd Pass, where

125

the division had suffered brutally two months earlier in the preliminary encounters that preceded the battle of Kasserine Pass. Patton issued orders to me to send a combat brigade through Aïn Rebaou Pass, and I picked the First Armored's Combat Command A, led by Brigadier General Raymond E. McQuillan, to carry out the mission.

McQuillan's advance was a little slow, but with good reason. The retreating enemy had sown the pass heavily not only with antivehicle mines but also with antipersonnel mines designed to blow off the legs of any man who stepped on one. Patton had come up in his scout car to watch the operation, and was outraged by the Combat Command's cautious pace. Brushing aside my explanations that the caution was justified, he relieved McQuillan on the spot and ordered him to the rear. I felt General McQuillan was a good soldier who was giving me excellent cooperation.

The movement through the pass brought the First Armored to the painfully remembered battlefield in front of Lessouda mountain. The plain was littered with the hulks of division tanks destroyed the preceding February when the Germans had come roaring through the pass; it was a desolate scene.

In the days since I had taken command of the division I had heard repeated references to the terrible beating it had taken at Lessouda. Since we were to remain in the area for a day or so, it seemed to me a good opportunity to urge my men to get this memory out of their systems. There is a real danger in war that a unit's confidence in itself, and thus its combat-worthiness, will be permanently impaired by recollection of a serious defeat.

I called a meeting of all the division's officers at 8 P.M. I believe in promptness. When the appointed time arrived and I discovered that about seventy-five officers were still not present, I told Colonel Dewey to take down the names of all the latecomers. These men would each be fined fifty dollars under the 104th Article of War, I advised my audience. The murmur from in front of me made it obvious this ruling was

126

not going to make me very popular in the short run. (And in retrospect I now think my severity was a mistake—a firm warning would have sufficed.)

Then we got to the main business of the evening. I shared with the officers a piece of information about the division that General Eisenhower had provided me: the British First Army carried the First Armored on its books as "noncombat worthy."

"I just don't believe that," I said. "I am confident that the 15,000 officers and men of this division are as good a cross section of fighting men as there is in the Army. I don't want to hear any more talk of the defeat at Lessouda. This battlefield no longer is going to be the graveyard of the First Armored; it's going to be the symbol of its resurrection."

The withdrawal of the enemy into northern Tunisia steadily reduced the size of the sector assigned to the II Corps. The presence of the British First Army on our left flank prevented us from shifting any significant distance to the north, and the advance of General Montgomery's British Eighth Army along the coast to the east of us each day further diminished the Corps' opportunities for combat.

Fortunately, General Eisenhower and other Americans in the Supreme Allied Command had insisted that the II Corps, the major U.S. force in the Tunisian theater, be assigned a major mission in the final mop-up of Axis forces in Tunisia. These strategists pointed out that Americans needed extensive combat experience not only to raise their morale but also to gain experience that would subsequently be of enormous value in training the only great body of Allied reserve troops, the force that was being organized in 1943 in the United States.

General Sir Harold R. L. G. Alexander, commander of the 18th Army Group, to which the II Corps reported, drafted a plan under which the Corps would be moved 150 miles north to the Mediterranean Coast and assigned the ultimate task of taking Bizerte, Tunisia's second largest city. The British were not enthusiastic about this plan. In one of his final acts as commander of the II Corps, Patton successfully beat down a British-inspired scheme to put the II Corps back once again under the command of the British First Army, led by General Anderson. I doubt that Ike ever understood the overwhelming unpopularity of that dour Scot with most Americans. Eisenhower concedes in his memoirs that Anderson "was blunt, at times to the point of rudeness," but then adds curiously that this trait was more annoying to other British officers than to Americans.

I did not share this view, and I cannot agree with Eisenhower that credit must be assigned to Anderson for "the smashing victory . . . finally attained in Tunisia." If such credit is to be assigned to anyone in particular, it should go to Alexander, not Anderson. The fact of the matter is that Anderson was a disagreeable man disliked by practically everyone.

The final Tunisian assignment of the II Corps was decided on April 14 in Haidra at a meeting attended by Eisenhower, Alexander, Anderson, Patton, and Patton's Deputy Corps Commander, Major General Omar N. Bradley. The Americans prevailed. II Corps was to move north.

Although tales of moving large numbers of men long distances are difficult to vest with the glamor that surrounds accounts of battle, the transfer of the II Corps was a feat worthy of note. Patton was succeeded as Corps Commander by Bradley on April 15, with Patton returning to Algiers to begin the job of planning the invasion of Sicily. Consequently it was Bradley who saw to moving 90,000 men along the two highways that ran from Tebéssa north to the Mediterranean. To add to the difficulties of the move, these roads crossed the two highways and the two railways used to carry supplies from Algeria to the Allied forces at the northern front. Meticulously careful timing of the operation was essential, so that the northbound troops could be alternated with the east-west supply traffic. About half of the First Armored (Combat Command A was left behind to come north by the other route) set out under my command on April 19. We were under orders to follow the British First Armoured Division and the King's Dragoon Guards on the road. We caught up with the tail end of the British column at that certain hour in the British afternoon; there stopped dead in the middle of the road they sat—drinking tea. Later I complained to Bradley about this incident, protesting that in wartime people shouldn't be creating mammoth traffic jams by taking time out to drink tea.

With a ghost of a smile, Bradley replied, "Harmon, instead of being so impatient, you should have gone forward and drunk some tea with them."

On April 22 the First Armored (minus Combat Command A and some other detached units) reached its preliminary destination, an area eight miles northwest of the village of Béja. The countryside in that part of Tunisia is rough terrain, peppered with sharp sandy hills, and is not well-suited to tanks. As a result I had an immediate struggle on my hands to hold the division together against those officials in the high command who deemed it most logical and efficient to attach the division's infantry regiment to the First Infantry Division and its artillery to still another division.

The British, in fact, had sought to limit the First Armored's strength in northern Tunisia to a single combat command. But a combat command is a flexible force. By finagling and ingenuity, I had managed to bring north in the initial column the entire division except one tank regiment and a battalion of infantry. Now I had to get my division into combat as a unit.

I argued this out with General Bradley and finally convinced him that the First Armored should be assigned a small sector of its own somewhere along the II Corps' 35-mile-long front. We would cover this sector with our infantry regiment, I said, supporting it with our artillery and such tanks as could be worked into the scheme. Then when the front had been pushed far enough east for the Allies to occupy the line of hills that overlooked Mateur, the First Armored could rush its armor through the gaps and make a quick dash to capture Mateur, a major town fifteen miles along the way to Bizerte.

Bradley liked the scheme and on April 26, after several days in reserve and three days after the opening of the campaign, the First Armored took its place in the line. To our right were the forces of the British Fifth Corps, to our left the First Infantry Division. Directly in front of us was a nasty range of hills, thoroughly infested by Germans. Slightly to our left was a fairly level valley that was quickly dubbed "The Mousetrap." The Mousetrap, which was the alluvial plain of the upper reaches of the River Tine, might have been good tank country were it not for the surrounding hills. As it was, neither Americans nor Germans could linger in the Mousetrap by daylight, though our patrols sometimes clashed there by night.

Shortly after the First Armored assumed its position in the line I had a visit from General Anderson, who as head of the British First Army was in effect our commander. (Technically, Bradley reported directly to General Alexander's 18th Army Group, but Anderson was authorized to issue the orders necessary to coordinate the II Corps' operations with those of the First Army.) I was at work in my tent when Anderson arrived, in the midst of a pouring rain. He looked me over in a rather supercilious manner and inquired what I planned to do with an armored division in that terrain. Pointing out the positions on the map, I explained the plan Bradley and I had worked out for the armored rush on Mateur.

Anderson waved his swagger stick vaguely and commented, "Just a childish fancy, just a childish fancy." With that he stalked out of the tent. I may have made some noncommittal response, but I confess that under my breath I muttered to myself, I'll make that son of a bitch eat those words.

My understanding with Bradley was that I could have my tanks ready to roll on Mateur on an hour's notice, but we had a wait of several days before the situation was ripe. These were days of brutally heavy fighting for the First and 34th Infantry Divisions to our left, who had the mission of taking the hills that overlooked the Mousetrap.

130

During this period one of my light tanks, on night reconnaissance in the Mousetrap, ran over a mine that blew its track off. The tank had some special range-finding equipment that I hated to lose. The next night I ordered a wrecker in to drag out the disabled tank. The men ran into a German patrol and were driven off after two or three of them were wounded. I asked for another attempt at salvaging the disabled tank the third night. The salvagers again ran into the enemy and one of our men had a testicle shot away. When word of this was brought to me, I said, "The hell with it, leave the tank out there. There isn't any tank in the Army that's worth a man's testicle." The word spread through the division like wildfire that the old man wasn't going to waste any of his men just to get a piece of iron out of the muck.

When the signal to unleash the First Armored's tanks finally came on May 3, the fall of the town of Mateur itself was almost anticlimax. The Axis, badly mauled and desperately short on supplies, withdrew with great speed from their strongpoints in the hills and hastened through Mateur to form new defensive points around Ferryville and in the hills south of the Lac de Bizerte. I had assigned the mission of taking Mateur to Combat Command B, under General Robinett. Colonel Dewey, my operations officer, and I rolled up in the tanks, leaving Colonel Rose, my chief of staff, with the main body of the division. We made it into town in an hour; the enemy was blowing up the bridges east of town as we arrived from the south and west. But with the exception of a few Germans and Italians we took prisoner, most of the Axis forces got away.

Shortly after we got into town, I was informed that the Command's advance guard had stumbled upon a cellar full of wine and had all got drunk. I blew my top and ordered Dewey to send out a new advance guard to cover us, get the offenders' names and have them shot at once.

Around sundown I asked if my orders had been carried out. Colonel Dewey replied that the new guard was out on duty and added, "General, I think we ought to let the men live

131

until sunrise. It's customary to give them that long to say their prayers and so forth."

I agreed, but added firmly that I wanted them shot at sunrise without fail for abandoning their mission in the face of the enemy. In the morning I asked again whether the men had been shot, but by this time I had cooled off. When Dewey confessed my order still had not been carried out, I just said the hell with it. Colonel Dewey knew me and my temper pretty well.

One of my first orders after we arrived in Mateur was to instruct the 16th Armored Engineers to get busy and rebuild the bridges over the river east of town that had been systematically demolished by the departing Germans. By mid-evening, I am proud to relate, they opened three bridges over the Oued Djoumine, although they had been forced to work in the midst of almost constant artillery shelling. I issued orders to division forces the next day, May 4, to begin reconnoitering north and east of Mateur.

As I sat on a little hilltop outside Mateur studying the situation that day, a British brigadier, a liaison officer from the British First Army, came up and asked what I planned to do. I knew what he hoped to hear; there was strong sentiment among some of the planners to mount the second phase of the attack immediately, before the Germans had time to establish defensive positions in the heights on the routes to Bizerte.

I had a different point of view. I told the British officer I intended to bring up the remainder of the division during the night, devote May 5 to reconnaissance and the issuing of attack orders. Then at dawn May 6 we would launch a coordinated attack and pound through the hills to Bizerte. One strong conviction I reached as a commander was that military success is achieved most easily when all one's fighting forces—and by that I mean step by step down the command structure to companies and patrols—understand what the overall mission is and how they fit into it.

"You mean you are going to sit here for thirty-six hours and let the Germans get set in front of you?" the brigadier inquired in a horrified voice.

I explained carefully that the attack could not be mounted properly until my engineers, artillery and infantry had the opportunity to prepare for a coordinated operation, but he still was dissatisfied. Finally I said, "If you don't like it you can go back and report to the people in the rear, because I have made up my mind. If they don't like the plan, they can relieve me." With that the brigadier went away—to complain to Corps headquarters, I assume.

At any rate, a few hours later General Bradley came to the front to see how we were doing. He and I were just greeting each other when a shell exploded nearby and Bradley hurled himself to the ground in the approved basic training manner. We had been shelled off and on through the morning, and as a result I scarcely flinched; I told Bradley to get up and dust himself off, there was nothing to it. He got back to his feet, grinning a little sheepishly, and we began to discuss the situation.

I outlined the plan I had described earlier to the British brigadier, and he said, "That sounds good to me, Harmon. Whenever you're ready to attack is okay with me."

I knew then I had Bradley's confidence and would not be dumped because some British liaison officer didn't like or understand what I was trying to do.

During the day Combat Command A, still under the temporary command of Colonel Lambert, finally arrived. I also received word that the division would be reinforced by three thousand additional men—the 39th Infantry Regiment from the Ninth Infantry Division, and a battery of 155 Long Tom Artillery. Late in the afternoon I called the key officers together and we went over the battle plan. Combat Command A would strike at the highest peaks on our left flank; Combat Command B, which was short of infantry, would move around the right flank on somewhat more level ground. The infantry reinforcements (expected the following afternoon) would be dispatched up the road to Ferryville on our left. Once we pushed beyond the formidable mass of hills in front of us, I knew we would have the Germans pinned on the flat plain of a peninsula surrounded by ocean on three sides; from there there could be no escape.

On the way back to his command post after the briefing, General Robinett was hit by a shell and badly wounded in the foot. I went to see him and knew at a glance that his combat days were over for the duration. I wished him the best of luck and placed Colonel Clarence C. Benson, a cavalryman I had known many years, in charge of Combat Command B.

At dawn May 6 the attack began, the first time in the African campaign the First Armored Division had been joined together and able to fight as a unit. From my command post I watched the battle unfold. At 10 A.M. I could see twenty-three of Combat Command B's tanks burning on the hillside; they were making little or no progress on the right flank. About noon Combat Command A forces had reached the hilltop and were on their objective. But there was still no sign of progress toward a small ridge on the right, the objective of Combat Command B. I called in Colonel Benson and Colonel Howze, who was now executive officer of the Command, and asked what the trouble was.

Benson said the men were worn out.

"They can't be worn out," I said. "They've only been fighting two or three hours. *You* must be worn out—you are relieved from command, go back and sleep in the tent there."

I then turned to Howze and asked him to explain the problem.

"The battle wasn't laid on right," he said, an observation that took considerable courage to make to the commander who had done the laying-on. I asked him to explain.

"There are some German antitank guns across the river at that point," he said, gesturing toward the location. "They weren't there when the battle began, but they have been moved in, and every time we go around the corner of the objective they open up on us. They will have to be smothered with artillery before we can move."

I immediately told him to stop the attack and be prepared to renew it at 5 P.M. after I had put extra artillery fire on the antitank gun emplacement. "You are in command of Combat Command B since it is clear you know how to fight this battle," I told him. "At five o'clock I want you to go around that corner and come up over the ridge in front of us or else don't come back at all."

At five o'clock, in the fading day, I watched as the Command's tanks moved around the corner out of sight. I waited anxiously. And then, to my intense gratification, our armor came rolling up over the crest of the ridge. We had gained the whole objective. I called General Bradley, happily told him we had successfully completed our first-day plan and would ready ourselves to open the second phase of the attack at daybreak. This was to be a double-pronged envelopment which was scheduled to circle the base of the next and final range of hills, as a bracelet or handcuffs circle a wrist. Combat Command A, supported by the 39th Infantry Regiment, would move on the left toward Ferryville and Bizerte, while Combat Command B, reinforced by most of the First Armored Regiment, would press round the right toward the sea.

But warfare is seldom as neatly packaged as all that. About 6 P.M. Colonel Robert I. Stack, the senior officer on the left flank, telephoned to say that German Tiger tanks had crept up the far side of the hill and driven our forces off the crest triumphantly won at noon. Complaints began to come in from Combat Command B that their men were being fired upon from heights they supposed were under the control of Combat Command A.

I went out to talk over the situation with Stack. He told me he thought he might be able to recapture the summit if he could get a few tanks up the steep slope on our side of the hill. I told him that he must win back the lost objective by daylight because I couldn't allow the next day's plan of action to be interfered with. They fought through the night. About 3 A.M. I received the call I was waiting for: the summit was ours again.

The news was quite a relief to me for I had fudged a bit in my communications with II Corps headquarters; I hadn't notified Bradley that we had been driven off our objective. Shortly after dawn I was able to call the Corps commander and announce that the second phase of the attack was under way. He asked how the night had gone and, mentally crossing my fingers, I replied, "We had a very pleasant, quiet night, sir. Everything is on the ball." I believe he found out later that we had one hell of a night, but he never spoke of it.

That day and the next were days of heavy fighting, but we steadily tightened our armored noose round the penned-in Axis forces. Forces of Combat Command A occupied Ferry-ville on May 7 and the following day two task forces of the Command began the sweep round the southern and eastern shores of Lac de Bizerte toward the sea. On May 8 Colonel Benson, now returned to command of Combat Command B, assigned a task force under the command of Colonel Howze the mission of severing the Bizerte-Tunis highway. Howze was confronted by two alternative routes; he could take a pathway along the edge of the Garaet el Mabtouh, a swampy flatland west of Protville, or risk a steep climb over a mass of hills five miles to the north. Howze, tempted by the alluring prospect of catching the enemy by surprise, chose the tricky and hazard-ous northern route.

It paid off. Toward the end of the day Howze and his forty tanks reached the final slope that descended to the highway. Though they were greeted by a barrage of German 88-mm shells, it was clear the enemy was confused and shaken by the appearance of Allied forces from such an unexpected quarter. The heights overlooked a major fork in the highway, where a side road veered off to Porto Farina and a German airfield. Throughout the night Colonel Howze, waiting for daylight to make his final advance, watched hundreds of enemy vehicles blaze on the plain while tracer bullets, prodigally expended

136

before the imminent collapse, laced the sky like streaks of summer lightning.

It was obvious to us at headquarters that the end was near. Early in the morning of May 9, accompanied by my aide, I set out in a jeep to see how our forces were doing. First I checked on the left flank where, standing on the crest of a hill, I saw our tanks drive into Bizerte. Then I moved round in the jeep to check on the right flank, a journey of some twenty miles. As I neared the front on the right, I came upon a cluster of tanks parked by the side of the road, firing bravely but not moving forward. There was fairly severe machine gun fire, but I got out and managed to pick my way to the tank commander; he told me his tanks were being held up by heavy machine gun and tank fire.

"All right," I said, "you follow my jeep forward," and I climbed back in the vehicle. This was sufficiently embarrassing to stir the young commander into action; the tanks began to move up. I continued on toward the south. I had been told that the road my aide and I were traversing was entirely under our control, but the information, as sometimes happens, was not quite correct. We drove over a little rise and suddenly found ourselves in the midst of a company of German soldiers, who were huddled in a cut by the side of the road attempting to shield themselves from American artillery fire. Directly overhead I could see the artillery liaison plane that was directing the fire. My aide and I hastily joined the Germans in the cut, hugging the dirt along with them.

Now I've really put my foot into it, I said to myself—a division commander captured by the enemy. I reviewed the circumstances and my situation with great rapidity. Then I began to yell for the *Hauptmann* (the German captain). When he crawled to my side, I said to him, "I must go back and have this artillery fire lifted and arrange for your surrender. Come with me."

And by golly he did. He and I ducked into the jeep, in the midst of the shelling, and drove back up the road. Within a

137

mile or so we came upon the forward observer for the artillery, where I ordered the shelling to be lifted and members of our infantry to proceed and take the German company prisoners. It was a close call.

I got back to my command post about 9 A.M. Immediately upon my arrival Colonel Rose, my chief of staff, advised me that three German officers had just come in under a flag of truce, inquiring the terms of surrender. All I could think of was what General Grant, my great Civil War hero, had said to the Confederates in front of Fort Donelson—"Unconditional surrender; we propose to move immediately upon your works."

There were no terms of surrender except unconditional surrender, I told the emissaries. I said they could have until ten o'clock to make up their minds; if they hadn't surrendered by eleven, I added, I intended to move the attack forward and drive them into the sea. The senior officer then asked if I would send one of my staff officers back with the group to report the terms to the German commander. I gave the task to Colonel Rose (a chore I don't think he much appreciated), and shortly Rose and the three Germans, now blindfolded, rolled off in a command car toward the enemy lines. I telephoned the news to General Bradley. He said the terms I had outlined were fine and asked me how many prisoners were likely to be involved.

"I haven't any idea," I replied, "probably three or four thousand."

Soon Colonel Rose's voice came in over the radio. The Germans accepted the terms and wished the firing to cease at once.

"How about those bastards on the left?" I shot back over the airwaves. The inquiry about surrender terms had originated with the enemy forces on our right flank; those on the left, toward Bizerte, were still fighting. I think Colonel Rose may have been somewhat taken aback at my phrasing of the question; at the moment I spoke he and the German commanders were in the midst of sealing the agreement over a bottle of champagne.

But he was soon back on the air with word that the left flank commander also accepted the terms. I ordered the cease-fire and the battle ended. The job of collecting the prisoners began. Soon I called General Bradley with a conservative estimate that we had taken at least twenty thousand prisoners. As the day wore on, the count continued to rise. Eventually we discovered we had bagged nearly forty thousand men—including six generals.

Our prisoners were neatly penned up by the local geography—the surrounding sea formed three walls of the pen and on the fourth side the guns of our tanks were pointed directly at them. Nonetheless, this suddenly acquired responsibility for such an enormous mass of men put a considerable strain on our resources. The enemy had exhausted his supplies of virtually everything, a major factor in the collapse of Axis resistance. (We learned later that Generaloberst von Arnim, the top Axis commander, and his staff of Army Group Africa were able to fuel their final retreat before the surrender only because a stray barrel of gasoline had drifted ashore near their headquarters.) Water and food were needed everywhere.

We managed this mass of prisoners by ordering them to manage themselves. Each unit was instructed to return to its camp; there the troops stacked their arms. Fortunately, the fight had gone out of most of them and they appeared relieved that for them the war was over. We trucked in rations, then tackled the logistics of moving the forty thousand to a temporary prison camp near Béja. From there they were marched westward across Africa and ultimately were shipped to POW camps in the United States.

That afternoon General Bradley, trailed by a number of war correspondents, arrived at what had recently been the front to inspect the scene of our triumph. I had stationed our covey of German generals on a little rise not far from my tent while we decided what to do with them. One of the correspondents asked permission to photograph me with the generals and I sent a sergeant to fetch them. All of them came quite willingly, except for a nasty little chap named General Willibald Borowietz. When the sergeant told me Borowietz had refused, I told him to go right back and bring him over dead or alive, I didn't give a damn which. I don't know what the sergeant said to him, but General Borowietz attended the picture-taking. I had another run-in with Borowietz later in the day. He had driven in to surrender in a little blue Opel. When we made ready to ship the prisoners, I told Captain Rooney that he and I would take charge of the Opel. General Borowietz protested noisily about riding in a truck with his troops, but I sent word that my decision was final. I told the guard to feel free to help him into the truck with a bayonet if necessary. That was the last I saw of General Borowietz.

I had a curiously prophetic conversation with one of the other German generals we had captured, an officer who had an American wife and spoke excellent English. After chatting a bit about inconsequential matters, he observed that it was a shame that Americans and Germans were fighting against each other instead of fighting together against the Russians.

"Later on you Americans will probably have to fight the Russians all by yourselves," he said.

Although the general was no doubt echoing the line being pushed then by Goebbels' German propaganda agency, I reflected on it from time to time in later years during our stickier Cold War moments with the Russians. But there in North Africa, fresh from a battle with the officer and his associates, I made what I am sure was the right remark for the moment.

"As far as I'm concerned," I said, "the last German can kill the last Russian. We'll take care of disposing of the survivor."

I confess I felt a twinge of annoyance at the speed with which Bizerte, which had been bought with American blood, was turned over to British occupation. The Stars and Stripes came down and was replaced with the British Union Jack before our jeeps were even off the streets. But that was part of the plan worked out by the High Command and I daresay it was sound. The forces of II Corps, including the First Armored, were to relinquish their equipment to the British and march back to Morocco for reoutfitting and filling out of our ranks with replacements. There we were to train for the forthcoming invasion of Italy. Tunisia as a whole was to pass into the control of British occupation forces.

Before we left there was a great victory parade in Tunis. First the British marched smartly past and then the French, who I noticed had a far greater contingent of troops in the parade than their contribution to the campaign warranted. A battalion from the gallant U.S. 34th Infantry Division shuffled past like Arkansas backwoodsmen, but I saw no reason to fault them for their lack of marching precision. They proved their valor in the bitter battle for control of Hill 609, the victory that opened the possibility of the armored drive on Mateur and Bizerte. Then came a battalion of my tanks. They were battle-scarred and dirty, and I was very proud of them.

Throughout the day I grimly awaited the victory dinner for the senior officers; I knew I would encounter General Anderson there and I intended to seize the opportunity to remind him of his comment about my "childish fancy." Finally the time came to present myself at the palace where the dinner was to be held. As I climbed out of my jeep, General Anderson bounded down the steps toward me, smiling. He pumped my hand and said with tremendous enthusiasm, "Well, you did it, didn't you? Congratulations!" Feeling a little foolish, I lamely accepted his good words.

TEN

★ ★

The Invasion of Italy

THROUGHOUT MY MILITARY career, being a leader of men interested me more than the brass-hat politicking that carried some otherwise mediocre soldiers to the top ranks of the Army. Still, it is difficult for me not to be a little resentful of the turns of fate, and on one occasion the unfair treatment, that forever denied me the third star of a lieutenant general.

It was not long after the First Armored and I left Tunisia that a third star seemed most nearly within my grasp. I had gone for a short visit to General Patton, who had been named to lead the U.S. forces in the invasion of Sicily. Patton greeted me with the news that General George C. Marshall, who was in the area, was seriously considering assigning me to command of the II Corps to succeed General Bradley. Bradley was about to be transferred to England to work on preparations for the invasion of Normandy. I dined with Marshall that night and he questioned me closely about the Tunisian campaign. Later, when I went to bed, Patton told me I had made a favorable impression on Marshall. I badly wanted the assignment, which ethics had already once denied me at the time I recommended the relief of General Fredendall.

In the morning the chance for the II Corps command disintegrated right before my eyes. I had written a letter recommending promotion of Colonel Kent C. Lambert, com-

142

mander of the First Armored's Combat Command A, to brigadier general. As General Marshall was preparing to leave, I asked in all innocence whether he had received the letter and added a personal expression of hope that he would act favorably on the recommendation. What I did not know was that Lambert had blotted his War Department record before he joined the First Armored by sneaking an uncensored letter to his wife through the State Department pouch at Tangier; Lambert had never spoken of the matter to me.

In a flash Marshall turned on me and said harshly that I should know better than to recommend a man like Lambert for promotion. Such an action, he added, made it obvious that I wasn't fit for a high command. With that he strode out of the room and drove away. I heard no more about being put in command of the II Corps. Later that morning, though, I told Patton that if I had it to do over I would still act the same. Lambert was an able commander and he deserved promotion.

I went back to my First Division and resumed the preoccupations that dominated our concerns for many weeks that summer of 1943—training, training, training, until every man of the division understood what a tank would and would not do. I had been regarded with a certain suspicion by many in the division when I first took command, particularly as it became clear that I intended to demand taut and snappy performances by the divisional officers. The low point in my relations with the division, I suppose, was reached in Tunisia a few days after I took command, when I fined the officers late to the meeting at Lessouda Mountain. I began to hear grumbling that Ward's relief was unfair and that Harmon had no real hard battle experience. Both charges were probably true. Some of the suspicion of me was wiped away by our successes in the Bizerte campaign, but I think an incident that followed the achievement of the Tunisian victory was almost as important in building up rapport.

The first American unit to march west out of Tunisia, the First Infantry Division, was assigned a route along the popu-

143

lous Mediterranean coast. The word quickly returned to
Bizerte that the First Infantry had left a trail of drunkenness
and debauchery all along the way. When I checked on the
route the First Armored was to take to Morocco I was
informed that we had been assigned a route through the arid
interior that passed through few cities and consequently
offered little temptation.

I immediately appealed to General Bradley for reconsidera-
tion and offered my personal guarantee for the good behavior
of my men. I said I thought my men ought to have the cooler
route for the long march; also, they had earned the opportunity for a little fun. Bradley agreed to my request, but warned
I would lose the command if there were trouble. I assembled
the division in a natural amphitheater among the hills and
told them exactly what I had guaranteed Bradley.

"I am going on ahead to Morocco to arrange for your
arrival," I continued. "If you want to get rid of your new
commander, you know exactly how to do it." With that Major
Rooney and I climbed in the little blue Opel we had liberated
from General Borowietz and started for Morocco. The division's first convoy set out May 23, the last, six weeks later. The
division was granted generous liberty time in Algiers, but
there were no significant incidents there or elsewhere. General
Eisenhower later wrote me a nice letter complimenting me on
the First Armored's good behavior.

Life in Rabat was not as easygoing as it had been when I
was there earlier in the year. The city had acquired a Corps
commander with very strict notions of soldierly discipline;
among other things he had placed the Medina, the Arab
quarter, off limits. This created something of a problem for
those men of the division who had been looking forward for
some time to visiting the Medina's well-known bordellos. I
called the division together and told them the bad news.
Orders were orders, I said, and I warned them that anyone
caught entering the Medina would be fined fifty dollars. Some
of the soldiers became quite adept at cloaking themselves in

Arab burnooses and sneaking past the sentries posted at the gates to the Medina, but there was always a long line of glum-faced men at the summary courts martial. Occasionally I went out and sat under a tree to watch the proceedings. When I would ask a man whether the adventure was worth the penalty, he usually grinned sheepishly and replied he didn't know whether it was or not, but it was fun trying to get away with it.

Relations between the men of the First Armored and the Arab populace around Rabat were uneasy, and I found myself trying to smooth over some unpleasant incidents. Although the Second Armored's soldiers had generally gotten along easily with the local people, the men of the First Armored—influenced in part by British attitudes, I think—had developed a lively dislike for Arabs. Experiences in Tunisia, where some of the Arabs had collaborated with the Axis and where we had run into cases of Arabs coming on to the battlefield to rob the wounded and dead, probably contributed to the ill will.

In any event, I was glad when we got the word a few weeks later to move over to Oran to begin heavy training for the invasion of Italy. In Oran, the division had the first real training it had ever received; the officers and men used the period to acquire skills that served them well later in the war. I insisted that every tanker learn to shoot indirect fire, employing his tank gun like an artillery piece to fire at an unseen target with the assistance of a forward observer. I also insisted that every artillery gunner become proficient at direct fire at moving targets.

Battlefield experience in Tunisia taught me that at least one of the tactics of armored warfare laid out by the stateside theorists was worse than useless. Operators of tank destroyers—light armored vehicles equipped with 75-mm guns—had been taught to advance aggressively on enemy tanks and knock them out. Tank destroyer units valiantly attempted to carry out such missions until we learned the bitter lesson that the 75-mm gun was little better than a popgun against the hide of a German Tiger or Panther tank. Worse, against the high velocity 88-mm guns of the German tanks, the armored wall of a tank destroyer gave our boys about as much protection as a slab of butter. Many gallant men died while we learned that the proper weapon with which to kill a tank is another tank; then the so-called "tank destroyer" passed into unmourned oblivion.

Throughout the war we suffered from lack of gun power. The Grant tank, with which we started the war, was obsolete by the time we got it on the battlefield, and even our best tank, the Sherman, lacked the gun power and the armored protection of the German Tigers and Panthers, although I think it was mechanically superior. In the long run the measure tipped in our favor primarily because our supply of tanks so far outran that available to the Germans.

In Tunisia Allied forces were harried almost continually from the air—something I think American troops who came into the European theater later never quite realized. Those later warriors, who arrived after the Allies had acquired superiority in the air, could march to jumping-off points by day or night without difficulty. But in the early days we suffered many casualties from machine gun strafing from the air and from bombing; aerial opposition cramped our style of battle and limited our freedom of movement.

One morning at breakfast in Oran the division surgeon remarked to me that he was disturbed by the increasing number of men who were contracting venereal diseases. He recommended that we counter the problem by opening a divisional brothel. The surgeon acknowledged that it was an explicit violation of the rules of the North African theater for the military to maintain houses of prostitution, but he said his responsibilities as a physician impelled him to propose the step. I considered his suggestion and decided to go along with it, winking at the rules. I specified that the house must have daily medical inspections and be discreetly run.

146

THE INVASION OF ITALY

I took no further notice of the brothel until a member of my staff happened to tell me that one of the ladies of the house had previously been employed as an opera singer and still sang nightly. He urged me to come and meet her. I demurred. But various officers continued to talk about this woman's superb voice until curiosity got the better of me. I agreed to attend a performance if it could be arranged at a private dwelling away from the bordello.

It was a remarkable evening. The singer was about twenty-five, a woman with flaming red hair and the ample figure one associates with operatic divas. None of the four or five of us in her audience was expert on opera, but we thought of enough requests to keep her singing without accompaniment for an hour and a half. I recall I asked for selections from *Madame Butterfly* and *Carmen*.

Afterward the young woman told us she had sung in the Paris Opera before the war and had made her way to Algeria after the fall of France. She scraped a living in Algiers by singing on the radio until the Allies took over the country and shut down the radio stations. Then, with her occupation gone, she had turned to prostitution in order to eat.

I thought it was a shame any woman with such musical talent should be reduced to earning her keep by prostitution. Shortly thereafter the French police reopened Radio Algiers and we saw to it that she regained her old job singing on the radio. I have never heard from her since.

As August turned into September, I began to await with increasing eagerness word of the date for the invasion of Italy and the return of the First Armored to battle. The invasion of Sicily on July 10 had come too soon for us to be in on it. New equipment from the United States arrived with painful slowness; my former command, the Second Armored, which represented the American tank effort in Sicily, was outfitted in part with equipment we transferred to them. Other units with higher priorities also relieved us of equipment; in late July I was forced to warn my superiors that the division's ability to train for combat had become seriously impaired. But finally the supply lines were unclogged and the First Armored returned to combat readiness. When the Allies completed the capture of Sicily I knew Italy would come next, and the First Armored would play a part in the action.

A strong indication that the First Armored would begin the Italian campaign as a second-class participant emerged with the announcement of assignments for the beachhead landing at Salerno. The 27th Armored Field Artillery Battalion and elements of the 16th Armored Engineer Battalion, units of ours, were detached for service in the invasion, which began September 9; but the rest of us remained in Algeria, in reserve. I am proud to record that the 27th was credited with knocking out sixteen German tanks by direct fire on the desperate fourth day of the landing. In the wheat field outside Oran I had trained my artillery for just such an emergency as the battalion faced when the fierce German counterattack nearly split the Allied landing forces in two.

General Mark W. Clark, who headed the Salerno battle as commander of the Fifth Army, wrote in his memoirs that the 27th's Battery B along with the 158th and 189th Field Artillery Battalions were chiefly responsible for halting the Germans' seemingly inexorable advance. (Clark records that he was so short of reserve troops to fend off the counterattack that he was forced to man one high point with a hastily armed regimental band. He christened the previously unnamed hill "Piccolo Peak" because "there was nobody there but the musicians.")

Eventually, after the Fifth Army triumphantly entered Naples, orders came to bring up the rest of the First Armored. By this time the Italians had surrendered and withdrawn from the war, but the surrender appeared merely to have reinforced German determination to retain military control of Italy. We sent off an advanced party to make arrangements for our arrival—drawing supplies and clearing the way for the debarcation and bivouacking of our troops—and the following day,

September 1, the First Armored sailed out of Oran. In my first glimpse of the Bay of Naples, cluttered with partially sunken ships resembling the half submerged backs of sleeping alligators, and now converted by the engineers into wharves, I caught sight of Mount Vesuvius in the distance wreathed in steam and smoke. For a moment I felt like a tourist. As we entered the Bay I recall looking down into the dirty, busy waters and discovering with surprise that Italians rowed facing to the front of the boat. Theirs seemed a much more sensible system to me. The tourist impulse was with me only briefly. Our advanced party had failed to arrive; the ship that carried them was attacked en route by Axis planes and had limped into Malta. The First Armored scrambled ashore in Naples in considerable confusion.

I reported at once to General Clark's headquarters, which were in Caserta, about twenty miles north of Naples, on the grounds of a palace built by a one-time King of Naples. Colonel Dewey, who was now my chief of staff (Colonel Rose had transferred to the Third Armored), and his assistants had the unhappy task of organizing the unloading of the troops. We were assigned to a bivouac area just north of Capua to await developments. Our future role depended on how the initial phases of the Fifth Army campaign unfolded.

Anyone who spent the winter of 1943 in Italy can tell you that one three-letter word serves to summarize the experience of the Fifth Army's slogging northward drive toward Cassino: the word is "mud." For tanks, the terrain was impossible. Rain and snow were incessant. While I sweated out the action in reserve, once again elements of my division were borrowed as support forces for other fighting units. Finally in early December Major General Geoffrey Keyes, commander of the II Corps, assigned tanks to drive the enemy off Mount Lungo, a massive ridge overlooking the village of San Pietro. The mission was not a success. The tanks ran into mines and heavy antitank fire and suffered from poor traction on the narrow terraces of the mountainside. Worse, we had the hideous

149

experience of helplessly watching several tanks roll off the precipices. Ultimately less than a platoon of tanks closed with the enemy.

My frustration deepened when General Keyes directed the formation of Task Force Allen, a force assembled from the Sixth Armored Infantry Regiment and other components of the division and placed under the command of Brigadier General Frank A. Allen, Jr., commander of the division's Combat Command B. For me it seemed like a rerun of the organizational problems I had wrestled with in Tunisia. Allen arrived from the United States to take charge of the command while we were training in Algeria. I argued strongly against the creation of Task Force Allen, insisting that the force operate under the division commander, but I was unable to dissuade General Keyes from his decision.

I had as little faith in the design of that operation as I did in its commander. The objective was Mount Porchia, the next to last of the range of hills that blocked the Fifth Army from the Rapido River, a major objective. Someone (I don't know whether it was Keyes or Allen) decided the attack should be made without artillery preparation in order to "surprise" the Germans. I was confident, and events proved me right, that chances were slight of surprising an enemy in control of the heights and on constant alert for Allied advance movements.

Even though I was not in command, I went forward with my troops as H-hour approached, 7:30 in the evening of January 4, 1944. I was not a happy man that night. I recall standing in a ditch about to drink a cup of coffee when the Sixth Armored Infantry Regiment, which was marching past, halted momentarily. I handed my coffee to the soldier who stopped abreast of me, but the march was resumed before he could finish the coffee and hand back the cup. One day in Cincinnati after the war, at a reunion of the First Armored, a man came hurrying up to me in the hotel lobby and enthusiastically shook my hand. "I've been waiting a long time," he said, "to thank you personally for that cup of coffee."

150

To reach the line of assault on the hill, the two attacking forces, the First and Second Battalions of the Sixth Armored Infantry had to cross two miles of flat, open land veined thickly with the many zigzag tributaries of the Garigliano River and heavily mined by the enemy. The Second Battalion, commanded by Lieutenant Colonel Elton W. Ringsak, moved briskly out to the first phase line, but the First Battalion, on its right, was slowed by enfilading fire from machine guns emplaced on two little knolls halfway across the valley. Through a mixup, an attack on the left by the British 138th Infantry Brigade, planned to be simultaneous with ours, never began at all.

The German artillery was thus able to turn its undivided attention on the Second Battalion, which waited nakedly in the night at the first phase line. An overwhelming volume of deadly accurate fire poured down on the unprotected men and scores fell, wounded or dead. Among those who lost their lives was Chaplain Arthur C. Lenaghan, the regiment's Catholic chaplain, who went out repeatedly with the medic teams to comfort the wounded and dying until he too fell, fatally wounded.

There were two days of bitter fighting before twenty-two soldiers—two officers and twenty men—of the Second Battalion reached the crest of the north end of Mount Porchia. A fierce counterattack by three companies of the Germans' Hermann Göring Division drove the twenty-two off the crest at nightfall on January 7. On January 8 the regiment's shrunken numbers were augmented by troops from the 48th Engineer Combat Battalion, who had been seeking under fire to repair the nearby railroad; at 3 A.M. that day the First Battalion of the regiment reported that the crest had been regained. The regiment attained its objective, but the cost was painfully high. Final casualty figures showed the Sixth Armored Infantry lost seven officers and 106 enlisted men killed or dead of wounds, 328 wounded and evacuated (including the valiant Colonel Ringsak), and 71 missing in action.

Three years later, when the war was over and I was commander of the Constabulary in Germany, I noticed during an inspection a soldier whose insignia indicated service in the Sixth Armored Infantry. I asked what battalion he had served in and he replied, "The Second Battalion, sir."

"Are you lying to me or were you one of the twenty-two?" I asked.

Tears sprang into his eyes as he said that he was indeed one of those who made it to the crest of Mount Porchia. I felt a little dew in my own eyes and I moved on quickly. To retain my composure I bawled out the next man in line.

A short time after the Task Force Allen debacle General Clark called me in and told me General Bradley had written him to ask that I be released from the First Armored. Bradley wanted me in England to take command of a new corps then being organized. (Bradley left the Mediterranean theater at the end of the campaign in Sicily to work on OVERLORD, the code name of the plan for the invasion of Normandy.)

"Did you have anything to do with this request?" Clark inquired sharply.

I told him quite honestly that I had not, although the request was not entirely a surprise to me. General Bradley had told me previously that he might seek my reassignment if the need for my abilities arose.

Clark slapped the letter down on his desk and said emphatically that I would remain right there in Italy. "I need an experienced armored commander and you're him," he said.

My thoughts fastened briefly on who it was who hadn't been allowed to command the assault on Mount Porchia and then flitted to my chances at the third star of a lieutenant general, once again flown away. But I am a soldier. I kept my mouth shut.

The capture of Mount Porchia and its sister peak, Mount Trocchio, brought the forces of the II Corps to the banks of the fast-flowing Rapido River. Beyond the river lay the village of Cassino, the entrance to the Liri valley and the road to Rome. Beyond the river's western banks lay also the enemy strongpoints the Germans called the Gustav Line; this defense line was skillfully dug into the range of towering hills that swept north from the Tyrrhenian Sea into central Italy, broken only by the entrance to the Liri valley. The terrain where the Gustav Line was built had been used for many years by the Italian War College as an example of an area defensible against almost any type of attack.

At a conference of his senior commanders held immediately after the securing of Mount Trocchio on January 15, General Clark outlined his plans for the next phase of the Fifth Army's northward drive. He proposed an immediate thrust across the Rapido by an infantry division. When a beachhead was secured on the west bank of the river, he said, the First Armored Division would pour across the Rapido and pound up Route 6 in the Liri valley toward Rome, ninety miles away.

The plan was promptly rejected by every other commander at the meeting. With unaccustomed unanimity, we all pointed out that such a tactic was impossible because the enemy controlled both of the ridges overlooking the valley. At least one of the ridges, we said, must be in Allied hands before there could be any reasonable hope of success. Clark overruled us. The 36th Infantry Division would cross the Rapido and establish a beachhead, he announced; then the First Armored would throw a bridge across the river and bring up its tanks.

What none of us at the meeting knew, but what Clark revealed in his memoirs, was that he was under intense pressure from the British—not only from General Alexander, his immediate superior, but from Prime Minister Churchill too—to intensify efforts to capture Rome as soon as possible. Churchill and his adherents were convinced that German morale would be dealt a severe blow with the fall of Rome into Allied hands. But it was obvious, judging from the slogging pace of the Allied drive up the Italian peninsula, that only a beachhead landing near Rome could speed up the

153

campaign. The place selected for the landing was a little seaside resort named Anzio.

The decision to bypass the Gustav Line by sea in turn raised other problems that someone like myself in a divisional command was only partly privy to. Of vital importance was a decision made by the logistical planners, who were charged with the responsibility of shuttling around scarce military equipment. They determined that the landing craft essential for the establishment and maintenance of a beachhead at Anzio could be spared for only a limited time; then the equipment must be rushed to England for the invasion of Normandy. Clark felt, rightly or wrongly, that an immediate, vigorous assault on the Gustav Line would tie down German troops that otherwise would be available to beat off the scheduled invasion to the north.

Historians must decide whether these seemingly neatly interlocked decisions were correct in the circumstances. I will confess that I was greatly relieved when still another shift in plans withdrew me from playing any role in the crossing of the Rapido, which I was convinced from the start was doomed to fail. When the gallant 36th Infantry Division launched its calamitous three-day attempt to cross the Rapido, and suffered 1,681 casualties, I was back at our bivouac area in Capua, organizing my men to sail up the west coast of Italy to serve as reinforcement troops on the new Italian front at Anzio. Waiting for action in the armored thrust across the Rapido that never occurred was General Allen and the First Armored's Combat Command B.

154

ELEVEN
★★
Our Bitter Days at Anzio

SO LONG AS Americans read American history, and military buffs fan the breeze around the modern equivalent of the coal stove at the village store, there will be controversy over the battle of the Anzio Beachhead. Was it, strategically, a sound operation? Were the substantially heavy casualties justified? Should we have fought a war of attrition with German forces in Italy when our major forces were already assembling for a massive invasion of France via the English Channel?

I led the First Armored Division into Anzio on January 29, a week after the original and unopposed landing by the American Third Division, the British First Division and various other units. So hot was the fighting when we arrived that some of our tanks rolled off the LSTs and, once their waterproofing had been removed, rumbled straight up the Albano Road toward the enemy.

Whatever else may be said about Anzio, it was the scene of one of the most courageous and bloody dramas of World War II. Anyone who doubts the abilities of the American soldier as a fighting man—his courage, his stubbornness, his ingenuity—has only to read the Anzio record to be convinced that, when the pinch is on and he believes in the justice of his cause, he has no superiors anywhere.

The American soldier—such is our tradition—is trained to be

155

offense-minded. He is taught to attack; and then to attack again; in the African and European campaigns he was always pressing forward. But at Anzio, through a variety of circumstances, some of them unforeseen, he was compelled to fight a long, bitter, almost despairing defensive action for a period of many weeks. Outnumbered by the Germans, beleaguered by day and bombed by night, he beat off every attack of Hitler's finest troops. In this unfamiliar defensive fighting, so distasteful to his impatient temperament, he proved once and for all his tenacity and the true measure of his stature.

Some military masterminds, Jovelike in their detachment, have assessed Anzio as a "minor operation." Like the troops I commanded, I was a combat soldier and barely on speaking terms with global strategy; I went where I was ordered to go and fought as best I could when I got there. But it seems to me that the importance of Anzio can be assessed better if we consider not what we won when we won the beachhead, but what we would have lost if we had lost it. For one thing, we would have lost at least 50,000 troops and their equipment. We would have lost the magnificent artillery which made Anzio tenable. We would have lost something else for the time being at least—the upper hand in the war. If the Germans had driven us into the sea at Anzio—and they almost did—the strategic reactions might have been profound. The Germans needed a victory. One of the reasons for the desperate fighting in that flat, marshy, difficult plain circled by mountains was that Hitler personally ordered that the beachhead be regained, whatever the cost in men.

The cost in men has been assessed, and it was a high and tragic cost. From January 22 to May 22 the combat casualties of the Allied VI Corps numbered about 30,000, including at least 4,400 killed and 18,000 wounded in action. Of these totals, American units lost approximately 17,000 men, including at least 2,800 killed and 11,000 wounded in action. The Germans reported the capture of 6,800 Allied prisoners, including about 2,400 American troops. There were also the men never found—the missing. But there were other enemies

156

besides bullets; sickness in the swampland was responsible for some 37,000 noncombat casualties. Although many of these recovered and returned to the line, in crises their absence was felt.

German casualties cannot be determined so accurately as our own. Captured documents of the German 14th Army seem to indicate that their total casualties for the period were roughly the same as ours, although the number of troops killed in action was considerably higher.

The story of Anzio is not an easy story to tell. It was conceived as a short-time battle but it developed into a murderous siege and a prolonged campaign. Let us go back a moment to the war rooms where the plan was hatched.

The autumn of 1943 in Italy was a miserable experience not only for those who had to fight there, but also for those who had planned the Italian campaign. In September, when the Fifth Army landed at Salerno and the Eighth Army, led by General Sir Bernard Montgomery, stormed into Taranto, the Allied strategists were flushed with excessive optimism induced by the fall of Mussolini and the subsequent unconditional surrender of Italy. There was much brave September talk of "Rome by Christmas." As we sat soddenly in our encampments not very many miles north of Naples on Christmas day, facing near-impenetrable German defenses, it wasn't easy even to crack jokes about such foolishness.

As early as November these sadder, wiser strategists began to study the possibility of a landing on the seacoast behind the German troops—in football parlance, an end run. The projected enterprise was given the code name SHINGLE. First it was thought that SHINGLE could be mounted simultaneously with a successful breakthrough at the Gustav Line. Troops from the SHINGLE landing would meet up with other troops of the Fifth Army as they poured up the Liri valley; together the united force would march into Rome. The events of early December made it obvious that any speedy breakthrough at the Gustav Line was a pipe dream.

Members of the Allied High Command, including the

optimistic Prime Minister Churchill, met in Tunis at Christmas to study the situation. Churchill, those who were there report, clung tenaciously to his advocacy of a thrust at "the soft underbelly of Europe." How he or anyone else ever conceived of the harsh, forbidding Italian terrain as "soft" I find impossible to understand. When the Tunis meeting concluded Project SHINGLE and the drive on Rome remained on the drawing board; only now the operation rested on fresh, new and equally fallacious assumptions.

Our intelligence experts had decided the enemy had "no fresh reserves and very few tired ones." In other words, they believed the Germans lacked sufficient troops to fight on two fronts, and that a landing at Anzio would be such a threat to their rear that they would be compelled to weaken Gustav Line defenses to meet the new challenge. A thinning of forces at the Rapido might make an Allied breakthrough there possible.

I have no desire to be a Monday-morning quarterback, and I have been a soldier too long not to know that hindsight is, inevitably, more fully informed than foresight. Yet honesty, and the record itself, obliges me to report that top-level Intelligence—G-2, in Army jargon—was responsible in this instance for some inaccurate crystal gazing. One error was in predicting there would be active opposition to an Allied landing. There was almost none. The Germans were so thin, as a matter of fact, that in one area a single company guarded a nine-mile front. But above all, there was one major error which made Anzio an unexpected battle to the death.

Allied Intelligence assumed—on what evidence I do not know—that the Germans were so hard-pressed they would not be able to bring reinforcements to Anzio quickly. As I recall the figures, it was conjectured that the Germans could not assemble reinforcements of more than two divisions from Northern Italy until at least sixteen days after the Anzio landing.

We know now—from the study of captured enemy records—

that the Germans had anticipated an amphibious landing. Although they did not possess precise knowledge of the port to be attacked, they had a flexible and ambitious program to meet the threat wherever we landed.

As a result, our hopes of immediately relaxing the pressures on the Gustav Line could not be realized; few if any troops were withdrawn from the southern theater. Instead, fresh units were brought in from Northern Italy, from Yugoslavia, from France, from Germany itself. And, despite the blastings of our air attack, they were brought in quickly.

Before sunset on the pleasantly unopposed Allied D-day, the Germans had 20,000 troops in areas from which they could drive on our beachhead. Two days later, they had twice as many troops and outnumbered us. In a few days' time there were 70,000 German crack troops assembled for the purpose of containing our invasion. These statistics may provide an answer to the persistent people who maintain that the VI Corps, immediately after the Anzio landing, should have swept up through the mountain passes and on to Rome. To be sure, it could have been done, and, in staff meetings at Naples, I proposed it. I am glad now I was overruled. Armor could have been in the mountains by sunset and in Rome the next day, but the fast-assembling Germans would have sliced our supply lines and chewed us up at their leisure. The Allies would have had Rome for twenty-four hours. After that the Germans would have had us.

The Anzio operation, it should be realized, was by no means a landing in heavy force. As I have already indicated, the planners of the Anzio invasion were locked in competition for LSTs and other landing vehicles with the planners of the forthcoming assault across the English Channel on Normandy. The British and American navies at Anzio did a grand job in every sense of the word, but sea lift was so limited that only two divisions and various specialized units could be transported for the original landing. Two other divisions—the American 45th and my own First Armored—had to wait in

159

Naples until the minor armada of landing craft and Liberty ships could return for us.

By the time the First Armored got there, approximately a week after D-day, all hell had already broken loose, and this was to be Anzio's persistent climate for a good many weeks thereafter. The twin resort towns of Anzio and Nettuno, about thirty miles directly south of Rome, had been swank bathing spas during the Mussolini regime, and the pink-and-white villas and the pastel-tinted hotels were mighty pretty until bombing and artillery fire reduced them to rubble. Back of the beaches was an area of reclaimed land on which the Duce had established Italian peasants in neat two-story stone houses.

The limits of this narrow coastal plain were the limits of our beachhead. Southeast of Nettuno were the age-old Pontine Marshes bordered by the Mussolini Canal. Northwest toward the Tiber was a region of rolling and wooded farm country. To the north and northeast were the mountains.

Reared in Vermont—and appointed to West Point from there—I have always had a loyal allegiance to rocky cliffs and green mountains. At Anzio I learned to hate mountains. The Colli Laziali, better known to English-speakers as the Alban Hills, rose abruptly from the coastal plain some twenty miles inland; some of the peaks, which ringed the crater of an extinct volcano, reached altitudes of 3,100 feet. The Pope, in happier times, had a summer residence at Castelgandolfo in the Alban Hills overlooking Lake Albano, the beautiful blue crater lake. To the east were the Lepini Mountains, which also gave German artillery a perfect bead on our flat-land forces. I can subscribe to the sentiments of an Oklahoma sergeant who said to another commander, "General, with them Krauts lookin' down from the mountains, I feel just like bacteria in a bottle."

I had my first glimpse of the landscape that Caesar and Vergil knew on a deceptively bright morning. The naval convoy which had brought the First Armored from Naples lay anchored four or five miles at sea.

160

There were so many sunken craft in the shallow bay that only one LST could be unloaded at a time. So, packing a few possessions in a musette bag, I went ashore in a motorboat. An occasional high frothy splash in the bay reminded me that German artillery was greeting the morning too. A jeep met Colonel Dewey and me, and guides led us through the masonry-littered streets to VI Corps headquarters, then located in a three-story building right in the middle of the urban shooting gallery that was Nettuno. A few days later the headquarters was to go underground into a cavernous wine cellar.

Major General John P. Lucas, the commander, rose from a desk in his map-hung office, laid down his inevitable corncob pipe, and shook hands. There was the sound of firing in the distance.

"Glad to see you," he said briefly. "You're needed here."

This was the situation as Lucas described it to me: During the first two days after the initial landing, the Allies pushed seven miles inland, but since that time German resistance had stiffened tremendously and it was plain the enemy was preparing an all-out offensive. In view of the rapidly increasing enemy build-up, General Lucas intended to drive toward the volcanic hills of the Colli Laziali before Allied forces were too far outnumbered. H-hour was set for the next morning.

The object of the Allied offensive was to seize strong natural positions in order to handicap the Germans in launching their attack. The American Third Division, a dashing, battle-tested outfit, was to capture the inland town of Cisterna. The British First Division was to crank up the excellent blacktop Albano Road, seize the important highway and railroad junction at Campoleone, and push forward as far as possible. The battle plan called for the First Armored to support the British by swinging wide to the left of the Albano Road and then in again toward Campoleone with the idea of a partial encirclement.

Beginning at noon, the First Armored came ponderously

161

ashore and by early darkness most of my tanks were biv-ouacked in a stretch of timber known as the Padiglione Woods. Generals have their troubles, but they don't have to worry about housing. When I reached the Padiglione Woods, my command post was set up. The telephone switchboard was working; I had a "goose-egg" chart which told me where all units were located; and the remodeled ordnance-repair truck I used as an office and bedroom had been magically transported from ship to shore. These are the miracles in housekeeping an efficient staff can perform. Some 12,000 men and their ma-chines had been quartered.

I made only one change in the housekeeping arrangements. I noticed there was a British field artillery unit only about twenty-five yards away, and promptly ordered my truck moved out of the woods and into an open field. I had seen too much combat in Africa not to know that an artillery battery draws counterbattery fire from the enemy, and I had no intention of dying on my first night in Anzio. It was a tough enough night as it was, a typical Anzio night. There were German air raids, and the charivari of ammunition dumps—our ammunition dumps—going up like skyrockets and coming down like lethal hail. My dinner was C-ration warmed up on a single-burner gasoline stove. The night was cold, and my commanders and I welcomed the heat from the gasoline lanterns which lighted us at our paper work. We were to jump off in the morning in unknown terrain. No one slept much.

The miseries of the VI Corps began at once. Reconnaissance reports indicated that the Germans held only delaying posi-tions in front of Cisterna and Campoleone. These reports—like so much of our intelligence in that early period—were errone-ous. The enemy was there in wholly unexpected strength, and, in fact, was not preparing, but was prepared to attack. On the right Colonel Bill Darby's Rangers spearheaded the offensive against Cisterna under cover of darkness. At dawn on January 30, the First and Third Rangers found themselves within 800 yards of the town—and in a German ambush.

162

As the sun rose, they were greeted by concentrated machine gun and mortar fire. There had been no surprise, and they were surrounded. The Rangers fought all morning from the cover of drainage ditches. At noon German tanks appeared and swept the ditches with murderous enfilading fire. For a half hour the Rangers fought the tanks with bazookas and sticky grenades, and then everything was over. Of the 767 men in the Ranger attack, only six escaped death or capture. I do not understand to this day why all the First Armored strength was assigned to the British sector. As I told Colonel Darby subsequently, fifty of my tanks in daylight support of the Rangers would have made this sacrifice of crack troops unnecessary. We could have gone in and got 'em.

But First Armored had its own miseries. There was no time for reconnaissance or exploration. In the early light of that same morning, our Sherman tanks and light tanks and the Sixth Armored Infantry Regiment trundled out of the woods and swung around to the left of the British, who were fighting hotly—and desperately—far up the Albano Road. There was one thing definitely wrong with the battle plan: the Moletta River section where we were supposed to operate was completely impossible terrain for tanks. Presumably our operation had been planned after a study of aerial photographs of the region. Unhappily, what seemed on the aerial photographs to be a series of dimples or minor indentations turned out, when my tankers got there, to be gullies fifty feet deep. When tank commanders attempted to skirt the gullies, they found themselves bogged down in mud. Off the limited network of hard-surface roads in the beachhead, the January rains had made the area a gluey morass.

Back at my headquarters, the discouraging reports came in. I remember one incident in particular. Four tanks were stuck in the mud. I ordered an armored wrecker to pull them out. The wrecker was ambushed by the Germans. I sent four more tanks to rescue the wrecker. Then I sent more tanks after them. Apparently I could learn my first Anzio lesson only the

163

hard way—and the lesson, subsequently very important, was not to send good money after bad. Because I was stubborn, I lost twenty-four tanks while trying to succor four.

This fiasco brought me boiling up to the Moletta River section in a jeep, so I could see the terrain for myself. Erosion had made it difficult all right, but I thought that by seizing an abandoned railroad bed that snaked its way through the gullies in a diagonal direction, we might proceed on built-up ground toward our objective. All effort was now lent to this enterprise, but the Germans did not cooperate. They were there in force, and it soon became evident that our infantry, backed up by tank fire, would have to do the job. Careful plans were worked out for tank-infantry team play, and the infantry pushed forward through a storm of mortar and machine gun fire. But this courageous and determined effort was vitiated by the fact that, in mid-afternoon, Corps headquarters ordered me to detach a battalion of tanks and send them to support the British elsewhere.

A day in the Moletta gullies convinced me that tanks should not be there at all, and that night I got General Lucas' consent to a change in battle plan. The British had made a two-mile advance, but in some places their plight was desperate. Enemy tanks and self-propelled guns were causing heavy losses on the upper reaches of the Albano Road. I believed if my armor rolled up that excellent highway in full strength, we would not only hearten the British but perhaps, in maneuverable territory, have a chance of busting through.

Next morning we gave it a try. During this advance we almost rang the bell. Allied positions were pushed so far forward along a narrow corridor that the salient became known both to the enemy and to us as "The Thumb."

It was on the day of my armor's farthest advance that I had the privilege of relieving a group of British soldiers who had held a position under the most punishing circumstances. They belonged to the Sherwood Foresters. I think my great respect for the bravery and fighting ability of the British enlisted man was born that afternoon. The Foresters had driven through to a bluff where they overlooked the whole German position at Campoleone Station. But they could get no farther, and lay under mortar fire all day. It was the absolute front line; between them and the enemy lay a gully and a steep railroad embankment.

I came up in a tank—a jeep wouldn't have lived long there—to watch my tanks, spread wide on the level ground to the right and left, trade fire with the Germans. I decided I would plow up the steep slope where the Foresters were entrenched. My tank climbed the hill, and then I called a halt and got out to walk. There were dead bodies everywhere. I had never seen so many dead men in one place. They lay so close together that I had to step with care. I shouted for the commanding officer.

From a foxhole there arose a mud-covered corporal with a handlebar mustache. He was the highest-ranking officer still alive. He stood stiffly at attention.

"How is it going?" I asked. The answer was all around me.

"Well, sir," the corporal said, "there were a hundred and sixteen of us when we first came up, and there are sixteen of us left. We're ordered to hold out until sundown, and I think, with a little good fortune, we can manage to do so." We got the corporal and his fifteen gallant comrades safely out of there and back to join up with other British troops.

The allied offensive failed. For three days we battered our heads against strongly manned and well-prepared positions. The Third Division could not take Cisterna, and First Armored and the British could not thrust through on the Albano Road. On February 2, General Clark radioed General Lucas to prepare for defense, and the battle of the beachhead entered its second phase. By this time British losses were so heavy in the Thumb sector that the American 45th Division, under the quiet and imperturbable Major General W. W. Eagles, had been sent forward to share the job of holding Albano Road positions.

A rugged month was ahead. Everyone knew the Germans outnumbered us and planned to drive through to the sea. We all felt captured and caught in our narrow coastline area. The pattern was established early. The German 240-mm railroad guns—any railroad gun was "Anzio Annie" or the "Anzio Express" to the troops—began their heavyweight depredations. The German Air Force, quiescent so long, was now out in strength, and concentrating its efforts on our shipping.

After the failure of our offensive, General Lucas placed me in charge of the beachhead reserve. Detachments relieved from front-line duty for rest or refitting reverted automatically to my command, and, as a result, I came to be well acquainted with every outfit, British or American, that fought at Anzio. Because I had command of the fast-moving mobile units, I was also the official troubleshooter. At any hour of day or night, the corps commander called upon me to send my armor or my self-propelled artillery forward to back up the infantry in any or all sectors. Night after night, my tankers stood what we call half-hour alert at our bivouac in the Padiglione Woods. Half-hour alert means the tank must be full of ammunition and gasoline, the engines warmed up, and the crew not more than fifty feet away. And night after night the tanks clanked forward to repel a raid or to provide additional artillery fire.

None of us, from GI to major general, slept much, and my telephone switchboard—located in a hole in a hill and manned by tireless noncoms—buzzed ceaselessly. Visiting newspapermen called me the Fireman of Anzio, and I suppose their judgment was substantially accurate. When there were "fires," the First Armored was called to put them out.

There is always humor, even in desperate circumstances, to help a man stay on his rocker. My truck still sat out in the open field, but the earth beneath the truck's wheels had been scooped out to make my roof line lower. The gravity of the battle could be charted by the height of that roof line. Every day the wheels were dug in a little deeper, until finally only a

166

foot or two of the truck could be seen above ground—a prudent acknowledgement of the mathematical accuracy of German artillery fire.

The members of my staff were quartered around me, mostly in dugouts. Colonel Dewey slept in a steel half-track, almost buried in the ground at the foot of a giant tree. Much of the division headquarters work was done at night, and a field generator had been brought forward to provide electricity for approximately seventy-five outlets. After a few evenings I suddenly noticed that my lights were dim and steadily growing dimmer. I called in a soldier electrician. He made a tour of inquiry and came back to report "Nothing wrong, General"—the generator was going full blast.

At that very moment the lights drooped to a faded orange which made it impossible even to read a map in my truck. The electrician left in a hurry. Eventually he was able to solve the mystery. The solution, in daylight, seemed pretty funny, even to me. Ingenious soldiers had tapped in on the Old Man's wires, and their theft was so elaborate that 250 of them had the luxury of electricity in their underground warrens. I must add, in the interest of truth, that the next night they slept in darkness.

At Anzio there was no quarrel between forward and rear-echelon troops. Everyone was in the front line. In that pocket-handkerchief area, German artillery or German air could knock off service troops as easily as combat units. Shoulder insignia was no protection: General Penney, British commander, was sent home wounded, to be succeeded by Major General G. W. R. Templer. Staff officers of the VI Corps were killed as they climbed the steps from the wine-cellar headquarters at Nettuno. The tent cluster on the shore which served as our evacuation hospital—we removed the wounded to ships as quickly as possible—became known as Hell's Half Acre; it was subjected to bombing and shelling throughout the campaign. There was no place on the beachhead which was not a target. The hazard of Hell's Half Acre was so well

167

known that many of my combat troops concealed their wounds in the hope they would not be transported to that plague spot. They preferred to stay forward. When I was reproved by a superior for having my command post too near the lines, I replied, with complete frankness, that I felt safer there than I would have at the rear.

I am a product of the Regular Army and am not a sentimentalist. War is hard and I believe in hard, rigorous training. Disciplined, toughened, well-trained troops live the longest. But there was something about Anzio which touched even my reputedly granite heart. There were no malingerers there, no goldbricks. Stevedores, DUKW drivers, ammunition passers, ordnance men, medics, quartermaster troops—all were brothers. Engineers were shoved forward into the front line to fight as infantrymen. Ski troops fought in swamps. Cooks dropped their skillets and picked up their guns.

It is true that all of us were in the same boat: we were there to stay or die. But it is not true that such a situation always creates brotherhood. I have never seen anything like it in the two World Wars of my experience. There was at Anzio a confidence in unity, an unselfish willingness among troops to help one another, that I never saw again. I have sometimes thought that this was, in the end, the electric force which made victory possible.

The Germans shoved us steadily back. The Cisterna sector was relatively quiet—if you can make such distinctions about the difference between a violent storm and a tornado—but there was nothing except trouble on the Albano Road. Attack and counterattack centered around a cluster of three-story and four-story buildings at Aprilia, built as models for Fascist farm settlements. This development, located on a rise of ground, dominated the countryside like a feudal castle, although it was known to our troops by a more American analogy, "The Factory." Eventually it became a pile of rubble, but to many veterans wearing tweed suits today the mere mention of the Factory will bring back recollections which are closely akin to nightmare.

168

The British and the Americans tried repeatedly to recapture the Factory and failed. This meant that the Germans—with Cisterna on the east and the Factory on the west—now had their positions for a major attack. In military terms, this is called a line of departure. By February 12, the Germans had 120,000 troops in the area. The combat units were the finest in the Reich's army—I was not to see their equal later in Belgium or Holland or Germany. When the attack came, it was propelled by Hitler's personal order that the "abscess in Italy" must be removed.

General Clark—who commuted by PT boat between Naples and Anzio—sent us replacements and reinforcements, but the beachhead was so limited in size that, ironically enough, there came a time when there actually wasn't physical room for many more. Our advantage was in artillery and in air power. I remember one day when 731 bomber sorties were flown. The fighters were active, too, in support of the VI Corps. But there were, of course, many days of evil, closed-in weather, and some of them were crucial days, when we slogged on with no air support whatever.

The major German offensive began on February 16. German prisoners later told us that even soldiers sick with dysentery were routed out of their beds and thrown into the line. Both daylight and darkness were hideous. Enemy troops infiltrated behind our forward points a few hours after midnight, and attacked from two sides at dawn. Counterbattery fire was so heavy in the early morning that I still wake up at home, when a spring thunderstorm growls over Lake Champlain, to wonder what section of the beachhead will presently need tank support.

On the first day the enemy attacked everywhere and made only slight progress. Then the power play developed again on the bloodstained Albano Road. Steadily the Allied troops were driven back until we stood at the last defensible line—a point above Anzio where an east-west highway bridged the north-south highway. The British called this bridge the "Flyover," the Briticism for what Americans call an overpass. Once the Fly-over and its high embankments were lost, German progress to the sea could not be interrupted.

Not only our line troops but many of our officers were despondent, and, as I could readily see, at the point of crack-up. Evacuation of any considerable number of troops in case of defeat would be impossible. Fortunately, there were among my brother commanders some sturdy characters who realized that if we were near exhaustion, the Germans must be tuckered too.

The crisis came on February 18 and 19. On February 18 I was called to a noon conference at Nettuno. Generals Clark, Lucas, and Truscott, commander of the Third Division, were there. At that time I proposed that elements of the First Armored should attack the Germans in the flank along a diagonal road known to the soldiers as the "Bowling Alley." This intersected the Albano Road at a point considerably behind German front positions menacing the Fly-over. I proposed that we knife through the Germans and try to cut them off. The plan was approved and set for the next morning. As the tanks moved in, my own Sixth Armored Regiment was to be on one side of the Bowling Alley and the 30th Regiment of the Third Division on the other. All the VI Corps artillery, arrayed behind us, was to attempt to make life unlivable for the enemy in front of us.

It was an eventful afternoon and evening as we prepared for the all-important slugging match. After darkness fell, tanks began to move forward into position. Most of the infantry-men—each man carrying 120 rounds of ammunition and a gun—had to march five miles in ankle-deep mud to get to their jump-off positions.

I thought I would try to grab an hour or so of sleep. At 2 A.M. the corps commander's office telephoned. The Germans had already begun a tremendous offensive which threatened to break through at the Fly-over. It was suggested that perhaps our sortie should be called off and the armor pulled back to meet the advance head on. I disagreed emphatically, and got permission to proceed with the original plan.

Two hours later I received a message which was responsible for the toughest decision I ever had to make. My chief of artillery reported that a battalion of the 45th Division, for reasons unknown, was in front of what we called the "No Fire Line." In other words, if we laid down our barrage we would kill our own troops. There are times when the responsibilities of a military commander are, in the true meaning of the word, awful. This was one of them. To order the artillery attack might mean the death of many fine, brave American soldiers. To abandon the artillery attack would be to abandon the sortie upon which, I was convinced, the saving of the beachhead depended. The brutal, naked choice seemed to be between the loss of some hundreds of men and the loss of many thousands. Backed up by headquarters, I gave the order to fire.

Subsequently I was to learn that the "doomed battalion" was not a battalion, but a platoon, and that the platoon, fortunately, was not where, in the confusion of battlefield communication, we were told it was. This, however, does not change the reality of the decision I had to make.

Our counterattack on the morning of February 19 broke the back of the German advance. We jumped off at 6:30, and by 3:30 P.M. enemy troops were disorganized; an hour later our infantry had reached its objective. Unbeknownst to us, a fresh German division had been on its own way down the Bowling Alley to strike at our lines when the tremendous Allied barrage began. The German division had been destroyed; ruined vehicles and dead and wounded men littered the landscape. We took 1700 prisoners. Allied artillery, in addition to supporting our advance, had plastered German rear assembly points. Naval guns on ships at sea, antiaircraft guns and more than 200 medium bombers and fighter-bombers concentrated on the same ground with deadly effect. An escaped American prisoner told us that while being marched up the Albano Road he had seen enemy dead stacked up like cordwood in piles of 150 each. Bulldozers were digging mass graves.

171

By the evening we knew we had won our battle. What a difference a will to win can make! The day before, the enemy seemed to be infiltrating everywhere, Allied communications had broken down, whole companies and battalions were cut off. Now it was the Germans who were disorganized, disillusioned, and at the end of their offensive strength.

There was to be desperate fighting for another fortnight, but the frontal rush down the Albano Road was never seriously renewed after the Bowling Alley counterattack. We no longer needed to worry about being driven into the sea.

TWELVE
★ ★
Breakout at Anzio

AFTER THE INITIAL phase, Anzio became a siege which will, I think, go down on the record as one of the most famous sieges of all time. Three centuries ago there was a celebrated military engineer named Vauban who directed forty sieges. I'm satisfied to have had a share in only one.

There are classic patterns for defensive fighting which are taught in the textbooks at West Point, but, as an armored-force commander and a one-time cavalryman, I hadn't expected often to put them into practice. But when my division dug in, along with the rest of the Allied VI Corps, it became quickly evident that a lot of improvisation would be necessary. I should say at once that there never was a time when mobile units were not on call, but there were certainly times when fire power was more important than mobility. My tanks were lent to any unit in trouble, and some of them were immobilized for weeks at a time. By knocking out one wall of the stone houses Mussolini had built for his Fascist farmers, we turned them into satisfactory strongpoints. We ran our tanks inside and poked their guns out the gaping, paneless windows. The crews changed, but the tanks stayed in one place.

One instance of our improvisation has gone uncelebrated. This was at a period of crisis when the sea supply line broke down because of bad weather. There were only six rounds of

173

105-mm ammunition per artillery piece left on the beachhead. There were, however, 100,000 rounds of tank ammunition available. Ordinary range for the 75-mm guns on a Sherman tank is 11,000 yards. We sent soldiers to the woods to cut down trees, and the logs were shoved beneath the forward sections of the tanks. This raised the elevation of the guns and increased the range to 14,000 yards. During the period of emergency 250 Shermans—intended to be used as mobile weapons for offensive warfare—were propped up on stilts and successfully carried out their assignments in defensive firing.

The American artilleryman wrote a page in history at Anzio. His aim was deadly, thanks to skilled spotting by fighter planes and smaller aircraft. And American T.O.T. (Time on Target) fire was devastating. T.O.T. fire is a devilishly ingenious method of obliterating a selected area. Slow guns and fast guns and heavy long-distance guns are coordinated so that their packages of destruction all arrive at the same time. This means that whatever was there in the first place is, when the smoke rises, no longer there. At Anzio we could concentrate the fire of at least 270 guns at any objective on the beachhead. In some places this capability of concentrated fire rose to 400 guns, our entire complement of artillery. T.O.T. fire is a first cousin of a natural catastrophe, and it probably was the greatest single factor in breaking down the morale of confident and well-trained German troops.

One of the finest of artillerymen was my own Lieutenant Colonel John W. McPheeters, commander of the 91st Armored Field Artillery Battalion. McPheeters, a Hoosier from Indianapolis, had distinguished himself at Maknassy, in Africa, and was a very determined character. I remember that, before the Anzio invasion, his artillery was supporting the Fifth Army in front of Cassino. Unarmed, he climbed a hill to study the landscape for future artillery positions. A German sniper fired at him and missed. McPheeters was annoyed. He had no pistol, but he picked up a stone and heaved it with an Indiana boy's accuracy. The German sniper ran.

Official records show that McPheeters' battalion fired 8700

rounds in a single day at Anzio. I think that 5600 rounds in a day was the American record for a battalion in the Pacific. On that day, when going was tough for infantrymen, McPheeters fired so often that he almost melted his guns. Not too long after, he was conferring with another officer three miles north of Anzio on what we call a "fire mission"; they were charting their targets. A shell struck the tree under which they stood. McPheeters was killed and the other officer badly wounded.

McPheeters' troops loved him. They arranged the most impressive funeral I ever attended. The Anzio cemetery lay down by the seaside; indeed, most new recruits had to pass the expansive field of orderly wooden crosses when they first reported for duty. It was grim introduction to Anzio and I guess accurate enough. Most of McPheeters' men were still at the front, but they persuaded the Signal Corps into an unusual and elaborate use of battlefield communications. There was a loudspeaker at the graveside. When the time came to fire the farewell salute, the 91st Battalion piped into the loudspeaker a memorable one. It was eighteen guns in battery, shooting live ammunition at the enemy. It was, in fact, the "fire mission" that McPheeters had charted. I can't think of a better requiem for a valiant fighting man.

At Anzio, during the siege, one eventually became accustomed to the continuous crash of artillery; it was simply a part of our landscape. One went on about his business as best he could in the midst of an unceasing lethal hail. Lieutenant Mickey Miller, an aide of mine who was a pilot, and I frequently went up in a little Piper Cub to fly along the front and study the enemy territory. One day at the airstrip, as we made ready to go up on one of these reconnaissance flights, I idly watched another of our planes taxi down the runway and take off. The craft became airborne and then suddenly disintegrated, leaving nothing but a shower of metallic confetti. The plane had flown into the trajectory of an American artillery piece behind the airstrip just as an unseen projectile was lofted toward some distant enemy objective.

After we stopped the German attack down the Albano

175

Road, the enemy made another attempt to crack through the beachhead. This attack, mounted in the first week of March, zeroed in on the sector of the Third Infantry Division near Cisterna. The First Armored hastily sent over one of our mechanized artillery battalions to assist in repelling the attack. Mechanized artillery is exceptionally useful for rapid reinforcement because the guns, which are mounted on armored carriers and don't need to be dug in, can be fired as soon as they arrive.

The battalion fired between 4,000 and 5,000 rounds in a single day, a splendid performance. When the men returned to the First Armored's sector, I went over to congratulate them. I came upon a naked young artilleryman who stood behind an oak bush washing himself with a helmetful of water. He was obviously embarrassed about conversing with his commanding general in such circumstances, and to put him more at ease I asked what his duty was.

"I just chuck them in," he said, meaning he was a gun-loader. I reflected on the hundreds of shells he must have "chucked in" his gun that day—quite a job.

A grizzled sergeant came up to the two of us at that point and I turned to him. "Your men did great today, sergeant," I said.

But sergeants are sergeants, I guess. "Well, they did fairly good," he grunted in reply. "After awhile they will learn to become soldiers."

Serious fighting—by that I mean hand-to-hand and gun-to-gun fighting—just about ended after the German attack in the Third Infantry sector.

The punishing fighting of January and February left both the German 14th Army and the Allied VI Corps in a state of exhaustion. Like hound dogs after a chase, both sides lay panting with their tongues out. For a period of more than two months the opposing forces were to content themselves with raids and skirmishes, and with artillery fire and air attack. During this phase, we played host at Anzio to many distin-

176

guished visitors, but gradually it was borne in upon me that few of them wanted to spend nights—those deadly, destructive nights—upon the beachhead. By sunset most of them found they had pressing business in Naples.

Ernie Pyle, the war correspondent, was one visitor to whom this characterization does not apply. He came to Anzio several times. He always came first to my headquarters for a little chat. But invariably he declined my offer to put him up in at least modest comfort. He would thank me, and then make his way to the dugouts at the front where he could get a closer feeling of the common soldier's war. Later he was killed in the Pacific. He was a fine gentleman and I was always glad to have him come around and see us.

From the middle of March until the breakout late in May, conditions at Anzio were reminiscent of World War I. Forward positions were stabilized and remained practically unchanged. The whole area was a maze of trenches, foxholes, and dugouts, a tangle of barbed wire and barricades. Protection from shellfire was more important than comfort. Some of the troops sank huge native wine barrels deep in the ground and used them as bed chambers. Many of my tankers preferred to sleep in their tanks or in holes dug under them. An ingenious aide of mine had a portable bed—an ambulance which he had "borrowed" in some mysterious fashion.

There is a haunting unreality about a battle area which is difficult to explain. Battle is a kind of nightmare, with alarums and excursions, bravery and hysteria, but many men adjust themselves to it. It is the juxtaposition of war and peaceful routines which bothers men most. Even in those first weeks, when our occupancy of the beachhead was most in hazard, sheep grazed calmly right beside my truck. Cattle and mules wandered, seeking grass, among the mine fields. We had invaded a peaceful and pastoral land, and, because we were hard put to it at times to feed our own troops, some 20,000 Italian peasants had been transported to Naples in our empty and home-going LSTs.

But there were others who chose not to go. A peasant and his wife regularly washed my clothes and, despite the hail of hellfire from overhead, never left their homestead. The wandering mules of Anzio fared well; off-duty soldiers made pets of them, drove them tandem in races. Cattle were protected by Army orders, but the life expectancy of beef dropped sharply. Canned rations are monotonous and fresh beef tastes very good. At Anzio, cattle seemed to have a habit of attacking soldiers. Anyway, the soldiers always maintained they shot in self-defense.

Recreation facilities, of course, were limited, but on quiet days there were track meets, horseshoe pitching contests, and baseball games. Men ducked for cover when a shell came over and then calmly returned to their sport. Some of my own troops discovered the remains of a pheasant preserve in a thicket about 400 yards from the German lines. Another officer and I crawled on our bellies across an open space to the thicket and, armed with the sawed-off shotguns used for guarding prisoners, bagged dinner for ourselves. There were ducks on the ponds near the Mussolini Canal, but the fishing, though many patient lines were dropped, was discouraging.

One day Major Rooney came upon a half-grown pig rooting around outside an abandoned farmhouse. He brought the young porker back to the command post in a mail sack, and we turned our captive into the occasion of a celebration. Lieutenant Dixie Walker, a Floridan who had operated a barbecue restaurant in prewar days, was detached from reconnaissance duty to supervise the proceedings. We rigged up a pit of coals, mounted the slaughtered pig on an improvised spit, and Walker used a broom to brush it with a basting sauce he had concocted.

I invited several of the beachhead commanders, including some of the British generals, over for the feast. One of the Britons brought with him the musicians of the Gordon Highlander band. As the band was about to begin to play, the general tipped me off on an old British custom that I had not previously encountered. In a moment, he said, the band's sergeant major would ask permission to play his regimental march. As I gave my assent, the general said, I must also hand the sergeant major a water glass full of whiskey.

The sergeant major, a great tall Scotsman, strode up with a great flourish and saluted me with his baton. I gave him the expected permission and brought the glass of whiskey I had readied from behind my back. His Adam's apple worked steadily up and down as he swallowed that whiskey—not very good quality, I fear—in a single gulp; without a flicker of an eyelid he then turned back to the band and struck up the music. The British seemed to have a lot of old customs. This was one of which I thoroughly approved.

Eventually we were able to obtain from Fifth Army Head-quarters consent for our soldiers—10 percent of them at a time—to have four days' leave in Naples, dependent on the availability of shipping facilities. My first disillusionment came when some of my boys went down in somewhat sketchy uniforms—all they had after fighting for their lives—and were jailed by MPs for being improperly dressed.

When I heard about this, I blew up. I told Colonel Dewey that I was determined to leave half my soldiers to hold off the Germans and take the other half down to clean up Naples. Dewey was able to dissuade me from this project, but my wrath still bubbled. A little later I went to Naples myself and was given a handsome villa for my quarters. My aide and I arrived about midnight and after we checked in at the villa we went around to a restaurant I had patronized before I went to Anzio. All was in darkness, but we hammered on the door until the proprietor sleepily emerged. When he saw it was me, he roused the whole family—an impressive turnout, for he had seventeen children and his wife was pregnant with the eigh-teenth. We all sat in the kitchen, as the wife and two of the older girls prepared a dinner while the proprietor led his younger children in song. Sometime after 1 A.M. we launched into a wonderful meal. I'm not the Cromwellian type of commander who despises luxury; I like it when I have a chance to enjoy it. Eventually, though, the contrast to the beachhead was too much. Every time I saw combed and polished rear-echelon troops standing in line eight abreast for a movie, I wondered what they would be standing in line for if the ragamuffins had lost Anzio—bread? After a few days, I cut short my leave in disgust and went home to my own.

I should add that we were able soon, through the efforts of the Quartermaster Corps, to take care of the matter of new uniforms. But I remained, throughout the Italian campaign, dissatisfied with the recreation facilities made available to combat soldiers on leave from the front. They had earned a good time. They had it too seldom.

Old settlers on the beachhead, however, recall this period almost as sentimentally as Harvest Home. In comparison to the nightmare of earlier weeks, these days of early spring seemed like the prize in the popcorn box. The sense of desperation was gone and soldiers of both armies seemed to be in a singularly sunny frame of mind. I remember that a drunken American soldier found a tall silk hat in an Italian villa, and walked squarely, if unsteadily, through fortified German lines. The Germans in that sector were fun-loving enough to readjust his silk hat, turn him to the proper point of the compass, and send him, unharmed, back to us. Why? I don't know. Armies are made up of people. And many of them are boys.

Troops on both sides were sure that no immediate offensive was contemplated. They were right. The Germans pulled out two of their best divisions, the 26th Panzer and the 29th Panzer Grenadiers, and established them as Army Group reserves in Rome. The crack Hermann Göring Panzer Division was sent north to Leghorn. The Allies also were busy with breathing exercises. There were many substitutions of units, but the most welcome was the arrival of the veteran American 34th Division. It relieved the Third Division on the Cisterna front; after sixty-seven days of consecutive duty, the Third was

180

sent to a rest camp south of Nettuno. One loss suffered by the First Armored during this period was that of Colonel Kent Lambert, commander of Combat Command A. Lambert was badly hurt in a fall and was evacuated to Naples; he did not return to the division. His command was assumed by Colonel Maurice W. Daniel, who had been division artillery commander.

Some 14,000 replacements arrived to fill the gaps left by the dead, the wounded, and the ill. We were, of course, building up for an explosion out of the beachhead. At last we were beginning to feel strong.

General Truscott succeeded General Lucas as commander of the VI Corps in March. Truscott was a fine fighting soldier, a man of will power, decision and drive. He saw to it that there was plenty of activity during the siege days; he inaugurated a vigorous retraining program. This was important. Defensive fighting and static warfare are insidious assassins of morale. The offensive spirit had to be recreated for the job ahead—the breakout from our beachhead prison.

One measure toward this end was the local raid. Almost every night—and often several times in a night—small groups of our soldiers penetrated enemy lines to destroy communications and take prisoners. These sorties harassed the Germans and gave the participants, many of them replacements new to the battle, combat experience.

Most persistent of the raiders were the men of the First Special Service Force, 2500 strong and commanded by the gallant Brigadier General R. T. Frederick, who won the Distinguished Service Cross four times. Our S.S. troops, like Arsène Lupin, left their calling cards behind them. They carried stickers with them on their night excursions—their own red-arrowhead insignia, with such messages as, "Beware! S.S. Will Get You Next." These were affixed to houses and barns and bits of masonry.

The derring-do of the S.S., their signs, the fact that they often painted or blackened their faces, gave them a reputation

181

among the Germans for both ingenuity and ferocity. On one occasion the Germans discovered a lane along the Mussolini Canal which the S.S. habitually used at night. The Germans laid shoe mines there and surrounded an S.S. group in the darkness. Thirty-two Americans lost legs or feet in that cruel entrapment. I remember another raid I watched in which all participants came home unscathed. Five of my tanks went along.

The Special Service Force had discovered a German infantry company located across the Mussolini Canal in an isolated stone strongpoint. They intended to crawl through the grass and sometime after midnight surround the place. At daylight the tanks were to come over with protecting fire. I was spending the night away from my command post with a First Armored reconnaissance outfit, and I decided I would get up early to witness the performance of my tankers. At about 4 A.M. I crossed a bridge over the canal and found the five tanks lined up there. A young lieutenant—a replacement fresh from the States—was in command, and he was plainly jittery and uncertain. I walked up the apron of his tank and talked to him as he sat in the turret.

"You go left along the road to the next crossroads," I said. "Then you turn right. You put two tanks on one side, two tanks on the other, and hold one in reserve. You go forward. The doughs will be lying in the grass, but don't worry; they'll get out of your way. Go as far as a moat. You can't cross, but the doughs will swim it. Send one tank around behind to prevent the Germans' escape. You fire like hell and you'll protect the GIs with your firing. That, son, is all there is to it."

The operation was completely successful, and sixty Germans were captured. In one raid that lieutenant became a combat veteran. The next day he came around and reported to me. "You made it all sound so simple," he said, "that I just went ahead and did it."

Italian weather is abrupt. By May 1 midsummer broke out all over. The sun shone valiantly. Trenches were dry. Marshy fields which had been sinkholes for tanks became solid and parched, and, for the first time since arrival, the First Armored could wheel and maneuver off the network of roads. Activities in Anzio awaited the spring offensive of the Eighth and Fifth Armies in the south, for this was to be a coordinated Allied movement. The reinforced British Eighth Army had taken over the Cassino front, facing the Liri valley; the Fifth Army was to sideslip toward the sea and come up the coast.

The Eighth and the Fifth kicked off on the night of May 11-12, and at Anzio we were knee-deep in preparations. There were three alternative plans for our beachhead breakout, but I don't think we need to consider the discarded alternatives here. The Germans were convinced we would attack up the Albano Road, which was the shortest route to Rome, and they had their best troops stationed there. We wanted them to think that. Actually, our plan called for a breakthrough on the Cisterna front. The rested Third Division, now commanded by "Fighting Mike" O'Daniel, was to engulf Cisterna while the First Armored broke through and cut Highway 7, the German supply line to Cisterna. In a second phase we were to push onward to the edge of the mountains to cut Highway 6, the main supply line of the German Tenth Army in the south.

To conceal what we were up to from prying German eyes in the hills, we created an artificial fog with beachhead smokepots and then we conducted a full-scale training exercise. I had worked out an attack plan in which four battalions of infantry, each supported by a battalion of tanks, would advance abreast. The infantry was my own Sixth Armored Regiment and the 135th Regiment of the 34th Division, which was attached to my command for the attack. In the dry run, each of the four forces ran through the exercise twice: two companies of medium tanks led the mock attack; a company of light tanks accompanied the following foot soldiers to help carry their heavy equipment and to protect them from the close-up fire of Germans who survived the waves of medium tanks. Field Marshal Alexander, who was our Army Group

183

commander, came to Anzio to watch these exercises. He was greatly impressed by them. I am convinced that these exercises contributed much to our successful breakout from the beachhead on the first day of the attack.

First Armored engineers were also busy. There were three mechanical devices that proved extremely useful in the breakout. Colonel John Inchkeep and his assistants devised two of them. The first was a method of propelling a section of steel bridge ahead of a tank so that, under fire, it could be laid across a creek without exposing men to rifle and machine gun fire. The second was a grapnel—a hook drawn behind a tank to clear a forward area of barbed wire, so infantry could advance. This has a modest sound, but it was tremendously important. The third device was a weapon rarely used in the war. It was called "The Snake," and, in appearance, was unimpressive. The Snake weighed about 6000 pounds and was 300 feet of jointed steel tube. The steel tube was filled with TNT up to about fifty feet from the tank, which first pulled and then swung around and pushed it into a combat area. When the Snake was in position, the tankers buttoned themselves in to minimize concussion, and exploded the TNT by fire from machine guns. I found this a potent weapon for breaking through the mine fields and strong points built up during a siege. Upon explosion, the Snake could be counted on to clear a path from 200 to 400 yards wide. Its limitations and hazards don't need much explanation. It could be exploded by enemy fire as well as our own, and TNT doesn't choose sides.

It has always been my idea that the more exact battle information you can give a soldier, the better he will carry out his assignments. The "theirs not to reason why" of Tennyson's noble six hundred is long out of date. The American soldier, in particular, wants to know the "why" of military movements. And if he knows why, and if the whole thing seems to make sense, he will carry out the most hazardous assignment without complaint. There is another factor: many battles are lost because senior officers are killed, and junior officers and noncoms do not know the objectives to be gained.

The value of well-briefed troops had been confirmed for me back at the landing at Safi, and I decided that all troops of the First Armored should be told the detailed plan of attack. I was criticized by some commanders on the ground that I was taking chances with military security. Well, that was the issue—security versus understanding. Tank warfare is complex at its simplest, and, with my eyes open, I chose understanding.

We did more than tell the troops the plan of attack: we made them study it. All company and platoon leaders were flown over the beachhead in small planes so they might survey the situation from the air. Then I had built near my dugout a terrain flat of the Cisterna-Cori-Valmontone sector, with every hill, every stream, every bridge, every road, even the color of rooftops reproduced on this model. We placed a boardwalk above the exhibit, which was about fifty feet square, and the troops, in installments, came to study it minutely; day after day I would see them, using sticks and twigs as pointers, tracing the routes their units were to pursue. This was vital information to them; the knowledge of where they were to be during battle might mean, in emergency, the difference between life and death.

For the first time at Anzio, my division was at full strength. Combat Command B, which had been supporting the Fifth Army, had joined us. We were finally committed to do the job for which an armored division is designed—to lead an attack and exploit territory. It was vitally important that the troops approach the task with confidence and courage, and I sped from place to place in my jeep talking with them. I pointed out that any weapon from a jackknife up was lethal to an infantryman, while the tanker had only three things to fear— mines, artillery fire, and antitank guns. Mines might shake him up and tear off his treadtrack, but were seldom fatal; and, if he moved fast enough, artillery fire was not too dangerous. That left the undoubted and deadly hazard of antitank guns. I

185

put a test question to my platoon commanders: Should infantry or armor lead? If they expressed the belief that infantry should lead or were, on cross-examination, shaky on the point, I relieved them of duty forthwith.

There is a great deal of nonsense talked about military deception. I have found it prudent to assume that the enemy knows just a little more about you than you know about him; actually, about all that can be concealed when armies face each other is the time and the place of an attack. For the breakout at Anzio, however, we were able to achieve a rather surprising degree of deception. It was especially surprising because field glasses in the mountains constantly spied on our daylight movements.

Corps artillery and my tanks were partners in the play acting. In mid-May the artillery began firing in concert. At early morning it would lay a powerful barrage over a certain sector, and the Germans would rally for a breakthrough there. Then nothing would happen. The next day the big firing would begin at noon, and concentrate on another area, and the Germans would rally there. This continued until the enemy was bored by the whole procedure. Captured records show that the German High Command guessed that nothing much would happen at Anzio, that the Allies really intended to make another amphibious landing close to or beyond Rome.

Tanks are noisy; they can be heard even when, as at night, they can't be seen. We began working on that. Every night and every early morning, Shermans would roar up to the lines, shoot off a turret load of ammunition and return. In the beginning, the tanks drew artillery fire, but the Germans quickly learned that our artillery people could chart the positions of their guns from the spurts of flame in the darkness. After a while the Germans got used to the fact that our tanks growled around pretty harmlessly all night, and didn't even bother to leave their dugouts. The wasteful and excitable Americans, they decided contemptuously, were simply whooping off ammunition.

186

All this paid dividends. About May 19 the Eighth Army crushed through at Cassino and moved slowly up the Liri valley against strong opposition. After three days of fighting the Fifth pierced the Gustav Line farther west and started north. At Anzio, more tanks went to the front, but fewer and fewer came back. They were able to camouflage themselves in the folds of the ground, so they could not be seen by the spotters in the mountains. And there they lay doggo. Some of my tankers, supplied with cold rations, lay there four days. They handled their assignment so expertly that they were never discovered. We hoped, however, that the watchful Germans in the hills were catching glimpses of the force of tanks that was building up in the vicinity of the Albano Road. These "tanks" were made of rubber inflated like balloons, but to a man peering through binoculars they were indistinguishable from the genuine article.

Under cover of night, we also quietly moved forward part of our artillery. Some of the big guns were emplaced as close as 400 or 500 meters of the front and cunningly draped with camouflage nets. Each crew was supplied 1,000 rounds of ammunition and told to keep out of sight until the attack began. Moving the guns up in this manner assured us maximum artillery support during the breakout in the critical 6,000- to 10,000-meter ranges before our advance required that we displace and send the guns forward. When artillery is displacing it isn't firing, and we needed as much fire power as we could muster in the early stages of the attack.

The big forward movement of troops and supplies for the VI Corps' attack—1,000 truckloads of ammunition were needed for the First Armored area alone—took place under great difficulties. All movements had to be made in darkness, and the road network was limited indeed. Truscott's staff had to know exactly who would use what road at exactly what time for three vital nights. I think possibly my greatest contribution to the attack was the logistical decisions I made about the use of these roads.

My operations officer presented me with charts suggesting

187

the time each unit would need. I studied these charts and asked him on what marching speed and what time length of marching columns he had based this movement at night without lights. He said he had drawn on the data in the Leavenworth textbooks.

"Take your charts back and figure again on the basis of half that marching speed and twice the time length on your columns," I told him. My experience in Africa had taught me that night movement is filled with the unforeseen: troops that missed the proper road, bridges blown up, and columns mixed up with each other because one wasn't on time at the starting place. The data we finally used put our last reserve battalion at the proper point only 30 minutes before H-hour; and we managed without any of the dreaded traffic jams which would have left infantry and armor exposed and vulnerable at daylight.

The jump-off was set for May 23. My staff had scooped out a bedroom for me in the side of a canal at the jump-off line. This dank, odorous place was supposed to be safe—and it was safer than my buried, sandbagged truck back in the Padiglione Woods. On the night of May 22-23, German artillery demolished that sandbagged refuge, and most of the officers left behind in the rear headquarters became casualties. Later we captured a German map that had an X marked with nice precision at the site of my command post. I can only assume the enemy delayed the strike on the post in hopes they could demolish the division's communications network just as we prepared to attack.

The jump-off came at 6:30 A.M. It was preceded by a 45-minute barrage which shook the ground like an earthquake; all artillery in the beachhead took part. The Germans, indifferent now to our katzenjammers, plainly didn't realize that an attack was headed their way. Their field artillery did not deign to reply. At H-hour, the First Armored pushed forward toward Highway 7 with eight companies of medium tanks abreast. We advanced over a sector only 2,000 yards wide, which meant

188

many tanks to an acre. After the Sherman mediums came four battalions of infantry interspersed with companies of light tanks which carried the infantry's heavy weapons and could be dispatched hither and thither to wipe out the points of minor resistance that the Shermans bypassed.

Simultaneously the Third Division attacked and at Cisterna was plunged at once into heavy fighting. The Special Service Force moved forward on the Third Division's flank along the Mussolini Canal, and ran into determined resistance. The 45th Division protected the First Armored's flank and, together with the British First and Fifth Divisions, made such a successful holding attack at the Albano Road and in the Factory sector that the Germans were convinced for some time that our major thrust was to occur there. This prevented the movement of the crack German outfits—the 65th Infantry and the Third Panzer Grenadiers—to the area of the breakthrough until too late.

Bad weather curtailed planned air support in the morning, but before evening hundreds of missions had been flown. Before evening also the First Armored had advanced 4,000 yards, crossed the Cisterna-Campoleone railroad and smashed the German main line of resistance. We had cut through their field artillery and captured most of it. That meant, in military terms, that we were through the crust.

Mine fields took heavy toll of tanks and tank destroyers. Strangely enough, most of the mines were American mines, laid when we held the territory in the early days of the beachhead. I was glad they were American mines, because they had only about half the explosive power of the German variety; many of the disabled tanks—there were 116 of them—could be repaired in a few days' or a week's time. There was one significant circumstance. Colonel Daniel, whose combat command attacked on the left, used the Snake to blast his way through mine fields and suffered a minimum of casualties. General Allen, on the right, failed to use the Snake, and his tank losses were high.

189

Dead and wounded among our own organic infantry and in the 135th Regiment totaled only 92 for the first day. These light casualties were due, at least in part, to our meticulous armor-infantry exercises before the attack. The 362nd German Infantry Division in front of us lost 50 percent of its fighting power, and two regiments of the German 715th were badly mauled. The American Third Division to our right, however, had found the going rough and their losses were very heavy.

I got a little sleep that night in a cave in a wheat field. On the second day, the First Armored plunged forward and cut Highway 7 between Velletri and Cisterna, and threatened the road between the towns of Cori and Valmontone. General Mackensen, we learned later, realized the precariousness of the German position, but the High Command refused his request for permission to withdraw to the base of the Lepini mountains. On this second day, however, the First Armored felt the impact of determined counterattacks on our left. Such excellent troops as the German Fourth Parachute were already moving over from the Factory area in an attempt to stem the tide.

But they were too late. The severing of Highway 7 led to a virtual encirclement of dusty, bloody Cisterna, and that evening defenses there began to crumble. The next day the Third Division captured the town and took almost 1,000 prisoners. The major bulk of the First Armored moved up into the hills and gullies before Velletri, where we were stopped cold by the Fourth Parachute. We held the door closed, however, while the Third Division raced through the valley called the Velletri Gap. A task force of my armor commanded by Colonel Howze dashed forward with them on May 26, assisted in the capture of Artena, at the base of the Lepinis, and the cutting of the all-important Highway 6, which ran down the Liri valley from Rome to Cassino.

This made the beachhead a thing of the past. After all the weary months of waiting and hoping and fighting, we had cracked the walls of our prison. We were out! Americans of

190

the Fifth Army and the French Expeditionary Corps had been moving up the coast for a period of days. In the early morning of May 25, although I did not know it at the time, a junction of the troops of the north and the troops of the south was effected on Highway 7 near Littoria, at the edge of the Pontine Marshes. General Clark, who had been with us at Anzio during the breakout drive, was able to greet personally his reunited forces.

I have always believed that, at this point in the battle, the First Armored could—and should—have rolled onto Highway 6 and been in Rome in an hour and a half. The Germans had not recovered from their confusion, the valley road was ideal for tanks, and there wasn't then much in the way of military strength between us and the outskirts of the city. Unfortunately, on May 26 General Clark changed the battle plan. First Armored was called to a temporary halt, and relieved for rest and refitting.

I studied the new plan glumly. Despite all our earlier difficulties with the terrain along the Albano Road, I was ordered to turn the noses of the tanks in that direction and scramble through the rugged hills of the Colli Laziali. It turned out to be, in terms of destruction of tanks and all-important tank crews, our most expensive operation in the Anzio theater.

My tankers returned to the struggle on May 29. All that day and the next, they and the 45th Division fought bitterly and unsuccessfully along the Albano Road. The 34th Division was stopped by stiff enemy opposition below Lanuvio. The Third Division was counterattacked by the late-arriving Hermann Göring Panzers near Valmontone. The Fifth Army drive seemed to be stalled.

But important events were in the making. The 36th Division, famous for its fighting at Salerno and before Cassino, had arrived at Anzio on the very eve of the breakout. Now Major General Fred Walker's sharp-eyed patrols before Velletri discovered that the Germans had left unguarded the

191

vineyard-covered slopes of Mount Artemisio in the Colli Laziali. Just before midnight on May 30, in the light of a pale moon, a section of the 36th began quietly to climb. It was a brilliant maneuver. By dawn next day these troops had made a deep penetration, flanked the Germans, and not a shot had been fired to herald their advance. When the enemy discovered them and counterattacked with frenzied determination, the 36th Division held.

There were to be three more days of fighting before the Germans decided the time had come to withdraw northward. The Sixth Corps offensive was successful, but it had been a hard-fought victory. Allied casualties for the breakout period exceeded 4,000—almost twice the number of our dead and wounded in the big German attack of February. German losses for the breakout period were never reported, but I do know that we captured 4,828 prisoners and destroyed or damaged an almost unimaginable number of guns, tanks, half-tracks, and other transport.

On the afternoon of June 3, General Truscott and I stood in the shadow of a factory on the outskirts of Rome. We were trying to straighten out the folds of a war map when suddenly a machine gun cut loose. We threw ourselves flat on the ground. By craning my neck, I could see that the machine gun was located in a stone outhouse in an open field.

This, I thought, was the ultimate anticlimax. The two of us, who had gone through so much together, were to be killed by fire from an Italian privy. As we crouched there, a Sherman tank came up the highway. I shouted and pointed. The Sherman tank didn't bother with its guns. It just turned at right angles and charged across the field and butted squarely into the building. When the tank had finished, there was neither machine gun, outhouse nor German.

The tank commander saluted from his turret and rolled on. Truscott and I picked ourselves up, resumed the tattered vestments of our dignity, and went back to being generals again.

192

1944 - May 20: In the Anzio area GIs enjoyed a brief respite from battle, while awaiting orders to move their tanks up for the next offensive.

1944 - June 4: In the Rome area, men of the 1st Armored Division halt to inspect a wagon load of German equipment, after the driver, a German sniper, had been slain.

1944 - June 9: This German tank destroyer was knocked out near the town of Viterbo, Italy.

1944 - June 6: Tanks of the 1st Armored Division enter Rome.

1944 - June 6: General Harmon hears the good news that his troops have entered Rome.

1944 - June: Scene at 1st Armored Division command post in the palace at Oriolo Romano, Italy.

1944 - July: Three-man patrol of 1st Armored Division enters the town of Mignano in Italy.

1944 - July: General Sir Harold Alexander decorates—"in the name of His Majesty the King"— General Harmon with Britain's Order of the Bath.

THIRTEEN
★ ★
From Rome to Arno

ON JUNE 4, 1944, there was little peace and no quiet in Vatican City. All afternoon and all night ponderous tanks, armored vehicles, self-propelled guns, towed artillery, half-tracks, and an almost endless caravan of heavy trucks roared and clanked and clumped along the stone pavements that bordered those sacred precincts. Troops of the First Armored had little chance to savor the delirious, flower-strewn reception Romans gave the entering Allied forces. We had been ordered to proceed beyond the Tiber and establish positions north of the city.

Some authorities have quarreled with my conviction that elements of the First Armored were the first American troops in the triumphal entry of the Eternal City; there is no question they were the first to leave. I was their commander, and I had only a glimpse at Rome in passing. I am not sure to this day whether or not our columns violated the neutrality of Vatican City en route. During the long struggle at Anzio we were equipped with the most elaborate military maps. When we arrived in Rome we were ignorant and uninformed country boys who did not know our way through the city streets. I chose, from a plausible auto map, a route through those erratic ancient streets which might, with good luck, take us across the Tiber. Luck was with us. It did.

A few weeks later I had an audience with Pope Pius XII,

193

and I owned up to the fact it was the First Armored that had invaded his privacy and deafened his ears. It takes twelve hours for just the combat vehicles of an armored division— spaced fifty yards apart—to pass a given point.

"Any time you liberate Rome," His Holiness said to this not-very-hard-working Protestant, "you can make all the noise you want."

We did not encounter German resistance until we were about ten miles north of the city. Although many of Europe's historic buildings and bridges were casualties of World War II, the Germans seemed as eager as we that the monuments of Rome should not suffer such a fate. Their speedy withdrawal from the city made unnecessary the heavy air and artillery bombardment that is a part of modern combat.

The immediate Allied objectives north of the city were the port of Civitavecchia, on the Tyrrhenian Sea, and the airfields at Viterbo. Combat Command B, following a path close to the coast, rolled past Civitavecchia on June 6 and the next morning the city fell to elements of the 168th Infantry Regiment of Major General Charles Ryder's 34th Division. In the Civitavecchia railroad yards the Germans had abandoned two railroad guns, the "Anzio Express" that so tormented us on the Anzio beachhead; bomb destruction of the railroad tracks to the north had prevented their removal. These 280-mm monsters, 65 feet long, fired projectiles weighing nearly 700 pounds. Our ordnance experts told us that with rocket assists they could be fired as far as fifty miles.

I was still dissatisfied with the performance being turned in by General Allen, commander of Combat Corps B. At my request, General Truscott, commander of the VI Corps, relieved Allen; shortly thereafter Truscott and the Corps command left the Italian theater to begin planning the invasion of southern France. I assigned Colonel Lawrence R. Dewey, my faithful chief of staff, to the command in Allen's stead.

Complete cooperation among the principal officers of the

194

division was of high importance in the type of fighting that characterized the battle northward toward the Arno River. That portion of Italy is striped with north-south valleys, all relatively narrow; frequently the First Armored was obliged to advance through three or four valleys simultaneously. We met the problem by deploying task forces in each valley for which we were responsible. Each force was subdivided into three attack groups sufficiently strong to overcome the resistance we encountered at the German strongpoints on the valley roads. As each defensive position was overcome, the two trailing attack groups could leapfrog ahead, ready to move on the next strongpoint to the north, while what now became the third group assembled itself again into marching columns.

The successful use of task forces as a tool of battle depends heavily upon the aggressive spirit of the men assigned as force commanders. The men I slotted for task force commands—Colonels Howze, Dewey and Daniel—were three of First Armored's finest combat leaders. I carefully constructed each of the forces so that the task force commander invariably was the senior officer in the area and there could be no doubt who was in charge.

Despite the task force technique, our advance was slow. We averaged about five miles a day. The Germans fought a skillful rear guard action and the topography was to their advantage. The precipitous hills that bracketed the valleys were impassable to tanks, and the roads were punctuated with frequent hairpin turns and the shattered, grotesquely twisted remains of bridges, all of them blown up by the retreating enemy. In such surroundings a small group of Germans equipped with a single 88-mm antitank gun could hold up an entire column for hours.

Infantrymen worked closely with us on this northward drive, men of our own Sixth Armored Infantry Regiment as well as infantry units attached from other divisions in the vicinity. In general their task was to protect us at night, when the tank—halted for refueling, maintenance, and resupplying with am-

195

munition—becomes a relatively helpless weapon, and to dig out enemy soldiers barricaded in cellars and other positions inaccessible to tank attack. In tough situations, we also employed infantrymen in a highly successful tactic adapted from horse cavalry days. As the infantry unit put down a pivot of fire, pinning down the enemy, tanks would move up on one flank or, terrain permitting, both flanks and probe for the enemy's soft, unprotected sides.

Infantry units lent by other divisions were always glad to fight with us because our tankers understood it was their job to take the brunt of the battle off the foot soldier. Repeatedly I told my tankers to see to it that infantrymen came into second base on their feet, not sliding and maybe getting hurt. It must be a point of honor with every tanker, I often said, that he never permit an infantry unit to be overrun by enemy tanks. At Anzio I saw two battalions of Rangers—767 men—overwhelmed by German tanks because no Allied tanks were available to storm in and get them out. Only six men came back. I never forgot it. I always insisted to my tankers that in their rolling fortresses they were secure from most of the hazards of battle, and postwar casualty figures for the European Theater of Operations bore me out: infantry divisions suffered 70 percent of the casualties, armored divisions 10 percent.

As the First Armored pressed northward we came upon a beautiful blue lake, Lake Bracciano, that I promptly picked at once as a perfect rest spot for the division. I knew we were soon to be pulled out of the line for rest and refitting—we hadn't had a chance to rest in nearly three months—and I promptly got General Clark to reserve the Lake Bracciano area for our use. On June 9 the orders withdrawing us came through, and we headed for our lake. To my exasperation I found a British advance party had preceded us; they claimed they had authority to reserve Lake Bracciano as a rest center for the British Eighth Army despite the fact it lay within our American Fifth Army zone. I insisted, only half humorously, that I intended to have that rest area even if I had to fight the entire Eighth Army for it. Fortunately General Clark backed me up, and bloodshed was averted.

Among the first items of business at Lake Bracciano was an assembly line bath for the division. We fixed canvas barriers in the lake, marking out a 50-foot path parallel to the shore through chest-deep water. Every man of the division stripped off his old clothing, discarded it and plunged into the water. When he emerged at the other end of the course, he was given a complete new crisp clean outfit.

Bathed and freshly clad, the soldiers' thoughts turned to the potential pleasures of nearby Rome. And I had made some arrangements along those lines as well. General Clark had told me to allow a maximum of 1,500 men a night to visit the city. I knew the rest stop would last no more than five or six days, not enough time under the Clark ground rules for every man in the division to have a night on the town. The security and police of Rome were under the immediate command of Major General Michael O'Daniel of the Third Infantry Division, and Iron Mike, fortunately, was an old friend of mine. He and I made a private agreement, unknown to Fifth Army headquarters, to lift the quota to 5,000 men per night. The MPs were instructed to deposit any overloaded First Armored men they encountered in a special enclosure we set up in the city. First Armored Division trucks ferried these detainees back to the rest camp, where they were either put straight to bed or tossed into the lake to cool off as the individual case required. In three nights every man in the division got into Rome once and some got there twice.

On June 16 we were attached to the newly arrived IV Corps, commanded by Major General Willis D. Crittenberger, and told to head north. Six days later, we were again leading the attack. On our left flank was the 34th Infantry, on our right the Second Moroccan Division. The French force was made up in part of Goumiers, the celebrated Moroccan mountain fighters.

197

The Goumiers and the First Armored arrived at a happy working relationship. The Moroccans would drive the Germans off the high ground into an intervening valley where our tanks could chop them up. As the tankers disposed of that batch of Germans, the Goumiers would pass behind us and push up the next ridge. Their appetite for combat seemed nearly insatiable. General A. L. Guillaume, commander of the Second Moroccan—a real fighting general—and I got along famously. Some days later, when the Allied front had reached Volterra, we had a breathing spell, and General Guillaume came over to our camp with a gift for me. In full Gallic formality he kissed me on both cheeks and presented me with a burnoose and a document stating that I had been created an honorary corporal of the Third Regiment of Goums. The emblem of this corporalcy is a tiny silver dagger that I still proudly wear; so far as I know I am the only American officer ever to receive the decoration. It is a high honor to a French soldier to be made an honorary corporal. Napoleon, France's greatest military leader, is remembered to this day as the "little corporal."

Tactically the second phase of the First Armored's push toward the Arno was much like the first. The narrow north-south valleys, the primitive roads, and the wide front assigned to the division required me to deploy my tanks in several parallel task forces. I constantly zigzagged by jeep from one task force to another to check on their progress, and I was always in a hurry. On one of these missions my driver and I found ourselves trailing a tank that had been delayed by a thrown track and was now lumbering up to rejoin its task force. I endured the clouds of choking dust kicked up by the tank a long while; then I told my driver to swing left around the tank and get in front of it. The driver, who had better sense than I, protested that it was impossible to see if anything was on the other side of the tank, but I bullied him into attempting the maneuver.

Just as we drew abreast of the clanking behemoth, the

198

tanker abruptly wheeled in our direction in the road in order to cross a narrow bridge just ahead that hadn't been visible to us. The tank smacked squarely into the side of the jeep, crushing and pushing it about 30 feet. As I painfully extricated myself from the wreckage, I looked nervously at the huge tank tread that had just missed mashing me flat. The horrified tank driver had stood straight up, half his body out of the turret, in an all-out effort to brake the tank to a halt. He had torn off his goggles; his face was flour-white from the road dust save for the dark rings around his eyes where the goggles had been. He looked, in fact, much like a raccoon.

"Who's the driver of this tank?" I roared.

"Corporal Jones, sir. But, sir, I didn't know it was a general in the jeep," he stammered.

"Never mind that," I said. "Any man who can stop a tank that fast is a sergeant. From now on you are Sergeant Jones, you understand? You did a great job."

I limped away and had some dressing put on my leg. I had lost most of the skin from my hip to my ankle, but I was glad to be alive.

Sometimes when the distances to be covered were lengthy, I shifted from a jeep to a Cub plane; that form of travel also had its hazards. Rarely did Lieutenant Mickey Miller, my pilot, and I return from one of these jaunts without bullet holes in the plane's wings. We had been fired at by Germans or possibly by our own troops, there was no telling. But the little plane nipped easily into and out of makeshift pasture landing strips, and I began to use it quite frequently for visits to forward command posts and for reconnaissance.

One balmy July dusk, as I studied my maps and planned the next day's attack, I realized the terrain ahead would lend itself nicely to a double-pronged advance, with the task force divided into two parts, one on each side of the stream that ran down the valley—if the stream could be forded. The stream was inked in blue on the map, but I knew Italian streams frequently dwindled to virtually nothing in the summer. Miller

199

and I flew up to take a look, and sure enough the stream was a mere trickle.

We radioed this information back to my command post, and then I conceived the foolish idea of flying up for an aerial tour of Florence, which was then still firmly in German hands. We two sightseers came over that lovely city at about 5,000 feet. As I gaped out the window at the scene below, I noticed red streaks in the air beside us.

"What's that?" I asked Mickey.

"Antiaircraft fire," he replied tersely.

I had a quick answer to that. "Let's get the hell out of here!"

"I'm trying to," he said, pushing the stick forward and banking steeply, "but this old crate will only go sixty miles an hour even when it's headed straight down."

We dropped as close as we dared to the ground and scuttled away for home. I found it an intense pleasure that night to climb out of the cockpit and plant my feet firmly on the ground.

Word came to me from Fifth Army headquarters one day during this period that Secretary of War Stimson was touring the front and would visit my command post for lunch. I had previously invited General Ryder, commander of the 34th Division, which was fighting on our left flank, to join us. When Ryder arrived, I drew him aside and warned him not to eat too much. We served regular rations to Stimson and his entourage; I thought that if the high brass from Washington were going to rough it at the front, they ought to share the culinary experience that was the fighting man's most of the time. Stimson seemed quite genial, and we had a pleasant conversation along with the light—very light—lunch. After the Stimson party departed, Ryder and I returned to the table; my cook then brought in two ducks I had bought from a peasant. The ducks had been roasting quietly in the kitchen during the first sitting. I saw no reason to put off a duck dinner with Ryder to another day just because the Secretary of War came visiting, but there really wasn't enough duck to feed the Stimson party and the two of us as well.

The pace of our advance toward the Cecina River and the heights of Volterra, about fifteen miles south of the Arno, continued to be painfully slow; the terrain was some of the toughest for tanks that I encountered during my armored experience; the fighting, though comparatively small forces were involved, was frequently bitter. Eventually the strain began to tell on many of us. In eighteen days of fighting we moved the front north only forty miles as the crow flies, though we covered three times that distance on the twisting roads of our sector.

Toward the end of this campaign, when the fall of Volterra was almost in sight, one of my ablest armored battalion commanders came to my command post and asked me to relieve him. His face was drawn and had a ghastly pallor.

"I'm no good any more, sir. You'll have to put in someone else to command the battalion," he said, in a thin and shaking voice.

The man was obviously physically and emotionally exhausted.

After a moment's thought, I told him to go and get into my caravan truck. "I am going to give you three bottles of whiskey and post a sentry at the door," I said. "You are not to come out for three days, except as nature's purposes require; I want you to drink all the whiskey and sleep."

Three days later he was rested, freed from his horrors, and ready to return to his command. He also had polished off the whiskey, as ordered.

Military commanders in World War II had widely differing views on the problem of combat fatigue. My friend George Patton, most of whose military wisdom I greatly admired, regarded combat fatigue victims with total contempt; he was convinced they suffered from nothing but cowardice.

I realize that some soldiers who claimed to be suffering from "combat fatigue" had never been anywhere near the front, but

201

it is my opinion that Patton's airy dismissal of the phenomenon as non-existent was dead wrong. The time comes for every man when his nervous system has been taxed to its capacity, and he must rest. For some, like the officer in my caravan truck, a few sleep-filled days will do the trick. Others, including a few men I had under my command during the war, can never return to combat at all. They had to be transferred to rear areas to train replacement troops or else shipped back to the United States. No matter how brave he is, a man can stand only so much grief; then he breaks like a spring that has been flexed once too many times.

On July 7 elements of Combat Command A crossed Highway 68 north of the Cecina River, on July 8 troops of the 88th Infantry Division passed through the ranks of Task Force Howze to overrun Volterra, and during the next few days these and most other units of the First Armored were relieved and sent back to a rest area near Bolgheri.

These were sad days for sentimentalists in the division, for a reorganization of armored divisions ordered by Washington months earlier finally became effective. The division's assigned strength was diminished from 14,620 to 10,937, forcing the transfer of many men who regarded the First Armored as "their" outfit. Three units of the division with distinguished lineages and traditions, the First and Thirteenth Armored Regiments and the Sixth Armored Infantry Regiment, ceased to exist except as names in the pages of military history. Ironically, these painful alterations were visited upon the First Armored and subsequently on other armored divisions because of our experiences in North Africa. Our battle reports from Tunisia taught the experts at the Pentagon that the "big" armored division had too many tanks for its assigned infantry strength and that regiments were units too large for effective armored combat. Two tank regiments and an armored infantry regiment became three tank battalions and three infantry battalions.

These were sad days for me as well, for my career with the

202

First Armored Division was at an end. Orders had come through for me to return to the United States to assume command of a newly formed corps. I could look forward to service in the Pacific or possibly a return to Europe as new American forces poured in. Major General Vernon E. Pritchard arrived from the United States to succeed me as First Armored's commander.

It was time to say goodbye, but the potential threat of an enemy air attack ruled out the possibility of a full division review. I was prepared to forego a ceremonial departure entirely, but request after request poured in from my men that I review them by regiment and battalion.

And so I did. As I searched the faces of my men, tough and confident, I reflected on how changed was their attitude toward me as we said our goodbyes from the suspicion and skepticism with which I had first been greeted. It had been a long time since I assembled the men of a demoralized division in front of Lessouda Mountain, site of their first great defeat, and promised them that the battlefields of Lessouda would be the resurrection of the First Armored and not its burying ground.

FOURTEEN
★★
Return to the Second Armored

BY MID-1944 the American effort to build the vast army necessary to bring the Second World War to a decisive conclusion was rolling in high gear. Week by week entire new divisions marched out of training ready for battle, and new command staffs were organized to lead them. My relief from command of the First Armored in July was in line with a policy laid down by General Marshall, the American Chief of Staff. Marshall had directed that experienced American field commanders be promoted from their division commands to lead the new corps staffs. As I flew back toward the United States on the circuitous route then followed from Italy—Rome to Algiers to Casablanca to the Azores to Newfoundland to New York—I reflected on the future I supposed was ahead: a corps command, then further service in Europe or the Pacific. With the North African and Italian campaigns behind me, I felt like a seasoned and veteran fighting general.

The flight across the Atlantic, my first air crossing, had little resemblance to the luxurious trappings today's jet travelers enjoy. Our craft was a stripped-down C-47; we passengers alternated between sitting on the floor and sprawling on a stack of sleeping bags piled in the center of the barnlike interior of the plane.

I had a memorable reunion with my family, who were waiting out the war in Vienna, Virginia, a Washington suburb.

204

The morning after my arrival I walked into the Pentagon to report to Lieutenant General Ben Lear, commander of U.S. ground forces. I had known Lear for a number of years and had never seen any reason to alter my initial impression of him—that he was basically a bully.

Lear had scarcely shaken hands with me before he noticed the little dagger on my lapel that General Guillaume had given me. He asked me what it was and I told him all about my honorary commission as a corporal of the Second Regiment of Goums.

"Do you have War Department permission to wear that insignia?" Lear asked me sharply.

I had to confess I did not.

"Take it off then," he said. "You're not to wear anything unless you have permission."

Provoked, I pointed to my Distinguished Service Cross. "Shall I take that off too?" I asked.

"Of course not," he snapped.

Having attended to the matter of my costume, Lear turned briskly to other matters he found pressing. "I want you to report here tomorrow morning and dictate a report of your battle experiences. We need them for officers' training."

I reminded him that I had been granted thirty days' leave, but he waved that aside. "You can go as soon as you have finished the dictation," he said.

A few minutes later I was summoned by telephone to General Marshall's office. As I strode down the corridor, smarting from Lear's high-handed manner and feeling a bit rebellious, I drew the little dagger out of my pocket and fastened it to my blouse again. If Marshall even noticed the irregular decoration, he did not speak of it.

The Chief of Staff greeted me warmly and, after chatting with me a moment, suggested that I was probably pretty tired.

"I want you to go out to White Sulphur Springs for a good rest," he said. "Take Mrs. Harmon with you, and play golf for a week. You can go out in my plane."

I reacted cautiously to his proposal, remembering White

205

Sulphur Springs as a costly resort, but Marshall chuckled at my hesitation. The Army, he told me, had taken over the resort. I would stay at the cottage that once belonged to the president of the Pennsylvania Railroad. My wife and I would have to pay for our lodging, he added—$1.50 a day apiece!

I mentioned General Lear's directive that I report the next day to begin dictating my battle reports. General Marshall reacted with obvious irritation. "No, you don't have to do any such thing," he said. "That's why we gave you thirty days' leave. I want you to go to White Sulphur Springs right now." He seized the telephone and told General Lear to forget all about me until I got back to town.

The following morning my wife, my brother-in-law, Wellman Tuxbury, and I took off for White Sulphur Springs. Following the Marshall prescription, I played golf twice a day and began to unwind. After twenty-one months overseas, much of it in combat, I was wearier than I had realized.

One morning, just as I was teeing up, one of the prisoners of war who were serving as greens keepers walked over toward me and said, "How are you, General Harmon?"

I looked at him in some surprise and asked how he knew my name.

"I was one of the men of the Afrika Korps that you captured outside Bizerte," he said.

We had a pleasant talk, and he told me he hoped to stay on in the United States after the war and become an American citizen. I took more notice of the greens keepers after that and encountered several others during my holiday who had served in the Afrika Korps. They were fine looking soldiers.

At the conclusion of my leave General Marshall gave me orders to report to Camp Bowie, Texas, to take command of the XXIII Corps. My aide Mickey Miller and I flew to San Antonio in an Air Corps plane and spent the night there. Next morning we were to fly on to Camp Bowie. But just as we were about to board the plane for the second leg of the trip, a soldier ran out of the Signal Corps shack frantically waving a

206

telegram for me. It was an order from General Marshall to return to Washington immediately.

All the way back to Washington I puzzled fruitlessly about this sudden shift in my orders. Next morning in Marshall's office I found out the reason. The Second Armored Division, my old division, needed a new commander; Eisenhower and Bradley had both asked that I be named.

"You don't have to go, you have earned your promotion," said Marshall. "It's up to you."

There was a silence while he waited for my reply. For me, it was a painful moment. Once again that third star of a lieutenant general, which had seemed almost on my shoulder, was flitting out of reach. But down deeper I knew that the job of getting the war won was more important to me than personal promotion.

"When do you want me to go?" I asked.

Marshall's face crinkled into a grin. "Since the day before yesterday," he said.

The next day Mickey Miller and I took off in a plane bound for Europe. The Second Armored was somewhere near the Belgian border.

My one glimpse of wartime Britain, I am afraid, was not very informative. We arrived at London in the midst of a dense fog. After a single night at a London hotel we took off for France to report to General Eisenhower at his headquarters at Versailles. Staff people at the Supreme Headquarters of the Allied Expeditionary Force and at the headquarters of General Omar Bradley's Twelfth Army Group, where I reported next, were heady with optimism in that September of 1944.

But as I got closer to the front, the predictions became more cautious—and more realistic. At the headquarters of the First Army, to which the Second Armored was then attached, the consensus was that V-E day would come the following spring, which was correct. My first impression of Lieutenant General Courtney H. Hodges, the First Army commander, was not too good; I had the strong impression that he did little without the advice and support of Lieutenant General J. Lawton Collins, a West Point classmate of mine, who then commanded the VII Corps. General Bradley describes Hodges in his memoirs as "one of the most skilled craftsmen" under his command. It's all in one's vantage point, I suppose. As long as I served in it, the First Army remained to me a typical infantryman's operation: slow, cautious and without much zip.

Hodges asked me if I thought I could take the Second Armored north of the Albert Canal, which knifes through the northeast corner of Flanders near Belgium's border with the Netherlands. He said the British, who were pushing slowly through the Netherlands toward Germany, had complained repeatedly of insufficient liaison between their right flank and the left flank of the First Army. Major General Edward H. Brooks, whom I was about to relieve as commander of the Second Armored, had answered a similar inquiry with the diagnosis that the countryside north of the Albert was unsuited to tanks, Hodges said.

I hadn't seen a map yet, didn't know how the land lay. I asked Hodges whether there were German tanks beyond the canal. He said there were.

"Well, then," I replied, "it's tank country. Wherever German tanks can go, American tanks can go too." The answer seemed to please Hodges.

I moved on then toward my new command, stopping en route to report to my immediate superior, Major General Charles H. Corlett, commander of the XIX Corps. The Second Armored was resting at Hasselt, Belgium, which it had captured three days earlier and which remained a rest and recreation center of the division for the remainder of the war. I greeted Brooks as I arrived and set out on a brief tour of the division's units.

I soon found my earlier tour with the division was not forgotten. As I steered my jeep cautiously down a street in one little Belgian village, I overheard a soldier on the sidewalk say

208

to another, "Don't you know who that man is? That's the son of a bitch who gave us the eggs at Mazagan!"

I stopped the jeep, walked over, and shook hands with the soldier. I asked him if he had been with me in Morocco.

"Yes, sir," he replied. "We are all mighty proud to have you back commanding the division again."

The Second Armored had added many distinguished pages to its history as a fighting unit since I had left it in Morocco. After service in Sicily, it had been shifted to Britain; on June 9, three days after D-day, the division landed on the beachhead at Normandy. In the three months between that landing and my arrival, the Second Armored had battled all the way across France to within striking distance of the German border. The average American tends to link the drive across France solely with the name of George Patton and his Third Army. But the Second Armored and the Third Armored, both components of the First Army, paced off nearly as many miles and fought with the same gallantry, even if the Third Army collected more headlines.

General Brooks turned over command of the division to me on September 12 and I got to work immediately on the problem of getting across the Albert Canal. It was a narrow body of water, but deep. Without a bridge, the canal was as impassable a barrier to tanks as the Atlantic Ocean. I began the standard textbook maneuver for a river crossing against enemy resistance: my artillery moved forward to support infantrymen who, crossing in boats, would secure a bridgehead and build a bridge as rapidly as possible.

But indelibly fixed in my mind was a problem I had wrestled with years earlier at the Army's Command and General Staff School at Fort Leavenworth. The problem was to plan a river crossing for an army corps. Among the specifics provided in the problem was one which its authors thought of as a red herring: twenty-five miles to the right of the corps' location, the student was told there was a ford across the river. The hypothetical corps included a cavalry division. In my solution I had seized upon the red herring, and if I might put it so, turned that herring into a succulent morsel. I said that I would send the division of mounted soldiers down to the unguarded ford under cover of darkness, cross the river there, march them back toward the objective, and rout the enemy with an unsuspected attack from the flank and rear. The heavy losses that inevitably would result from a frontal attack would thus be avoided, I noted. In the schoolroom, however, my instructor was more interested in extracting the answer he desired than in student ingenuity. I argued in vain to shake his decision that my answer was wrong. I was firmly advised that I had evaded the intent of the question, which was to quiz my knowledge of the technique of a frontal river crossing.

The more I looked at the Albert Canal, the more I knew I had been right back at Fort Leavenworth. When reconnaissance elements reported to me that British forces held a crossing over the Albert Canal at Beeringen, about fifteen miles to our left, I promptly sent the Second Armored's Combat Command A, led by General John H. Collier, off to cross the canal. During the night they dropped back down the far side of the canal toward our position. While we poured on the artillery fire from our position in Hasselt, Collier's command attacked the astonished Germans from the rear and gave them a terrific shellacking. As the dust cleared two days later, the Second Armored had bagged several thousand prisoners, suffered only a handful of casualties and controlled all the land between the Albert Canal and the River Meuse. On our left as we faced the Meuse we made contact with the British Second Army. Some of our mopping up was done—in most workmanlike fashion—by a battalion of Norwegian infantrymen. They were fine soldiers.

Both before and after the crossing of the Albert Canal the Second Armored was operating in a situation of considerable fluidity. The Allied advance had been so rapid that pockets of German troops seeking to retreat to their lines were turning up in our midst every day. General Brooks had assigned an

210

infantry company to guard the division headquarters from attack by these German stragglers. But the Second Armored was still organized according to the table of the "big" armored division—heavy on tanks, light on infantry. In that circumstance, I didn't feel the infantry company could be spared for headquarters guard duty; I sent them back to their battalion.

Next morning I wasn't sure my decision had been a sound one. As I stepped out of the van that was my bedroom and office, I almost trod on a German who had come in during the night and was sound asleep underneath it. Fortunately he was delighted to be taken prisoner.

Snipers in the area also posed an uncomfortably common hazard. I dropped the custom, acquired in North Africa and Italy, of traveling by jeep in favor of using an armored car most of the time. It was just as well I made the switch. Several times as I traveled through the countryside from one command post to another I was shot at by unseen Germans. This irritation was relieved in part, by the knowledge that the local populace was fighting with us. On one of my rare excursions by jeep, I was stopped in a tiny Flemish village by a group of excited women. I could not understand what they were chattering about, but they all pointed at an outhouse in a nearby field. I sent my driver over with a carbine, and he flushed a German who was hiding inside. We promptly took him prisoner, and hauled him away on the hood of the jeep. Our prisoner probably came out well in the bargain. The women were well armed with rolling pins, kettles and frying pans. Had we not happened along when we did, I am sure those Flemish housewives would have captured the unfortunate German themselves—and probably a good deal less gently.

In the midst of this campaign, General Bradley reduced the long sector for which First Army was responsible and assigned its northern half—in which we were fighting—to the newly arrived Ninth Army, commanded by Lieutenant General W. H. Simpson. This was a switch much to my liking. Simpson, though little known outside military circles, was one of the

211

truly great leaders of the European theater, a real general's general. As the change in rear echelon command took place, the XIX Corps—and the Second Armored—continued the drive eastward across the Meuse into Holland's Limburg province. Fifteen miles further east lay the border of Germany, homeland of our enemy.

I cannot claim that the Second Armored were the first Allied soldiers to fight their way into the territory of the "Thousand Year" Reich. That honor goes to the Third Armored Division. The Third broke through the purportedly impenetrable Siegfried Line ten miles south of Aachen on September 13. The Second Armored didn't make it until five days later, rolling unopposed into the little village of Wehr. My first sight of Germany was this tiny town. Not a soul was on the streets. All doors and ground level windows were locked and barred, and from nearly every second-floor window hung a white sheet that meant surrender. The German army had fallen back to make its defense at the Siegfried Line, which hugged the east bank of the Wurm River in that part of the country.

The gallant 30th Infantry Division had established a small bridgehead across the Wurm, but was making little progress at enlarging it. I got permission at noon to send my tanks across the bridge at Palenberg. My plan called for Combat Command B to move east one mile to Übach, where the 30th Infantry was fighting, and then swing north through and behind the Siegfried Line to blast the pillboxes out of commission. As soon as we had wrested sufficient maneuvering space, Combat Command A would cross the Wurm also and push south toward Baesweiler and Oidtweiler.

The Germans put up ferocious resistance both from their stationary defenses and from a substantial force of tanks; elimination of the pillboxes was slow and dangerous work. Some we disposed of by firing tank shells or 155-mm rifled artillery through their gun slits. Others, held by particularly determined defenders, fought on until tank-dozers heaped up

212

earth around their rear doors and buried the occupants alive.

We lost about eighty tanks on the first day of the attack, more on the following days, victims of the painfully effective German antitank guns. I could reach my front lines only in a tank, for the lone bridge across the Wurm was pounded by a steady hail of German artillery fire. Fortunately for us, whoever built that masonry span built it strong and built it well. When the battle finally ended five days later the bridge was scarred, but still standing and passable.

I was fascinated by another monument of German architecture there on the Wurm, a lovely castle that belonged to a baron. One day I stopped for a moment to inspect it more closely. Its interior seemed to be from a storybook; marvelous tapestries hanging upon the walls and splended carved wood furniture and magnificent silverware gave mute testimony to the good life someone once had lived there. My orderly wanted me to take an electric warmer we found in one of the bathrooms to install in my caravan, but I refused. I was always very strict on the matter of looting with everyone in my command, including myself.

Late that afternoon when I passed that way again I saw a number of trucks belonging to rear echelon and Air Corps units parked outside the castle. The vehicles were piled high with the baron's possessions. Throughout the war looting by men stationed behind the front lines was truly scandalous. Very little of such pillaging was done by combat troops; their discipline was higher, they had no way to transport booty, and perhaps most important, they were too busy fighting to have time to steal other people's property.

In fact, the Germans kept us very busy at Übach. Progress for the first two days of fighting was painfully slow. At nightfall October 4 Combat Command B's three columns were only about 1,000 yards beyond the town. Things went a little better the following day for the columns on the right and left, but the center column made virtually no headway. The center column commander reported his forces—principally the 3rd

213

battalion, 67th Armored Regiment—had run into a murderous crossfire from dug-in antitank guns and artillery. No doubt this was true, but I also felt that his spirit was not sufficiently aggressive. I relieved him and put in a new man, Major Clifton B. Batchelder, with orders to capture Waurichen, a village about a mile to the northeast.

The change in command may have made the difference. At 11 A.M. October 6 a company of light tanks, maneuvering rapidly in muddy fields that had bogged down medium tanks, broke through the German defenses. At thirty-five miles an hour they raced through fortifications, dug-in infantry troops armed with bazookas, and took the high ground that contained the last fringe of the Siegfried Line. Evidently the quick, mosquitolike shifts of direction that the light tanks were capable of were more than slow-moving German gunners could deal with. The German lines began to dissolve, and our medium tanks stepped up the force of the attack.

Once pierced, a fixed defensive line is like an earth dam that is breached. After the initial crack appears, the chance of sealing off the leak is slight. What had initially been a trickle of American tanks through the Siegfried Line became a flood. I ordered Combat Command A forward to begin the drive to the south. Beggendorf fell into our hands that same day; in the following two days we added Baesweiler and Oidtweiler to our tally and dug in on a defensive line that we held for the next five weeks.

1944 - Enlisted men of 2nd Armored Division stand guard over captured German troops.

1944 - General Harmon with captured German officers.

1944 - Members of a 2nd Armored Division patrol enter Belgium, the first American troops to enter that country during World War II.

1945 - January: General Harmon and General "Pee Wee" Collier discuss Bulge Battle.

1944 - At Cologne, vehicle bridge (foreground) substitutes for destroyed bridges that linked the city.

1945 - June: Field Marshall Montgomery and General Harmon inspect the Krupp works in Germany.

1946 - In France, General Harmon says goodbye to NCOs of the 2nd Armored Division.

FIFTEEN
★★
The Advance to the Roer

THE SECOND ARMORED'S twelve-day drive to the Roer River gets little space in the history books although some believe it was the most titanic U.S. tank battle of all time. It certainly was the toughest fight of my military career. But the Allies were not able to capitalize on that salient we so painfully drove toward Germany's industrial heartland. Shortages of supplies, and possibly tactical mismanagement as well, delayed the capture of the all-important Roer dams to the south of our sector. Then the great German counteroffensive in the Ardennes—the Battle of the Bulge—threw all Allied strategy topsy-turvy, and our advance to the Roer became little more than a footnote to the military record.

We jumped off on our offensive on November 16 after holding a defensive line more than a month just east of the little German towns of Oidtweiler, Baesweiler, Beggendorf, and Waurichen. The distance from our line to the Roer, our initial objective, was less than 10 miles, but as it turned out those were to be bitterly contested and bloody miles.

During the lull that followed our punch through the Siegfried Line, General Bradley had reshuffled the positions of the Armies under his command. The northernmost segment of his sector, where we were operating, was assigned to the Ninth Army. This brought the XIX Corps (and of course the Second

215

Armored) under the direction of General Simpson. Bradley confesses in his memoirs that he moved in Simpson, his greenest Army commander, in the expectation that Montgomery would soon succeed in wangling transfer of the U.S. Army nearest him to his British Army Group. That bit of high brass larceny did not occur until later, however; and so far as I was concerned, Simpson's appearance as my superior was a rich reward. He was a pleasure to fight under.

The XIX Corps' commander, General Corlett, had been having increasing problems with a stomach ulcer, and shortly after the corps was assigned to the Ninth Army, Simpson had to relieve him for health reasons. The three division commanders in the corps—Major General Charles H. Gerhardt of the 29th Infantry, Major General Leland S. Hobbs of the 30th Infantry, and I, all seasoned veterans—hoped one of us might be promoted to the command. All three of us were disappointed. Major General Raymond S. McLain, a National Guard officer, arrived from France to take over the corps. Simpson told me later that General Marshall had personally selected McLain for the post to silence protests from National Guardsmen that too few of their number had received top commands. Despite his relative inexperience, McLain proved to be an able commander.

It was during this October lull that a soldier of the Second Armored earned the first and only Congressional Medal of Honor awarded to a member of the division in World War II. On our right flank the 30th Division had been battling to overwhelm a tenaciously held German garrison in the town of Würselen. Finally, on October 13, our 66th Armored Regiment joined forces with men of the 30th to mount a coordinated infantry-tank attack on the town.

Captain James M. Burt, who had learned his military science at Norwich University, was commander of the Regiment's Company B. On the first day of the attack Burt saw a group of foot soldiers run into a murderous volley of small arms and mortar fire some 200 yards in front of him. Dis-

216

mounting from his tank, he darted forward to a rise beyond the infantrymen and, ignoring the fire instantly turned in his direction, calmly motioned his tanks into a position where they could defend the pinned-down soldiers. As the attack gained momentum, he returned to his tank and continued to direct the operation from an exposed position on the rear deck. Throughout this period he was continuously under heavy and almost point-blank German fire, and finally was painfully wounded in the face and neck.

Despite his wounds, he continued to display similar aggressive leadership for the next eight days. The official battle report that accompanied Burt's Medal of Honor citation observed: "Captain Burt's intrepidity and disregard for personal safety were so complete that his men, and the infantry who attached themselves to him, were inspired to overcome the wretched and extremely hazardous conditions which accompanied one of the most bitter local actions of the war."

Our push toward the Roer was part of a coordinated eastward offensive Bradley had ordered all up and down his 140-mile front in what he figured was likely to be the last major campaign possible before spring. The weather was not on our side. As the Second Armored moved into the final stages of preparation for the offensive, clouds laden with biting autumn rain swept in. For three days and three nights the rain drummed down on us. Each day the high command called off the air strike that was to soften up the enemy before our attack. Finally the ground became so sodden I had grave doubts that our tanks would be able to maneuver in the quagmire. My staff, even more dubious than I, urged me to notify General McLain, the Corps commander, that our attack would have to be postponed until the ground dried.

To settle the question, I hailed a tank that was maneuvering in the rain about 800 meters back from our line and climbed in with the driver. He and I drove around together for a while, and I asked how he thought our armor would fare when we began the attack. He reflected briefly, then said the tanks

217

would have to drive in lower gear than usual but would have sufficient traction to plow through the mud. I returned to my command post at Baesweiler and reported to McLain and Simpson that the Second Armored was ready to attack when ordered, with or without the preliminary air strike.

But the morning of November 16 dawned clear. As noon drew near we could hear the sweet drone of approaching Allied bombers during pauses between rounds of artillery fire. The Belgium-based fighter-bombers pounded Immendorf, Floverich, Loverich, Gereonsweiler, and Ederen with a saturation attack. At 12:45 P.M. our tanks and infantry swept forward. Operation QUEEN was under way.

For the opening stages of the campaign the Second Armored had been reinforced with the infantry and artillery of the newly arrived 102nd Division. (This was in line with General Marshall's directive that green soldiers get their first combat experience fighting at the side of battle-hardened units.) Aerial reconnaissance had disclosed an ominous looking tank ditch not far east of our jumping-off point that was defended by numerous antitank gun positions. It looked to me like we had a very tough fight on our hands.

My plan of battle called for the initial attack to be mounted by three task forces of Brigadier General Isaac D. White's Combat Command B. As the tanks moved east the infantrymen of the 102nd Division were to be placed in the line, regiment by regiment, to hold our lengthening northern flank. When our attack, and the coordinated attack of the 29th Division on our right to the south, had gained sufficient ground, I intended to bring up General Collier's Combat Command A to wheel around behind the German strongpoints in front of us.

Our attack began with deceptive ease. The antitank ditch had cast an impressive shadow on our reconnaissance photographs but it turned out to be only a foot and a half deep, scarcely any obstacle to our tanks at all. Floverich, Loverich, Immendorf, and Puffendorf fell into our hands before the

218

afternoon was over, and when we took a count at day's end we found we had captured 570 enemy prisoners. Both on the opening day of the campaign and on the following two days our attack forces had the support of Allied fighter-bombers. This kind of close tactical air assistance was a new experience to me. The decks of our tanks were draped with brilliant orange sheets so the pilots wheeling above us in the sky could spot the front line; air liaison officers riding in the tanks kept in touch with the fliers by radio, directing their bombs and machine gun fire toward troublesome enemy strongpoints.

By the second day of the campaign, however, the Germans were ready to launch fierce counterattacks. The brisk pace at which we stepped off the first day slowed to a crawl. I brought a task force of Combat Command A up from their assembly area on the east bank of the Wurm and assigned them the mission of driving east from Puffendorf, but savage tank and antitank fire and repeated artillery barrages stalled their advance almost at once. On the northern part of our front Combat Command B was doing little better.

Matters did not improve on the third day of Operation QUEEN. It became clear to me that we could not accelerate our advance until I was able to throw the full power of Combat Command A into the line for my projected flanking maneuver. But that maneuver required jumping off from Setterich, a small town just south of the Second Armored's zone in the sector assigned to the 29th Division; and Setterich, largely bypassed by the 29th, remained in enemy hands. As I studied my maps, the reason why became obvious. Although possession of Setterich was crucial to my attack plan, it was of virtually no tactical significance to the advance of the 29th. The 29th was picking away at Setterich's defenses with just two battalions of infantry while the bulk of its force was fighting elsewhere on its front.

This experience taught me an important lesson: when a piece of terrain is essential to the success of your attack, don't count on "coordination" with another division to put it in your

219

hands; insist on its being added to your sector, even if such a transfer does widen your front. I successfully convinced XIX Corps headquarters to switch Setterich into my sector on the morning of November 19. In two hours I had infantry and tanks in there and the town was ours.

The weather by this time had closed in on us again, cutting off air support, but the fall of Setterich cleared the way for us to launch a major attack. The next morning we swept out in five task forces aimed at the three fortified towns of Freialdenhoven, Ederen, and Gereonsweiler. Although the Germans resisted fiercely, our increase in force and maneuvering space turned the trick. A small British force, two troops of the First Fife and Forfar Yeomanry, supported our tanks and infantry with the Crocodile, a flamethrowing tank; they were of great assistance in flushing diehard enemy snipers who had taken up cellar positions in Gereonsweiler, the largest town on our agenda for the day.

In the midst of the day's battle, General Bradley and General Simpson dropped into my command post near Baesweiler to see how we were faring. They picked a good day to come; the near-stalemate of earlier days of the operation was clearly broken. Heavy German tank and antitank fire was disabling many of our tanks (though our able mechanics put many of them back into service again, most within twenty-four hours), but we were making steady progress toward our objectives. Bradley and Simpson both seemed greatly pleased with what was going on. In fact, in late November 1944 all eyes in the Allied high command were watching the eastward movement of the pins on the big mapboards that stood for the Second Armored and other divisions in our immediate vicinity. We were the only forces on the long western front that had broken through the Siegfried Line and were pressing on toward the plains of the River Rhine, the great industrial heartland of our enemy.

That night I leaned back comfortably in my caravan and reviewed the day's accomplishments. Our front had been

220

pushed out more than a mile both to the north and the east. The troublesome enemy positions in Gereonsweiler, Ederen, and Freialdenhoven would trouble us no longer. All three towns were ours. I was feeling pretty good.

My day was further enriched in those pleasant, after-the-battle moments of the early evening by an unexpected visit from a very tired, very dirty young soldier, my son Robert. Bob at that time was serving in a tank battalion attached to an infantry division that was fighting not far from our sector. It was obvious from his appearance that he had been pretty busy himself and hadn't had much opportunity to get cleaned up. I asked my orderly to scare up some clean clothes and supper for him; those amenities attended to, we sat down in my caravan to talk.

With some reluctance, Bob told me how he happened to be on leave in the midst of the November campaign and thus free to pay me a visit. A few days earlier, he said, he had been driving a tank when an enemy shell pierced the turret, killing the commander and setting the tank afire. He had managed to escape unscathed from the flaming tank. Then two or three days later, he was commanding another tank when it too was struck by German gunfire and set ablaze; that time the driver was killed. Bob's battalion commander, I suppose, decided enough was enough. At any rate he gave the young man three days' leave.

I mulled over these revelations and decided for the first time in my career to use my influence for personal reasons. Picking up the telephone, I called General Bradley and asked him if he would transfer a soldier, serial number so-and-so, to my division, no questions asked.

"Certainly," replied Bradley. "Any time you want me to."

I confessed then that it was my son I wanted reassigned and that I wanted the transfer right away.

"No problem," said Bradley. "Let the boy stay right there. It may take a month to get the paperwork done, but eventually the confirming orders will come through."

221

Feeling much better, I hung up the phone and turned to Bob. I told him he was now transferred to my division and would be assigned to a supply battalion. "Two escapes like that are enough," I said. "I'm going to put you somewhere where you won't be shot at so quickly."

Bob was not pleased with my plan. He is a very stubborn character. "If I'm going to stay with your division," he said in a tone of voice not generally acceptable when noncoms address general officers, "I want to be assigned to a combat regiment."

By this time both of us were a little angry. "All right," I said in exasperation. "Tomorrow we're going to resume the attack. I'll put you in Company A of the 67th Armored Regiment. They're going to lead the attack." And a little later Bob went off in the night with a guide to join his new regiment.

I wouldn't have admitted it to Bob at the time, but I worried a lot about him privately. I made a quiet arrangement with my orderly, one that lasted as long as I was with the Second Armored: every morning the orderly was to check on the grapevine and report back to me whether my son was still alive. Stubbornness didn't hurt Bob as a soldier. He stayed with the 67th Armored Regiment until the end of the war and ultimately became the first sergeant of a tank company.

My oldest son, Halsey, was also stationed in Europe, an engineer attached to First Army. In March of 1945 his 1264th Engineers Combat Battalion built the tank pontoon bridge across the Rhine that permitted the continued reinforcement and supply of the Allied bridgehead beyond the river after the battered Remagen bridge finally collapsed.

I suspect it's not easy for a soldier to be a general's son. Long after the war was over I got a letter from Ernest J. Connelly, a librarian who lives in Hopewell, Virginia, who told me that early in the war, when he was stationed at Camp Edwards, Massachusetts, he had assigned another of my sons, Ernest, Jr., to KP duty. Young Ernie, said my correspondent, was turning in a commendable performance in the kitchen,

222

when suddenly a captain burst into Connelly's office.

"Connelly, Connelly," he shouted, "what in the hell do you mean putting a general's son on KP?"

Puzzled, Connelly replied, "Captain, I'm sorry, I didn't know there was a general's son within a thousand miles of here. Tell me which one is he?"

"Harmon's his name," was the reply. "His father is a famous general. You'll be the cause of all of us losing our commissions if you ever do such a thing again. Take him off KP this instant and send Private Harmon over to my office."

Connelly reported that Ernie, Jr., told him ruefully, after he was pulled off the duty and was on his way to receive the captain's apology, that the same thing happened to him everywhere he was stationed.

When he completed his training as an amphibious engineer at Camp Edwards, Ernie, my youngest son, was sent to the Pacific Theater. At age 18, as engine man on an LCM he helped get our troops ashore at Guadalcanal and participated in the operations around Manila Bay and Leyte in the Philippine Islands. He came home at the end of the war an unscathed corporal!

The sun was still battened away in the unbroken clouds when I stuck my head out of my caravan early on the morning of November 21 to check the weather. Once again we would have to fight without air cover. Despite the lack of support from the air, however, General White's Combat Command B made a respectable advance; by noon they had driven a mile north of Gereonsweiler and seized a hilltop overlooking the town of Linnich two miles to the east. That high ground gave us our first view of our ultimate objective, the River Roer.

In the southern half of our sector Combat Command A pounded east as far as the outskirts of Merzenhausen, but determined enemy resistance prevented us from entering the town until the following day. By midday the skies had cleared sufficiently for German planes to be in the air, though ours unfortunately were still buttoned down on their bases in

223

Belgium. Several reports flowed into my command post of enemy bombing and strafing of our positions. But an antiaircraft battalion attached to the Second Armored saw to it that the Germans were not harassing us from the air with impunity; out of one enemy flight of fifteen planes, the AA boys reported, they shot down three craft, two Folke-Wulfs and a Messerschmitt.

That day was the end of the offensive for Combat Command B. On the following days they reverted to a defensive posture, and one by one their units were replaced by elements of the now-blooded 109th Infantry Division. Three days later we yielded complete responsibility for what had been the northern half of our sector to the 109th. But on the south, elements of Combat Command A continued to inch forward against sturdy German resistance. It was not until November 28 that we beat our way through the village of Barmen and succeeded in securing all of our sector west of the Roer.

Later, after the German counteroffensive in the Ardennes began and I had the benefit of hindsight, I wondered whether I should have guessed why the enemy put up such fierce resistance in that tiny toehold we had in Germany west of the Roer, an area that appeared to have relatively little strategic significance. I had one clue: our intelligence told me that there were unusually heavy concentrations of German armor east of the Rhine. But at the time I did not know what the concentrations presaged. In the succeeding weeks the reason became clear enough: vast armies were on the move as Field Marshal Gerd von Rundstedt prepared for a counterattack far more powerful than the Allied high command realized he could mount. Understandably, von Rundstedt wanted no American forces close enough to the plains of Cologne to realize what was afoot.

As things turned out, there was no chance that the Second Armored could have been the Allied force that spied out the land to the east and uncovered the Germans' plans. The tactics of war are like an interlocking jigsaw puzzle, and a

piece of the puzzle vital to further Second Armored advance
was missing: to the south of us General Hodges' First Army
had failed in its mission of taking the two huge Roer dams. In
our area the Roer looked innocent and unprepossessing
enough, but our experts informed us that any time the
Germans chose to blow up the 180-foot Schwammenauel dam,
a wall of water twenty-five feet high and a mile and a half
wide would rage down the Roer valley. There could be no
hope of supplying or reinforcing any Allied advance force
unfortunate enough to be east of the Roer when such a tide
roared passed.

The bitter battle of Hürtgen Forest, Hodges' attempt to take
the Roer dams, is not a part of my own story. But I have often
pondered the lesson of that bloody and ultimately futile effort.
The battle of Hürtgen Forest gets little space in the history
books, possibly because no one cares to dwell on how three
gallant American infantry divisions—the Second, the Fourth,
and the 28th—had the heart chewed out of them. I am
convinced that other strategists, who better understood the
value and fighting qualities of tanks, could have organized the
capture of those dams—and at far more modest cost in human
life. Maps of the area show clearly that it is good tank
country. Heavy armored columns advancing on either side of
the forest could have performed a double envelopment of the
dams that would have made the infantry action unnecessary.
Instead, foot soldiers fought through the woods from tree to
tree and many, too many, did not return.

Since crossing the Roer was barred to the Second Armored,
we shifted to the defense, began to tally up our score sheets
for the campaign and to restore our men and machines to
fresh fighting trim again. The record proved to be one any
division could take pride in. Our casualties were 203 dead
(including one battalion commander, Lieutenant Colonel
Charles E. Etter), 198 missing, and 1,104 wounded. But we
took 2,385 Germans prisoner and killed an estimated 830
more. Possibly even more significant, in view of the increasing

shortages the enemy was suffering in supply, was our destruction of 86 German tanks, nearly the entire tank complement of a Panzer division. Of our own tanks 80 were disabled in the course of the twelve-day battle, but more than half of these were subsequently repaired and returned to service.

On December 16 I was notified that the Germans had launched a major counteroffensive to the south of us in the Ardennes. The Second Armored was put on double alert while we waited to learn what role, if any, we would be assigned in beating back the attack.

226

SIXTEEN
★ ★
The Battle of the Bulge

DECEMBER 21, 1944, was a dark and overcast day. The military news that reached my command post in Baesweiler was also dark, and profoundly confused. An enemy penetration like the one that was sweeping through Belgium to the south and west of us demolishes communications; when that happens your rumor is as good as mine. The Germans' offensive had already been under way for five days, and generals and GIs alike knew the situation was grave. Rumor made it graver still. Germans in American uniforms—or so the story went—were wandering the countryside and fooling everybody. The fact is that Colonel Otto Skorzeny—who stole Mussolini from his Allied captors—and his mysterious 150th Brigade had hoped to do just that. They had the American uniforms all right, but the fluent English of the German parachutists was neither slangy nor profane enough to deceive Brooklynites and Kansans. Most of the parachutists were caught.

The Allied high command, alarmed almost to the point of panic by the Germans' explosive thrust through the weakly held Ardennes, had hastily rearranged the command structure. The enemy attack had pierced Allied lines at the midpoint of the long front assigned to General Bradley's Army Group; his American forces north of the Bulge were turned over to the command of Field Marshal Montgomery. The exact intentions of Field Marshal von Rundstedt were of course unknown to us, but their broad outline seemed clear enough. His spearhead was directed at Liège, but his eye was cocked at Antwerp, the principal terminal for Allied war supplies on the continent. If von Rundstedt seized the Antwerp storehouses, thirty-two Allied divisions—half our forces in France and the Low Countries—would be cut off from supplies and close to suffocation by the Germans.

When word of the sudden German thrust into the Ardennes reached us in the Ninth Army's sector, we were at first afraid the action that had begun might be only the southern half of a two-pronged drive also aimed right at us. Both Simpson and I were painfully aware of how weakly held the Allied front was in the area just northeast of Geilenkirchen, where the Ninth Army sector joined that of the Second British Army. In a worried conversation, he and I speculated on the swiftness with which a German attack might slice down the soft seam that joined the U.S. and British sectors; sweep past Geilenkirchen and Maastricht; and join the southern German attack force somewhere around Liège. Finally I proposed—and Simpson agreed—that we send Collier and his Combat Command A back to the west side of the Wurm in the hope that Collier could at least slow, if not stop, such a German thrust if it came. I still believe that if von Rundstedt had included in his plan of attack the northern thrust that Simpson and I greatly feared, he might have succeeded in capturing the prize he sought, the port of Antwerp.

We now know far more than we did in that bleak December just how the German high command conceived their Ardennes counteroffensive, an action personally ordered by Hitler to snatch victory from defeat. In broad outline, their plan was simple: two powerful Panzer armies, the Fifth under General Hasso von Manteuffel and the Sixth under the notorious General Sepp Dietrich, a fanatical Nazi but an incompetent soldier, would strike suddenly through the Ardennes, sweep across a previously captured bridgehead over the Meuse near Liège, and drive on from there to Antwerp. Meanwhile a third German army, the Seventh under General Erich Brandenberger, would protect the attackers' southern flank by keeping Patton's Third Army at bay. The bridgehead itself was to be seized by Skorzeny's paratroopers. But, unknown to us at the time, von Rundstedt's plan began to go awry almost at once with the abject failure of Skorzeny's brigade to accomplish its mission.

On that morning of December 21 I was again summoned to Simpson's headquarters at Maastricht. I figured I knew what the summons meant: we were to pull out of our positions in Germany and plunge into the Ardennes battle. When I reached Maastricht, I discovered that Simpson was attending a highly important war council some miles away, and that he had left instructions for me to await his return. That made me doubly sure. I promptly got my own headquarters on the telephone and, in a guarded conversation, advised staff officers to make preparations for movement.

It was four in the afternoon before General Simpson returned. He was gloomy and preoccupied. Second Armored had been shifted from the Ninth Army to the First Army and attached to VII Corps, commanded by my old friend and West Point classmate, General "Lightning Joe" Collins. We were to proceed seventy miles over narrow, icy highways to an assembly area in the bend of the Meuse River near the town of Havelange, Belgium, and we must roll before midnight.

The movement of an oversize armored division in a congested combat area is invariably one hell of a traffic problem. It was no simple job for First Army to select routes directly across its battle front and lines of communication. We had a roster of 14,000 men, 3,000 vehicles of all types, and 450 heavily armored mobile units. On a single road with vehicles separated by at least the regulation fifty yards, we made a column more than 100 miles long.

It is difficult now to recreate the atmosphere and uncertainties of that day. Bad weather had prevented Allied air observation of the Ardennes area—a factor, we learned later, von Runstedt had counted on. As a result, no one had a very clear picture of where the Germans were or where they might be tomorrow. It was not yet dark when I left Maastricht and jeeped over to General Collins' headquarters. I was nervous; I still did not have those all-important routings and I knew several hours would elapse before they would be available. Collins sketched in what was then known: the Germans were still pouring westward, aiming at a crossing of the Meuse River. British units guarded the Meuse line. VII Corps and Second Armored were to steer clear of the fight for the time being, in order to be in readiness to hit the enemy an overpowering blow in the flank at an opportune moment.

It was 8 P.M. before the routings came through, and I left at once for my headquarters at Baesweiler. My principal commanders and the thirty officers of the reconnaissance battalion were assembled when I arrived; it was then ten o'clock. Second Armored's combat units were to be divided and to travel by two separate routes. There was no time for the formality of written orders; we must be on our way. Hurriedly we marked the routes on thirty maps, and at 10:30 the light vehicles of the reconnaissance battalion moved out. They were to lead the way on both marches. To minimize mistakes in direction and to prevent wrong turnings, I ordered these advance units to drop off a soldier at every crossroad. This provided a living set of markers all the way to Havelange.

Military historians have nominated the Second Armored's advance as one for the books. The main columns began to move at 11:30. All military identification on vehicles had been obliterated in the interest of secrecy. The night was pitch black. The roads were slippery with sleet and ice and clogged with traffic. There was an unremitting drizzle. The convoys traveled under complete blackout restrictions over roads they had never seen. The routes which began on the east of the Meuse River, led through the rubble that once had been the

230

city of Aachen, and thence turned south and west through hilly wooded country. Tanks growled through the outskirts of Liège as German buzz bombs droned overhead.

Meanwhile, Second Armored's supply trains were moving down the west side of the Meuse, assigned to load up new supplies of gasoline and meet up with the combat units at Huy. This way we were able to refuel our armor as soon as it arrived in the new area.

I decided to remain at Baesweiler for what was left of the night. I rose at dawn, snatched breakfast at a field kitchen on the road, and, by driving over uncongested if roundabout highways, was able to be at Havelange at 8 A.M., as my troops began to arrive. By noon the major combat elements were there and—at the price of 60,000 gallons of gasoline—we were ready for battle.

By the evening of December 22 we were successfully bivouacked in our new area. I still consider that seventy-mile march a truly remarkable achievement. No one lost his way. Despite ice and darkness, only eleven vehicles failed to be in at the finish. They had skidded off the roads on treacherous turns or grades. This was the pay-off for organization, troop morale and the intelligence of junior officers, noncoms and the men in ranks.

My chief of staff at this time was Colonel C. S. Mansfield, and much of the credit must go to him. Mansfield was a fine soldier; I had known and liked him for years. His death, a little more than two weeks later, was a profound tragedy for me. Mansfield had repeatedly requested command of a combat regiment, and eventually I gave in. At the head of the 66th Armored Regiment, he distinguished himself in some particularly difficult jobs at a very difficult time. It was my habit to carry in my pocket a few Silver Star decorations, so that when I visited the front lines I might reward deserving soldiers on the spot. On the morning of January 9 I decorated Colonel Mansfield with the Silver Star for gallantry in action. About five minutes later, he was killed by a direct hit from a

German .88. When we picked him up, the Silver Star was still pinned to his blouse.

My first job at Havelange might be classified as diplomacy. The Belgian farmers in the area were understandably frightened; they had met Germans in the past, and they knew Hitler's legions were already moving along the banks of the Lesse River, only twenty miles to the south. Their natural impulse was to pack up possessions and flee north with their families. But if the military roads in the area were clogged with refugees, our troops would not be able to function efficiently. I forbade all civilian movement and promised the peasants that the Germans would never get through. The promise was kept.

The morning of December 23 dawned cold. There were a few snow squalls. My new headquarters was located snugly in a beautiful small chateau. I left the chateau very early in order to call on General Collins at his new post. I discovered that not only the countryside but the entire American Army was in a high state of alarm. There were roadblocks everywhere. Sign and countersign were needed to get through them, and the passwords were frequently changed. This was supposed to trip up the German parachutists; on this particular day it almost tripped me up. I didn't know the countersign. I was stopped by a stubborn outpost sentry, but apparently my cuss words had an authentic American ring. He listened with a music critic's ear to the sulphurous rhythms and, grinning, let me pass.

Collins now was located about fifteen miles from Marche, Belgium. His newly assembled corps consisted at the moment of Second Armored, the 84th Infantry Division and the unvetted 75th Infantry Division, which had just arrived from Normandy. Collins had unexpected news. His 84th Infantry Division, which was located at Marche, was already heavily engaged with the enemy. This, apparently, was the picture: the Germans, driving west, constantly tried to swing north toward Namur and Liège. When they turned northward near

Hotton, their Sixth Panzer Army encountered our Third Armored Division. Then they sideslipped to the west again in the hope of finding softer territory and there ran smack into the 84th. Collins, however, was still hopeful that the original strategy—to punch the German with an unexpected blow at his flank—could be carried out at least in part. Second Armored was to lie quiet and hold for a surprise counterattack. It seemed to him likely that we would not be committed to battle for a week or ten days.

I passed this good news on to my officers when I arrived back at Havelange. They stayed for lunch, and all of us relaxed. It was left to a faithful lieutenant to play the role of the specter at the feast. We were drinking our coffee when the mess sergeant informed me that a young officer was demanding audience. Lieutenant Everett C. Jones came in. He was excited and he had a bloody bandage on his head. Marshal Montgomery's wait-awhile-and-hit-'em-later strategy vanished right there. The Germans had already hit us.

This was Jones' story: He was in command of one of the reconnaissance patrols which had been sent to the south of the assembly area. At the village of Haid—just an hour before—his patrol had been fired on by a group of German vehicles which included two Mark IV tanks. His own armored car had been hit, but he and the crew had escaped. A look at the map showed that Haid was just ten miles to the south. The implications were obvious. The German spearhead, evading the fight at Marche, had turned north again and was once more on its way to the Meuse.

It was plain to me that this was a time for action. Secrecy was a thing of the past; the contact at Haid had officially notified the Germans we were in the area. The house was on fire and somebody had to put the fire out. I ran across a field to a grove of trees where a tank battalion had gone into bivouac. I asked a tank captain how long it would take him to get moving. He said that if radio silence was lifted, he could be on his way in five minutes.

"Radio silence is lifted here and now," I said. "You get down that road to a town called Ciney. The enemy is coming up from the south. You block the entrances and exits to Ciney and start fighting. The whole damn division is coming right behind you."

Within five minutes seventeen Sherman tanks were headed south with throttles wide open. My second bit of sprinting led me to Lieutenant Colonel Hugh O'Farrell, commander of the tank battalion. He said he could get his outfit underway in fifteen minutes, and I ordered him to secure Ciney and to hold it until the rest of the division could arrive. With just these two verbal orders Second Armored jumped up to its armpits into the Battle of the Bulge.

I immediately telephoned General Collins. He agreed that the action I had taken was necessary and justified. Montgomery's previous orders to remain unobserved and quiet had been superseded by events—war, historically, is odd that way. Soon the main road was filled with tanks and armored cars hastening troops to the battle. Artillery prepared for action in nearby fields, and Cub planes buzzed above us to guide the artillery's blasts.

Ciney was important because it was the focal point of the road network between Marche and the Meuse, so I was taking no chances of being overpowered. I have always felt that if a situation calls for a toothpick, a baseball bat may serve even better. When the tanks reached Ciney they found the enemy had not yet got there. The town was immediately organized for defense, and General Collier's Combat Command A pushed on.

At about 9 P.M. Collier made contact with the Germans at the town of Leignon. It was only a skirmish, but we had to attack in considerable force to possess the town. Collier told me he would proceed on south at first light in the morning. This was not good enough. General Collins had made a point, in our telephone conversation, of the importance of the village of Buissonville, about eighteen miles south of Ciney. It was unprotected, and it needed to be occupied in order to secure the flank of the beleaguered 84th Division. I directed Collier to march immediately on Buissonville. Tanks normally fight only in the daytime, and Collier was a little incredulous when I ordered him to attack all night with his blind column. Very properly, he asked me to repeat my order. I repeated it. Collier may have blinked a couple of times, but, like the superb soldier he was, he said only, "Yes, sir, we will be on our way."

It was Colonel O'Farrell who led the column in the darkness toward Buissonville. As the fast advance patrols skittered along ahead in their jeeps, they heard the noise of a German armored column moving toward them. O'Farrell, one of the finest combat fighters I ever knew, immediately capitalized on his advantage. He split his outfit and put it into position in the shadows of big trees that crowded both sides of the road; darkness shrouded the waiting tanks. He was to manage something rare in modern warefare—an armored ambush. When the German column appeared two hours after midnight, our machine guns, cannons, and mortars cut loose. It was, rather grimly, the blazing gasoline in the German tanks hit by our shells that made the accuracy of American marksmanship so satisfactory in the darkness. By this extraordinary light, the slaughter continued until almost the entire German column was destroyed. It was four in the morning before Combat A, its own losses negligible because of the surprise element and the force of its attack, could coil up by the side of the road. But at 8:30 A.M. the advance was again resumed both on the highways and cross country. There were several minor tank fights, but by 2:30 P.M. Buissonville had been occupied.

Combat Command B, led by General White, took over the defense of Ciney in the meantime, and extended patrols to the north and west. Reports from these patrols and from air reconnaissance—the skies cleared magically on the day before Christmas—indicated there was another large German column in the vicinity of Celles. The French and Belgian underground

235

brought us word that this Panzer outfit was short of gasoline. The German hope of replenishing fuel from captured stocks had not materialized.

At dark on Christmas Eve our position had been clarified and looked encouraging. All that noisy day Allied planes roared through the cleared skies, swooping down on enemy units and wreaking havoc among them. I proposed to continue our attack at first light on Christmas Day. This meant carrying on—fifteen miles apart—two more or less independent battles. Collier would press on south toward the Lesse River while White struck at Celles. The fifteen-mile gap between the forces was held successfully throughout the struggle by the 4th Mechanized Cavalry (reinforced by some Second Armored artillery and tanks) under that dour and imperturbable Scot, Colonel John C. MacDonald.

I had moved from my comfortable billet at Havelange to an abandoned chateau in the wood in order to be nearer the battle. I remember we were almost suffocated by smoke when we started fires in the sooty old fireplaces. I did not then know that, three weeks later, I would look back on these rude quarters with nostalgia while I watched my personal staff dig a three-foot layer of cow dung out of a Belgian stone stable, so I would have a roof over my head for the night and a place for my telephones.

A seasonal sentimentalist, I was more than a little dismal as I sat in a drafty room on Christmas Eve and watched a wet and unwilling Yule log sputter. If I were home, I reflected, it would be time to start decorating the family tree, but my three boys, Army men like me, were also somewhere else tonight. Back in the States there would be carol singing and colored lights and the resinous smell of evergreens. Christmas had always been a big day at our house, but now it seemed a million miles away. I knew that it seemed a million miles away to my GIs—homesick, too—huddled in their bivouacs.

Mounting the Christmas attack required some rather serious finagling with military orders. First Army headquarters had

236

prescribed that we move back and assume a defensive position, but General Collins and I were both convinced that we had the enemy in the bag and that an attack was imperative. Ultimately Collins took it on his own shoulders to give me authority to attack. To me, the whole experience was a clear demonstration that the high command, surveying the scene from forty miles away, was too distant to sense the real situation at the front.

All troops jumped off at dawn on schedule. We now knew the Second Austrian Panzer Division was in front of us. This was an old enemy the Second Armored had met in no-decision battles in France. We hoped to settle scores once and for all. We knew also that the outcome of the whole Bulge battle might be riding in our turrets. The weather was clear and cold. White's Combat Command B attack on Celles had annihilation of the enemy as its aim. One column swung to the southwest to cut off the retreat of the Germans, and the other columns moved down to surround them from the northeast and west. The attack was brilliantly executed and by 5 P.M. Celles was taken, with an undertermined force of German armor and artillery surrounded in the forest northeast of the town. Several attempts to counterattack and provide an escape out of the pocket had failed, and two attempts by German columns approaching from the south to relieve Celles had been beaten off successfully.

On the left flank, however, Collier's Combat Command A pushed forward slowly and met increasing resistance. A task force made a night march on the town of Humain on Christmas Eve, and gained it early on Christmas Day. The task force was a small one, and it was heavily counterattacked and driven out at 7:30 in the morning. Our infantry made two efforts to recapture the town during the day, but elements of the German Ninth Panzer had rushed to the aid of Second Panzer and held on stubbornly. The town of Humain was to become a serious military problem for us.

On Christmas night, as I returned from battlefield inspections, the situation seemed rugged but promising. I felt sure that White could withstand the periodic attacks launched to relieve the beleaguered enemy caught in the Celles pocket. Collier's problem was something else again. The Germans were still determined to go north to the Meuse. The air observers reported a heavy German build-up aimed squarely at Humain. I told Collier to get set, hold his position, and be prepared to attack on December 27th.

It was 10 P.M. before my staff and I had time to eat dinner. In the press of events, I'd forgotten we had something rather special in store. The day before, I had spotted a large swan swimming around in a chilly pool near the chateau. I had never eaten swan nor heard of anyone eating swan, but I had an intuitive feeling that it was closer to a proper Christmas dinner than C-rations. I told my jeep driver to shoot the swan with his carbine and take it to the mess sergeant. The driver said swans weren't good to eat. The mess sergeant agreed. I ordered it cooked anyway.

That enormous bird came in on a platter, and my weary junior officers looked at it dubiously. I pitched in, and the others, a little hesitantly, followed suit. It tasted much like duck, and I found it excellent. So, apparently, did everybody else. When I went to the kitchen for a midnight snack, I looked sadly at the devastated carcass; nothing was left but the sturdy bones.

The next two days saw heavy slugging. At Celles the Germans tried Trojan Horse tactics on us by leading one of their sorties with captured American vehicles. After that, extreme care had to be exercised to avoid firing on friendly units—since all vehicles were suspect until identified. The enemy's stubborn resistance can be measured by the small ratio of prisoners taken to Germans killed. The battle turned into a hundred little battles. Each dug-in position had to be reduced individually. Each enemy tank, when it ran out of fuel there in the woods, was transformed into a stationary pillbox.

Although the German troops were hopelessly surrounded,

238

the German command continued its efforts to rescue them. The most disturbing attack from the south came shortly after noon on December 26. It was led by Mark V and Mark VI tanks. Experience had taught us that these monsters were almost impervious to the fire of our lighter Shermans. Dive bombing would have saved the day, but there were no fighter planes immediately available.

General White knew the British on the Meuse had some rocket-firing Typhoons in their arms and, while our artillery attempted to delay the advance, he hustled over to Dinant. The British were most anxious to cooperate, but now a new difficulty presented itself: Second Armored had no radio capable of communicating with and guiding the planes. White had an answer; our artillery-observation Cubs had precise knowledge of the enemy's whereabouts.

A little later, American soldiers on the ground were treated to an odd spectacle. A squadron of Typhoons appeared in the sky, led by one tiny, unarmed Cub. It looked like a butterfly leading a squadron of buzzards. The Cub dived on Tiger and Panther tanks coming up the road toward Celles and then made tracks toward our lines. The Typhoons screamed down, rockets zizzing from their wing runners, leaving devastation in their wake. What was left of the German column retired with our troops in hot pursuit.

In General Collier's sector, fifteen miles away, the Germans attacked tirelessly and in strength. Company I of the 66th Tank Regiment, supported by two platoons of the 41st Armored Infantry, wrote a paragraph in history with its heroic resistance at the village of Havrenne, which lies a mile and a half below Buissonville. This group, commanded by Captain Henry Chattfield, was assaulted twice by greatly superior forces. The Germans were determined to break through to the north. The first attack came in the dank morning mists, and, despite heavy losses from accurate American fire, continued until the enemy had showed up to within one hundred yards of our position. At that point the Germans withdrew, leaving

239

their dead and their blasted tanks and their burned-out half-tracks scattered on the field. Later they came on again, and again they were set back with heavy casualties. There were fanatical drives all through this area, but it seemed to me they grew weaker as the first day waned.

Combat generals have to be gamblers. I decided that December 27 was the day we'd throw in everything we had. While Collier's other columns drove south with everything they had, I sent the division's Reserve Combat Command, under Colonel Sidney R. Hinds, into the battle to capture Humain. The artillery laid shells in there from 7 to 8 A.M. Then a task force of tanks and infantry went around the town and attacked from one side while a battalion of infantry attacked from the other. One of the penalties of artillery fire is that it provides rubble to use as barricades for a determined foe. These soldiers of the Ninth Panzer—whom we had also met the month before in our battle to the Roer—were determined. The fight lasted from early light until darkness.

The Germans' last gasp came just after sundown. A few survivors had found refuge in a thick-walled castle on the edge of the town. They resisted all efforts to get them out and refused to surrender. Then a flamethrowing tank belonging to the British Fife and Forfars was brought forward. It advanced into the open and belched its geyser of flame into a large tree just in front of the castle. In a moment the tree was a high torch that lighted the courtyard like day, and very shortly it had shriveled to ash.

This spectacular exhibition proved to be effective propaganda. A few minutes later, 200 German soldiers marched out into the courtyard with their hands held high. They had seen enough.

Second Armored's part in the Battle of the Bulge was, of course, simply one element of an immense action that involved many gallant troops. South and east of our sector, forces of Brigadier General Anthony C. McAuliffe held besieged Bastogne against determined German attack; McAuliffe earned

240

his place in anthologies of military phrases by his immortal rejection of the German demand for surrender—"Nuts!" Still farther south, troops of Uncle George Patton's Third Army pounded up seventy-five miles from the Saar to throw themselves against the southern flank of the Bulge.

But fortune placed the Second Armored square in front of von Runstedt's vanguard division, and in that great three-day action the division that called itself "Hell on Wheels" proved it was just that. It pounded the Second Panzer to pieces and halted the Germans' westward advance.

At nightfall December 27 the division was in complete control of the north bank of the Lesse River from Houye on the west, where we had made contact with British forces, to a point some distance east of Rochefort. At a cost of 220 wounded and fewer than half that number of fatalities, we had killed 550 Germans, destroyed the full tank complement of an enemy division and captured 1,200 prisoners and quantities of German materiel.

We were pulled out of the line on the 28th for a rest and refitting, but the Battle of the Bulge was not yet over. Now that the enemy's advance had been halted, his retreat had to be made as costly as possible.

In the midst of swirling snow on New Year's Day, 1945, Second Armored received orders to sideslip thirty miles east to Grandmenil and prepare for new action. Grandmenil lies almost due north of Bastogne, where Patton's forces had now broken the siege. Allied strategy called for VII Corps to push south to meet Patton's northbound troops; if we were fast enough we could slam the exit door on the German forces seeking to escape from the arrowhead of the Bulge.

The weather, poor during our Christmas campaign, had turned savage. Snow was followed by rain; the rain was followed by a hard freeze that glazed the narrow, twisting, hilly roads in that part of the Ardennes into near-impassibility; then it began to snow again. It took most of three days for the division to complete that thirty-mile move to its new zone.

241

Our steel-tracked tanks and tank destroyers were particularly vulnerable. The moment one of these armored vehicles missed a precise straddling of the high-crowned road by as little as an inch or so, its tracks lost their purchase and the machine slid inexorably off the road into the adjacent ditch. Our telephone lines were laid in these ditches; a tank sliding into the ditch usually fouled and broke them.

Finally I ordered that the steel tracks be exchanged for rubber. This was no simple task; the two tracks on a Sherman tank weighed a ton apiece. But our mechanics labored willingly on the job in that bitter weather, working on only two or three tanks at a time so the attack could continue without interruption.

On January 3 we launched a coordinated attack along an eight-mile front, initiating thirteen days of the most difficult campaigning I have ever experienced. Heavy snow fell continuously, blotting out all light like clouds of fog. In many places drifts reached waist height. Visibility was so poor—some of our armor still had not arrived from Havelange—that our forward artillery observers were able to work only an hour. We considered asking permission to postpone the operation, but finally decided to go ahead.

Our advance on that and following days was slow. We encountered not only determined resistance from the enemy, but we were also plagued by a succession of minefields. Some of the mines had been laid the previous month by American forces as they withdrew; but they had been laid so hastily that there were no proper charts of the mines' locations. We had to search out each mine individually. Once we got past our own minefields, we got into fields the Germans had planted. A particularly nasty German device we encountered was the plastic mine, undetectable by our metal-sensing mine detectors. Frequently a scattering of plastic mines lurked unrecognized for hours or even days under the thick ice covering the road, until steady passage of traffic finally touched off a lethal detonation. Then, of course, we had to block off the road and painstakingly locate and remove every one of the mine's unexploded companions.

Snow, ice and cold were more brutal enemies than the Germans. We had sent in requisitions for winter clothing, but through some foul-up cigarettes and other nonessentials came off the ships long before overshoes were unloaded. The battle was over before sufficient winter garb arrived. Consequently, our men, chilled to the bone, improvised, camouflaging themselves in sheets and mattress covers for want of white snow uniforms, and wrapping their feet in torn pieces of blanket. I watched the toll of frostbite and trenchfoot steadily rise. By the end of the battle Jack Frost had put more than twice as many of my soldiers in the hospital as German guns.

I soon discovered that a lot of our men were trying to conceal mild frostbite and trenchfoot because they knew that once a soldier was evacuated to a hospital it was almost impossible for him to get back to his original unit. I had an answer to this. Acting on my own authority, I took over an abandoned chateau back of our lines and set up an unofficial "rest camp" for treating minor frostbite, trenchfoot and combat fatigue cases. One of our dental officers presided, doling out medicinal whiskey and making sure the patients got plenty of hot food and rest. We found most of our patients were ready for duty again after three or four days of this treatment.

After their fright at the German counteroffensive wore off, medical people back at the Supreme Headquarters became aware of what I was up to and took offense at a line officer's interfering with their procedures. I received a peremptory order to shut down my shop. But a general fighting a battle is a busy man. Somehow the order got lost among my other papers and wasn't attended to until the battle was over and we no longer needed the rest camp anyway.

One way or another the men at the front managed to make do, in spite of the bitter weather. We tried to keep hot food moving to the lines, but frequently battle conditions interdicted that luxury, and the men had to get along with battle rations. If the rations were frozen, as was often the case, the men thawed out the packages on the exhaust manifolds of their tanks. Despite efforts by my staff to dissuade me, I insisted on making frequent visits to the front to see for myself how the ordinary soldier was making out and to spread a bit of encouragement. I at least was able to creep in a barn to sleep at night, and I found—under the circumstances—that the aroma of the dung left behind by the previous occupants was not in the least objectionable. The combat soldier had to bed down right out in the open.

One day, near nightfall, I met up with a soldier who was standing guard behind a bullet-scarred tree. His buddy, who had a load of pine boughs in his arms, was busy kicking at the snow on the far side of a little knoll a few yards to the rear. I asked the young man if he was getting along all right. He seemed a little shy; possibly he was surprised to find himself talking to the division commander. He said he was making out fine; he had had a hot meal that afternoon, he told me, and luckily his buddy was a Minnesotan who knew how to lay down boughs to make a bed in the snow.

Perhaps he noticed I was shivering a little. "General, you ought to take care of yourself," he concluded reprovingly. "An old man like you shouldn't be milling around in the open in weather like this."

And I thought I was the one who was supposed to be cheering people up!

It was tough fighting. But each day we pressed closer to our objective, the village of Houffalize, and the juncture with Patton's troops who were battling northward.

During these thirteen days Peewee Collier, who had triumphed so dramatically at Buissonville by sending his Combat Command A in on a night attack, continued to rewrite the classic texts on techniques of armored warfare. He opened his attack toward the village of Devantave by night and, after hours of bitter fighting, completed his seizure of the town about noon of January 6. The following day, again fighting at night, the Command captured the village of Cochamps. After two such successes, I thought that our chances of surprising the enemy with still another night attack by tanks would be slight. But when we arrived three days later outside the key town of Samrée, which was heavily defended by German armor, Collier asked authority to launch another night attack. A little dubiously I assented.

In the meantime forces from White's Combat Command B, which had been pushing south on Collier's left, pivoted around Samrée to the east to plug up the town's eastern and southern exits. Collier's tactic of night attack worked perfectly still another time. His tanks roared into Samrée fifteen minutes after they jumped off. After recovering from the shock of their surprise, the Germans—several battalions of infantry and about twenty Panther tanks—defended themselves with vigor. But their case was hopeless; few of the infantrymen escaped and the tanks we didn't destroy we seized. Following the capture of Samrée and a day's respite for reorganization, maintenance and repairs, our southward pace quickened. The German defense was beginning to crumble. A reconnaissance battalion attached to Combat Command A captured a German battalion command post and took prisoner the battalion commander and his entire staff. The division's 41st Armored Infantry Regiment led by Colonel Hinds, captured another enemy command post; their feat included the recapture of a sack of American mail previously bagged by the Germans. The sack contained a special delivery letter addressed to Hinds himself.

At 9:30 A.M. on January 16, in a field just west of Houffalize, a patrol of the 82nd Armored Reconnaissance Battalion spotted another patrol making its way toward them from the south. Our patrol held its fire; as the other party of soldiers cautiously came closer, the patrol commander recognized them as Americans. They were forward elements of the 41st Cavalry Squadron, Eleventh Armored Division. We had met up with Patton: the pincers had closed, the Battle of the Bulge was over.

SEVENTEEN
★★
Corps Commander

A FIELD COMMANDER in the midst of a major battle is so busy just doing his job that he doesn't have time—or at least shouldn't have time—to worry about whether his superiors are taking proper note of his performance. Still, praise for a job well done is very pleasant, and I enjoy it as much as any man. Consequently, I was much moved in early January when General Collins passed on to me this memorandum from First Army headquarters.

5 January 1945

SUBJECT: Enemy Equipment Counted in CELLES (P-0675) Pocket

TO: Commanding General, 2nd Armored Division

THRU: Commanding General, VII Corps, APO 307

1. The Second British Army has reported that the final

246

count of enemy equipment found in the CELLES pocket is as follows:

Destroyed or Captured

    81 tanks
     7 assault guns
   405 vehicles, all types
    74 guns

2. It is believed that the bulk of this equipment belonged to the 2nd Panzer Division and that the tanks probably represent almost every operational tank in that division, since the German Panzer Div now contains a total of 100 to 120 (maximum) tanks. The 74 guns represent the normal complement of over six battalions and would account for the complete divisional artillery and AT battalions normally under a division.

3. The action of your division therefore destroyed the 2nd Panzer Division as an armored division. This division has always been composed of first-class personnel from Austria, and therefore its overwhelming defeat by your division is regarded as an outstanding and distinguished feat of arms.

4. Please accept my heartiest congratulations to you personally and convey them to the officers and men of the 2nd U.S. Armored Division.

> Courtney H. Hodges
> Lieutenant General, U.S.A.,
> Commanding.

Even more pleasing than this formal letter of commendation was the postscript penned below in a cramped English hand. It said simply, "My very best congratulations to the 2nd Armored Division." It was signed "B. L. Montgomery, Field Marshal."

A few days later, as the Second Armored secured a defensive line along the Ourthe River around Houffalize and began the clean-up and rehabilitation chores that mark the end of battle, General Bradley told me I was to be relieved as the division's commander and promoted to command of the XXII Corps. The news came to me as something of a blow; over the months I had lost my heart to the Hell on Wheels Division. I told Bradley that the war was obviously going to come to an end within a few months and that I preferred to stay with the division until the last.

But Bradley replied that I had earned my promotion and should accept it. "Perhaps your corps will be sent out to the Pacific after things are wound up here," he said.

So, sadly, I let it be known to the division that I was leaving. "I have always looked forward to the day when I could march the Second Armored in a returning victory parade at home," I said in my farewell message to my officers and men. Many tokens of affection were given to me: perhaps the most touching was a gift I received from three or four soldiers of our 41st Armored Infantry who were still coated with the mud of battle, a beer stein they had captured at Barmen. I knew it was a souvenir they themselves prized greatly. On January 19 I relinquished command of the division to General White, who had been commander of Combat Command B.

My aide and I drove off to pay a farewell call at the headquarters of the First Army, located at Spa, Belgium, about forty miles away. We arrived just before dark, and I reported at once to General Hodges. I found Hodges sitting by a cozy fire; he rose and greeted me without enthusiasm as I entered the room, but then he complimented me on the Second Armored's performance in the recent battle.

Abruptly he fell silent and I saw he was staring at my shoulders. "General, where are your green patches?" he asked.

"Green patches? What green patches?" I replied in genuine perplexity.

Hodges frowned. "Haven't you read the orders?"

248

"General, I have been busy fighting a battle for the past four weeks," I said. "I don't know anything at all about any green patches."

Hodges explained in fussy detail that orders newly issued called for commanders to wear green patches under their shoulder insignia to distinguish them from officers without commands.

"Then I don't need any green patches," I said briskly. "My people know who's in command of my outfit."

Hodges made no direct reply, but it was evident from his expression that my flippant comment annoyed him. We moved on to other matters. As I prepared to leave Hodges invited me to return later in the evening for dinner.

"I hope you will find some green patches to put on before then," he said.

I walked out fuming inwardly at the absurdity of scolding a general who had just successfully completed a crucial battle assignment for a trivial irregularity in his uniform. But I borrowed the required patches from Hodges' aide and appeared at my dinner engagement in irreproachable military rig.

Next morning my aide and I set out on a two-day trip to Vouziers, a village in the Ardennes department of France southwest of where we had fought the Battle of the Bulge. There I picked up my new corps headquarters. (Unlike a division, a corps has no combat units of its own; until it is inserted in the command structure and assigned divisions— usually three or four—it is simply a head without a body.)

The first view of my new staff was a distinct disappointment. Many of the officers were getting on in age and were sadly deficient in battle experience. Moreover, the corps had been without a commanding officer since November, aimlessly adrift with nothing in particular to do. Bradley had assigned XXII Corps to the newly formed Fifteenth Army, commanded by Lieutenant General Leonard T. Gerow; at the time it appeared that the Fifteenth might have a major assignment in the upcoming Rhine campaign. I realized at once that I would have to execute a major overhaul of the staff, and replace the older men who lacked the stamina to endure the hard work and sleepless nights of battle.

It was a painful task. Among the men I had to remove was one of my West Point classmates, a man who had grown soft after too many years of stateside duty in the coast artillery. I replaced him and other officers who didn't pass muster with alert younger men from division staffs whose work had caught my eye. As my chief of staff I selected Colonel Samuel Williams; earlier in the war he had been relieved, unfairly I thought, as an assistant division commander because of the disappointing performance of his division at Normandy.

Within a few weeks the Fifteenth Army was moved forward to the Rhine, but the war had progressed so rapidly that we were no longer needed as a combat force; XXII Corps' assignment was to hold a defensive line along the west bank of the Rhine from Dusseldorf to Cologne. I had under my command three airborne divisions—the 82nd, the 101st, and the 17th—the 20th Armored Division, commanded by Major General Orlando Ward, my old friend from Kasserine Pass days, and the 94th Infantry Division, a real fighting force.

On March 24, to the north of us, and on March 26, to the south of us, the Ninth and First Armies set off on a gigantic pincers movement around the Ruhr. The Battle of the Sack, designed to pen in the enormous force the Germans had deployed to defend the Ruhr industries, was under way. But the only duty of the Fifteenth Army—and XXII Corps—was to hold a defense line at the Rhine, the fulcrum of the pincers.

During a visit with me at the time the battle plan was worked out, General Bradley told me that my airborne divisions were destined for transfer fairly soon to the Pacific theater. Consequently he ordered us to limit our forays across the Rhine to forces of platoon size or smaller; this would ensure that our casualty losses were kept low. I passed this

250

word on to my division commanders. A day or so later the commander of the 82nd Airborne, a very young major general named James M. Gavin, telephoned me to report he had sent a battalion across the river. The battalion had encountered so little resistance, he said, that he planned to follow it up with a regiment that night.

"What did I tell you about limiting your crossing forces to platoon size?" I asked with considerable irritation.

Gavin blustered a bit at first, arguing that the opposition was so slight that his entire division should be permitted to cross the Rhine. I reminded him of Bradley's edict and issued a direct order that he withdraw his entire force at once to its assigned area on the west bank. The point Gavin had overlooked was that even though the hazards might be slight there was no strategic advantage to his division's advance: there was nothing of value to us in the immediate area he proposed to move into.

For a brief period at the beginning of April it appeared that I would return to service as a division commander again. Major General Maurice Rose, my chief of staff in Tunisia days, who had become commander of the Third Armored, was killed in action on March 31 near Paderborn, Germany. The Third Armored, which had set the pace for the First Army advance, had almost reached the point where it was to join forces with units of the Ninth Army and seal off the Ruhr.

I was saddened by the news of Rose's death, which struck me as tragically unnecessary. Rose and his aide were killed, and others on his staff were wounded, when a staff vehicle—moving forward at night—encountered a German tank that was attempting to escape to the German lines. A burst of fire from the tank's machine gun and Maurice Rose was dead. I have always taught that the commander and staff of a rapidly advancing division should never move toward the front at night because of just this type of danger. During a rapid armored advance, there are almost always enemy stragglers in hiding or maneuvering to return to their own lines before they

251

are captured or killed. Unhappily Rose decided to take a chance; it cost him his life and left the Third Armored without a commander at a critical moment of the campaign.

The morning after Rose was killed Bradley telephoned and asked me to step down from my corps assignment to take command of the Third Armored. I accepted the change of orders without hesitation; the combat situation seemed to demand it. However when I arrived at Third Armored headquarters and looked things over, I found that the officer who had been assistant division commander, Brigadier General Doyle O. Hickey, had everything well in hand. I notified Bradley that the Third Armored's command structure was in better shape than he had supposed, and I recommended that Hickey, an extremely competent general, be given the command.

Two days later my recommendation was approved, and I went back to XXII Corps. As a result of the two-day sojourn, however, I can claim—for those who enjoy odd facts—that during World War II I commanded the First, Second and Third Armored Divisions.

On April 2 forces of General Simpson's Ninth Army linked up with First Army units at Lippstadt, a village not far from Paderborn. The Allied ring around the Ruhr was closed. It took till April 18 to quell all resistance in the sack and to find just what had been bagged. It was an impressive tally: 325,000 prisoners of war. I regretted that XXII Corps' role in the action had been a passive one, that we had had no opportunity to demonstrate our battle-worthiness. It was obvious, as we watched the German defenses crumble in the waning days of April 1945, that the end of the war in Europe was very near. But Bradley continued to assure me that XXII Corps would have an assignment in the Pacific; neither he nor I knew anything about the development of the atomic bomb and thus we had no way of realizing how close was the conclusion of the war against Japan.

The officers and men (and women) of XXII Corps had the

252

proper material to toast the achievement of V-E day when that great day arrived. An engineer unit, poking about in the ruins of Cologne, had uncovered a network of underground tunnels. The tunnels contained an enormous cache of spirits and wine. When word of the find was reported to me, I did a little hasty calculation—number of bottles of liquor, number of persons under my command—and issued orders that every private soldier in the Corps should be given one bottle, every noncom two and every officer (including nurses) three or four, depending on his rank. As I recall it, I set aside a case for the commanding general—myself. In the circumstances I believe only a purist would regard my directive as irregular; given the choice of distributing such spoils of war among my own men or allowing those in the rear, to reap the benefit it seemed to me eminently more just to make sure the liquid refreshments wound up in the hands of combat soldiers.

News that the Germans finally had surrendered reached me on the morning of May 6, brought in to me by a delighted Signal Corps officer. The surrender was to take effect at midnight May 8. I was elated that the war in Europe was over, but was only too aware that peace would bring me not respite but a new flock of responsibilities. A huge civilian population was now wholly dependent upon me and my men for its survival from day to day.

Until you have actually witnessed it, it is difficult to imagine the chaos that exists in a nation where government has utterly collapsed; but chaos is the only word that comes to mind to describe the Germany I saw in May, 1945. The German people themselves, accustomed to obeying government directives without question and numbed by the magnitude of their defeat, were abjectly eager to carry out any orders we gave them. It was up to us to figure out what must be done to reestablish the basic elements of civilization as speedily as possible so that normal life could be resumed.

The roads were clogged with thousands upon thousands of wanderers. They could roughly be placed in three categories.

Most desperate among the multitudes and in a minority were the sad-eyed, skeletal, hate-filled victims of the Nazi slave labor camps. Very few of these survivors from hell retained the physical strength to walk out and away from their prisons on the day the gates opened and the SS guards tore off their once-formidible uniforms and took off in panic-stricken haste to escape the advancing Allied armies.

There were also vast bands of Allied prisoners of war who were immediately freed by our victory; they swarmed everywhere attempting to hitch instant plane rides that would miraculously deposit them back with their own outfits, present whereabouts unknown to them. These penniless, unshaven veterans in threadbare Allied uniforms, overjoyed at the suddenness of release, were rounded up for their own safekeeping by Third Army orders. To the quite understandable indignation of the youthful, would-be celebrants, they were temporarily penned in open fields enclosed by wire entanglements and were fed cold emergency rations until one by one they were properly identified, sorted out and dispatched to the correct destinations.

Then, too, in the swirling crowds of traffic afoot were Germans far from home and kinfolk (if there were still kinfolk and a home to go to), graying wives in search of long missing husbands, yellow-haired young women hopeful they might locate long absent sweethearts. Children who had stepped on mines or had been injured in bombing raids hobbled on makeshift crutches, side by side with the elderly, the ailing. One last recollection of total civil disorganization: Along the population-swollen roads for mile after mile stretched cherished but over-heavy family possessions abandoned in mid-journey; cartons and barrels of dishes and kitchenware, suitcases crammed with clothing, linens, bedding, boxes of tools, etc., heaped in clumps and covered as best as could be for protection from the weather. Each left-behind clump of personal belongings stacked at the roadside bore the evidence of typical German methodicalness, for to each was attached

254

a neatly lettered sign. Inscribed on the sign was the name of the owner-in-transit who presumably expected to return to the spot sometime in the future and pick up his goods, but rarely was any address listed on the label. Apparently the vanished wayfarers didn't know just where their travels would end.

Allied planners had of course laid out the design for a military occupation government, but there was no time to wait for formally delegated officials to arrive and settle in at their jobs. In consequence Army generals, very recently involved in planning and executing combat operations, found themselves at work improvising and imposing a rough-and-ready system of law and order, restoring a minimum network of transportation, and struggling to stave off mass starvation of civilians. I was made military governor of the Rhineland provinces, an area that included both what had been the XXII Corps zone before the final Allied campaign and much of the Ruhr basin.

Few of the officers and men under my command had prior experience as government officials, but I have only the highest praise for the skill and sensitivity they brought to this new kind of task. I can explain it only by assuming that a talent for government comes naturally to Americans because of their long experience with democracy and grass-roots decision-making.

In the Ruhr basin alone lived 6,000,000 people who were wholly dependent upon the occupation forces for their daily food. I wanted to feed these people so far as it was possible with local supplies, in order to avoid being tied to supply lines that stretched back across the Atlantic to the United States. I searched about and soon discovered that 80,000 tons of potatoes were available in Bavaria—if I could arrange the transport.

This required taking immediate steps to resuscitate the prostrate railroads. I speedily located the man who had directed rail operations in my area of Germany before the war ended. He was of course a Nazi, and I knew only too well that my orders specifically prohibited the employment of Nazis.

255

But I wanted those potatoes. I sent the railroad man off on a quick survey; he reported back that if I reopened enough of the Krupp steel works to make sufficient steel for repair of sixteen demolished railroad bridges, I could get the potatoes to the Ruhr area in four or five days.

"Go ahead and get it done," I said. And then I warned him, "As soon as you finish, I'm going to have to kick you out, you know. I'm probably going to catch hell anyway for employing a Nazi."

He grinned at me and got the job done. He knew what the score was.

We estimated that there were in the Rhineland provinces about 600,000 displaced persons. More than half were Russians who had been kidnapped from their native provinces to work in German factories and on the farms. Thousands were running around the countryside with nothing except the rags on their back and what they could push along the roads in carts, baby carriages, wheelbarrows, bicycles and anything else that would roll.

They were looting and stealing, and who can blame them? But the result was anarchy. My first job in establishing order was to collect these wandering thousands and install them in camps where they could be properly fed and cared for—many were so emaciated that their own skin fitted as loosely as a badly tailored suit—until there was sufficient transportation to get them back home. Even after the first of our trained military government officials began to arrive in the Rhineland, we found there were not nearly enough to go around. The trained teams took over the governing of the large cities; it fell to my combat officers and noncoms to run the small towns and the displaced-persons camps. In a short time there were more than 300 of these camps in my sector alone; each was a separate headache. In many ways this period was the most trying of my entire military career.

We separated people, as best we could, by nationality. Besides the Russians there were perhaps 100,000 Poles; the

256

remainder were Jews who had survived the holocaust, Italian and French factory workers, and the lost people from the Baltic states—Latvia, Lithuania, and Estonia. Then there was a constant stream of western nationals—Belgians, French, and Dutch—who had to be assisted in reaching their own countries. All of them had to be fed. American Army food, supplemented by captured German supplies, stocked the kitchens.

Our main problem—since they were the greater part of our displaced persons population—was the handling of the Russians and the Poles. No doubt it is treading on some toes to say so, but I must express my opinion that the Poles were the toughest to handle and the least amenable to discipline.

The Russians gathered in our compounds were largely peasants from small primitive villages, simple, unlettered, credulous folk with almost no formal education. There was hardly an ounce of ideology in a carload of them. Personally I found our Russian charges likable, friendly and, in the main, cooperative. They understood following orders and they expected discipline. They also expected from the governing authority a fatherlike attitude, and they counted on indulgence when, on occasion, they busted off the reservation. They accepted most of our camp rules and regulations without question. Unfortunately, they were completely ignorant of hygiene, and they were stubbornly unwilling to learn it.

This was a sore point with my soldiers. They had been taught the hygienic value of the latrine trench, and its usefulness in preventing epidemics. Personal cleanliness was part of their background and training. On this occasion their standards acted as something of a brake on international understanding. My soldiers' antipathy to the Russian peasant was based on refugee-camp experience. They couldn't understand why a person *in extremis* would surrender at the side of his bed, rather than take the extra few steps outside which would land him at the properly engineered location.

At first, with so many people to look after, it was impossible to guard the camps closely enough to keep everybody within

257

limits. We were in a country which had been fought over; earnest prospectors could find abandoned rifles and ammunition in almost any field. The German people gave us little trouble; they were defeated and they knew it. But there were a few bad actors among the liberated populations who were busy at murder, rape, and larceny of every variety. We instituted night and day patrols, and we were rather abrupt with the marauders we caught—the majority we shot on sight, perhaps 150 in all. In a reasonably short time there was more order than anarchy, but of course our score was not perfect.

At Aachen we had a camp which took care of 14,000 Russians. With great difficulty—in a combat area cattle are hard to find—we gathered up forty cows to furnish fresh milk for the children of the colony. One night all hell broke loose in the Aachen camp. Some apt, if untutored, chemist had devised a method of making liquor out of potatoes—and the result was the biggest and dizziest drunken orgy I have ever observed. When the tumult and shouting were finished, 4,000 people had broken out of the enclosure and were loose on the countryside.

Believe it or not, our patrols returned them all without bloodshed. The Russians came back down the road under the custody of our soldiers, laughing and singing and making jokes. They acted like children caught in some wonderful mischief. It had been a fantastic carnival, and the men and women had thoroughly enjoyed it. They had, to be sure, butchered, cooked, and eaten the forty cows that provided their children with fresh milk, and there were no more cows to be had.

The camps were supposed to govern themselves. They elected their own councils, and, as governor of the area, I listened closely to them. In the beginning, most people were satisfied. Then the Communist functionaries showed up to needle them into complaints. A visiting Russian general complained solemnly to me of ill treatment of his nationals at one of the camps. The whole thing, after investigation, boiled

258

down to twin facts: one of my sergeants had kicked a Russian soldier in the seat to make him behave, and someone had found a loaf of bread with sawdust in it. This particular loaf happened to be German bread taken from German army stocks to fill out that day's menu. The Russian general heard my report without comment. There was not a word of gratitude for the tons of American food carried across a very wide ocean to fill the stomachs of thousands of his stranded and destitute nationals.

I remember another complaint that brought a Russian liaison officer storming to my door; my Rhineland command, the liaison officer said, had refused Soviet citizens the right to fly their nation's flag. This is one of those matters of international protocol which can have grave repercussions. I hurried to the camp in question. The sergeant in charge was a serious young man.

He and his Russians could not agree on the troubled question of sanitation, and, in deadly fear that plague might sweep through his compound, he had set up his own system of reward and punishment. He had made the right of the Russians to fly their flag a privilege. If they policed the camp according to his directions, they were permitted to raise their flag next morning. No cleanup, no flag. I told the young man that I understood his problem in trying to keep things clean, but that he must develop some new formula—or get me court-martialed.

Our efforts to maintain public health also stirred criticism in other quarters. American medical officers, determined to prevent a typhus epidemic, established the natural barrier created by the Rhine as a *cordon sanitaire*. Thousands of German refugees, most of them women and children, were eager to cross the Rhine westward from Cologne and return to homes they had abandoned when the Allied armies pounded in; we were equally eager to see to it they brought no unwelcome traveling microbes with them.

Controlling the river crossings was a relatively simple matter

259

since the only bridge anywhere near Cologne was the pontoon bridge built by American Army engineers. All other bridges had been destroyed, victims of bombs, artillery fire, and demolition by the retreating Germans. Military transport priorities forced us to limit the use of the bridge by refugees to the hours between 2 A.M. and 4 A.M. We required the refugees who desired to cross to wait in detention pens at the river bank where they were fed, checked through, and sprayed with DDT to kill typhus-carrying body lice.

One day I was visited at my headquarters, a pleasant villa in the village of Hilton, by Dr. Joseph Frings, the Archbishop of Cologne. The prelate told me he had three requests to make of me. First, he asked permission to reopen the religious schools. (General Eisenhower had ordered the temporary closing of all public institutions, including schools.) I reflected briefly, then told the Archbishop that America too was a Christian nation and that his request was granted. Second, he asked permission to resume publication of the church newspaper, which carried notices of marriage banns, weddings, deaths and other matters of concern to church people. This request also I acceded to, waiving the temporary ban on newspaper publishing Eisenhower had ordered.

Finally we arrived at Archbishop Frings' third request: that I put a stop to "degradation of German women by American soldiers." I bristled and reminded my caller of the amount of time we were devoting to police work to protect civilians from marauders in their homes and on the streets. The Archbishop said he was aware of our efforts and was grateful; amplifying on his third request, he explained he was concerned that German women were forced to disrobe in the presence of soldiers so they could be sprayed with DDT.

"Archbishop Frings," I said, "I understand your position, but we don't have anyone else to do the job. Have you any suggestions?"

He had. He said he would provide German women to do the spraying. He was as good as his word—next morning his communicants were on the job. Our own soldiers were only too happy to be relieved of the duty. One of them remarked dryly to me: "After you spray 15,000 of the ladies, it gets to be a rather commonplace job."

In their dealings with refugees and the civilian populace, our noncoms and officers were almost without exception fair and just. They worked under great difficulties, and little by little a measure of order and hope returned to Germany.

Eventually a fleet of American planes was made available to start our 300,000 Russian refugees on their journey home. This produced a new and painful problem for us, for thousands did not wish to go. Some eluded our patrols and disappeared in the woods; others were collected and marched to the planes protesting bitterly. But we in the Army had no choice in the matter. It was a political decision.

Fortunately, for the sake of the men obliged to shepherd them to the airfields, most of the Russians went stolidly and without remonstrance. They arrived at the fields with sewing machines, bicycles, fur coats, gas ovens, grandfather clocks, oil paintings and all other forms of loot. Our C-47's had a capacity of twenty-five, and each passenger was limited to thirty pounds of luggage. The Russians were determined that none of their possessions should fall back into the hands of the Germans. When they learned of the baggage restriction, the spoils they couldn't take along they dragged to the edges of the fields and set afire. This will give you some idea of their bitterness.

Although most of these people, I am sure, had never been in an airplane, they climbed aboard without argument or show of fear. I asked one C-47 pilot how his passengers had made out.

"They gave me no trouble," he said. "I just sloshed down the center of the plane with a bucket of water, and was ready for another load. These Russians haven't got nerves, but they certainly get airsick."

In June the Allied high command had progressed far

261

enough with the onerous task of breaking down what had been a thoroughly multi-national staff into its national components to divide the administration of Germany into the four national sectors prescribed by the Yalta agreement. The Rhineland provinces over which I had presided lay within the British sector; the American zone lay to the south and east, in Bavaria, with a small enclave in the north at the port of Bremen so that the U.S. supply line was allowed.

I received orders to turn over my command to the British and move my corps headquarters to Pilsen, Czechoslovakia, as relief for V Corps, which was going home. I hated to part with my lovely villa at Hilton; after months at the front, I relished the opportunity that handsome house and its magnificent garden provided for living the good life. I suspect my British successor felt much the same way; he moved in as I moved out.

As the British troops entered the area, the American divisions under my command were returned to the Twelfth Army Group for assignment elsewhere. I began a round of farewell ceremonies, including one at which Major General André Dody, against whom I had fought in Morocco but who later became my friend, decorated me on behalf of the government of France with my second Legion of Honor. In the haste of the moment French officials were unable to locate the proper ribbon for the decoration. Dody gallantly solved the dilemma by removing his own Legion of Honor medal and fastening it about my neck. Later, when I received my own medal, I returned his to him.

The Stars and Stripes was hauled down from the flagpole in front of my headquarters and the British Union Jack went up in its place. The corps staff and I boarded trains to journey to the east. Our party included about a dozen Russian girls who had worked in the headquarters mess at Hilton. They were eager to return to their own people, and it was evident that remaining in Germany after our departure would create difficulties for them. At the recommendation of a colonel on my staff, I arranged for them to accompany us to Pilsen and to be escorted on from there to the Russian lines.

EIGHTEEN

★★

Face to Face with the Russians

MY EXPERIENCES IN Germany in the first months after the war in Europe ended provided me with the first ominous hints that the Russians might prove in the long run to be remarkably unfriendly Allies. By the time I arrived in Czechoslovakia and assumed command of 110,000 American troops, lined up face to face with the Russian Army along a demarcation line that knifed through Bohemia fifty miles west of Prague, it was evident that our wartime alliance with the Soviet Union was already breaking up.

I make no claim to any particular expertise in international affairs, but I can relate what I saw in Czechoslovakia in those waning months of 1945. I formed firm friendships with some of my Russian military counterparts, notably Colonel General Zadov, the top Russian commander in Czechoslovakia and Lieutenant General Lebedenko, commander of the northern of the two Russian corps that faced us along the demarcation line. (Commander of the southern corps was Lieutenant General Baklanov.) I also saw the shrewd, smooth Soviet political operatives and their Moscow-trained Czech associates maneuver Communist functionaries into one key government post after another until the final conclusion was inevitable: collapse of the democratic regime of President Eduard Beneš and its replacement by a pro-Russian Communist government.

The Czechs had reason to bear ill-will against both the

Americans and the Russians on V-E day. The American Third Army, commanded by George Patton, entered Czechoslovakia from the west on May 4 and rolled toward Prague at a pace that would have put it in the capital city in twenty-four hours. But Uncle George was under strict orders from SHAEF* to go no further than Pilsen; the Yalta agreement specified that Czechoslovakia was within the Soviet sphere and Russian military officials told Eisenhower that an American push beyond Pilsen was unacceptable to them. Unfortunately, the diplomatic niceties of Yalta were unknown to the Czechs. Patriots rose against their Nazi masters in Prague in anticipation of the Americans' imminent arrival. While Patton's forces cooled their heels fifty miles from Prague, the German garrison mowed down the ill-equipped rebels by the thousands.

The loss of life that resulted from this misadventure quite understandably led the Czechs to regard the Americans thereafter with a certain reserve. But the Russians initially were no more successful than we in demonstrating to the Czechs that they came as friends. The original Soviet troops to enter Czechoslovakia were Siberians and Mongols under the command of General Malinovsky, and they left a trail of pillage and devastation behind them. Moscow, anxious to woo the Czechs into the Soviet orbit, hastily replaced these vandals with Zadov's well-disciplined Fifth Guards Army. Zadov, who was one of the defenders of Stalingrad, made every effort to treat the Czechs with consideration, but the Russians there, as elsewhere, lived on the country—which never wins anyone a popularity prize.

Although technically my corps was attached to Patton's Third Army from the time I arrived in the ancient and beautiful city of Pilsen to take command of American forces in Czechoslovakia, his headquarters at Bad Tölz in Bavaria were a long way from my command post. The XXII Corps was what is known in military parlance as an "independent corps,"

*Supreme Headquarters, Allied Expeditionary Forces.

265

meaning that I received general letters of instruction from Patton, and found myself pretty much left to my own devices. And I found I had plenty of problems.

First to catch my attention were the cumbersome, time-consuming procedures the Russians had set up to grant clearance to Americans who requested permission to pass through their lines and go to Prague. It was necessary for me and members of my staff to visit Prague frequently to confer with Czech government officials, and I realized at once that the existing Russian pass system was intolerable. I requested a conference with Zadov.

When we met, I suggested to my Russian counterpart that we issue folder passes, printed in Russian, Czech and English, which would automatically permit crossing of the demarcation line if signed by either of us or our chiefs of staff. Somewhat to my surprise, Zadov agreed, stipulating that visits be cut to a minimum and made only for official business. I had no objection to the limitation, though it stirred protests among some people under my command who had hoped to sample the pleasures of Prague. Frankly, I didn't fancy the idea of Russian soldiers coming into Pilsen, getting drunk, and brawling with GIs, and I understood that Zadov probably felt the same way about Prague.

This first meeting with Zadov near Prague was a pleasant one. He had his headquarters in a handsome villa—mine were in a one-story building formerly used as a barracks—and he was guarded there by many soldiers armed with machine guns. The sight of these grim bodyguards posted at vantage points in the open and lurking behind bushes was offset by the general's affability and courtesy. When I finished my business, there were several glasses of vodka and a light lunch. I was to see a good deal of Zadov during the next months, and his bearing was always that of the professional soldier. Both of us were very conscious of the fact that we were not now governing conquered people, but were setting up camp temporarily in a liberated nation.

266

I must, however, report on my first journey from the American zone through the Russian zone to Prague. Crossing the border was like suddenly stepping from a bright sunny morning into dusky twilight. On our side cattle were grazing in the meadows, flocks of geese waddled fatly over the highways, farmers worked with machines in the fields. In the Russian zone there were neither fowl nor livestock to be seen anywhere, and the peasants sullenly broke the soil with antiquated implements. Their food was feeding the Red Army; they had no gasoline for their heavy machinery. The Americans were giving; the Russians were taking.

An incident that occurred not long after my session with Zadov made plain to me that a major Russian concern was to ensure that their soldiers receive no opportunity to meet GIs—and hear about the pleasant life enjoyed by the average man in the United States. One day I got word that General Lebedenko wished to come to see me. A conference was arranged, and he arrived with a large delegation of aides and interpreters. Lebedenko was a rough, tough trooper who had risen from the ranks to the grade of lieutenant general. In personal appearance he had a striking resemblance to our own unlamented Al Capone.

Highway 94 ran northwest-southeast between his lines and mine. Lebedenko abruptly proposed that I move my troops five kilometers back from the highway. I immediately refused.

"If I did," I told him, "I would wake up in the morning and find your troops on my side of the road, and next day you would want me to move back again."

After an hour of unsatisfactory exchanges through interpreters, I came out directly and asked the general to explain the real reason he wanted us to move. Lebedenko was terse enough. He said that he did not want his soldiers fraternizing with my soldiers; he said that on inspection tours he had often found them chatting together, and that this practice was not good for discipline.

I grasped his problem. The possibility of an exchange of

267

ideas between Easterners and Westerners scared him. Well, I had a solution. I proposed that he move his troops 300 meters back from the road and I move mine back 300 meters. The highway would be neutral territory and used by either side for inspection and supply in daylight; all roadblocks on the highway would be removed and no one would use it after dark. Lebedenko agreed and we separated in a friendly mood.

Two days later I rode up the highway and ran into a Russian roadblock. I got past that one but then ran into another, and, at the point of a gun, was forced to turn back. I was very angry. I thought the Russians had broken their agreement. I told Colonel Sam Williams, my chief of staff, that I was going down that road the next morning in a tank and that any Russian in my way would be run over. Sam knew I meant what I said, but he had already established a working friendship with Lebedenko's chief of staff, and he hustled over to see him. The Russian officer insisted the agreement had been carried out. However, he was willing to go to see for himself. When he came upon the roadblocks, Colonel Williams told me, he leaped from his car, grabbed the Russian lieutenant in charge by the nape of the neck and literally kicked him for a hundred yards up the road. Then he personally removed the obstructions.

I am now convinced that inferiority of Russian communications, rather than intent, was responsible for this breach of faith. Their communications were notoriously poor. For example, I had ninety-two telephone circuits in my headquarters switchboard; Lebedenko had four or five. I noticed that after an agreement had been made topside, there was always an exasperating delay before the word went down by chain of command to the subordinate leaders.

As time went on, Lebedenko and I became quite friendly. I gave him an American .45 automatic, and he gave me a double-barrelled 16-gauge shotgun which I suppose he had liberated from some German. I also exchanged visits with the other Soviet corps commander, General Baklanov. Baklanov was an extremely handsome man and a stimulating conversationalist. Again the custom of exchanging gifts was observed; my present to him was a wristwatch, his to me a Russian .45 automatic pistol (U.S.-made—lendlease, I imagine) suitably engraved with my name.

The Russian armies I saw were not, from an American point of view, well equipped, and high-ranking officers I met were sensitive on this point. The Russians had tanks, and good ones, but most of their transport was still horse-drawn. Neither their air forces nor their mobile artillery was in the same league with ours. I don't overlook one thing: in my experience the Russian soldier follows orders and will fight to the death. Discipline was very rugged; there was a caste system in the Russian Army that made any other army look like a free democracy—which no army can be.

Nevertheless, by off-the-record counseling between the chiefs of staff, most of our military problems in Czechoslovakia were worked out amicably. We agreed upon "ports of entry" along the demarcation line and manned them with Russian and American officers who spoke each other's language. Here stray Americans or Russians who were AWOL in the other fellow's lines were gathered up, exchanged, and sent back to their own units for disciplining. And we were able to keep incidents to a minimum.

On at least one occasion an incident that on its face would appear certain to prompt a major international flap was virtually brushed off by the Russians. An American sergeant from the 26th Division had made the acquaintance of a Czech lady of doubtful virtue—almost certainly by comparing notes with Russian noncoms, since the lady lived in a village well behind the Soviet lines. Unbeknownst to his superiors, the sergeant developed a regular routine of visiting at the lady's residence when he was off-duty.

Unfortunately the lady in question was also maintaining a liaison with a Russian captain who was commander of a company stationed in the vicinity. One night, while the

269

sergeant was calling, the captain—accompanied by a Russian lieutenant—discovered the American visitor and the lady *in flagrante delicto* in her second-floor bedroom. An altercation developed. The sergeant shot the captain dead, and the lieutenant prudently departed the room by the window, breaking his leg. The sergeant then returned to bed and spent the rest of the night.

A couple of days later the Russians produced the sergeant, who seemed remarkably unremorseful under the circumstances, at one of the ports of entry. We charged him with being absent without leave; the Russians charged him with murder. I assured General Baklanov we would convene a proper court martial to deal with the murder charge, and he promised to produce the witnesses. Before the trial could be held, the 26th Division was moved to Austria, but in due course the proceeding began in Vienna. Thirteen Russian witnesses came over for the trial. Possibly they had not cared for the captain. At any rate, all thirteen testified the sergeant acted in self-defense and the sergeant was promptly acquitted of all charges except being AWOL, for which he was punished in the normal American manner.

It seemed important to me, in our relations with the Russians, to make sure they had a clear picture of our military power. On V-J day, August 15, I staged a big celebration in Pilsen, to which I invited the principal Russian generals and their staff officers, and the Czech cabinet ministers. I invited General Zadov to bring a battalion of troops to take part in the parade and I furnished trucks for the soldiers' transport. I wanted to observe our mutual celebration together. For our part, we had there three infantry divisions and two armored divisions with supporting artillery, and our soldiers made a fine appearance. I insisted that all tanks pass the reviewing stand—which made the parade last several hours. The Russian military men were much impressed.

It was a great day, filled with a comradeship between Russians and Americans and a spirit of good feeling that

270

became impossible soon thereafter. Inevitably the day included a great banquet. Even before the toasts began, Zadov and I fortified ourselves with samples from a bottle of bourbon I had at hand. Then, as those at the dinner began to salute their countries and the victory with their glasses, Zadov—who twice had been awarded the gold medal of Hero of the Soviet Union—suddenly took off his Fifth Guards badge and prepared to pin it on my blouse. He was weaving from side to side in his chair, and his fingers fumbled.

I tapped him on the shins with my booted toe and whispered, "Stand up, Zadov, everybody's looking at us."

Zadov chuckled as he completed the pinning and then announced loudly to the company that I was "mean and tough enough to be a Siberian general." I think his comment was a compliment; at any rate I still have his badge.

After the banquet there was entertainment in a Pilsen theater; I had arranged for a large number of our soldiers to attend. During the course of the show, General Zadov told me he had never had the opportunity of speaking to American soldiers, and would like to do so. I was willing, if a little apprehensive, and the interpreters were handy. I needn't have worried. Zadov gave only a short talk. He told of the bitter days at Stalingrad, and how encouraged the Russians then were to know the Americans had entered the war. He said also, looking down from his box, that the Russians could not have succeeded in their drive against the Germans without American assistance.

General Lebedenko insisted on speaking when Zadov finished, and Lebedenko was truly a soap-box orator. My troops gave both of them thunderous applause. I still recall the conclusion of Zadov's speech. "If matters of peace and war could be left to the soldiers," he said, "there would always be peace between my country and yours."

My relationship with both Zadov and Lebedenko was that of soldier with soldier. I kept my agreements and they kept theirs. We had our last meeting in the autumn. I arranged for

271

a game of American football to be played in a Prague stadium. This was the first and only time that United States troops, with flags flying, ever marched over the historic and handsome Charles Bridge in Prague. Some 2,000 American soldiers watched the game from one section of the field, 2,000 Russian soldiers from another section. Most of the players were former American college stars, and it was a grand game. The Russians liked American football. Perhaps they didn't understand the strategy of advancing the ball, but they had a hearty appreciation of the jolting body contact and the virile roughness of the game.

In early September, Lawrence Steinhardt, the new U.S. ambassador to Czechoslovakia, arrived in Prague. His arrival was a great pleasure to me, for it relieved me of any further responsibility for American diplomatic relations with Czechoslovakia; I became simply the U.S. military commander in the republic. The reopening of the American embassy on a peacetime basis, and the restoration of the steady round of parties, banquets and receptions that seem to be a staple of diplomatic life, also gave me an increased opportunity to become well acquainted with the Czechs themselves.

Dr. Beneš, I felt, was perhaps the ablest statesman of Europe in that day—learned, patient, tolerant, a true patriot. Beneš was convinced that it would serve the interests of the Russians to maintain Czechoslovakia as a nation open to both East and West. He might have been right, but the Russians didn't see it that way. Subsequent events made it clear that the minions of the East in Czechoslovakia never intended to live with the West; they were simply biding their time.

Beneš and most of the other Czech democrats sprang from a cultivated, well-traveled, highly educated class; nearly all of them spoke French, many spoke other Western languages as well. In many ways they were remote from the great mass of the Czechs and Slovaks, Slavic peoples who looked to Russia as the primary source of their culture and their historical past. Communists had led the anti-Nazi underground during the

272

German occupation, many had suffered in German concentration camps, and they were heroes in the eyes of the people. It was not surprising they received posts in the government as Dr. Beneš set out on his doomed tightrope walk.

Others in his official family I held in less esteem. Prime Minister Fierlinger struck me as a shifty-eyed opportunist. Foreign Minister Jan Masaryk, son of the founder of Czechoslovakia, was genial and thoroughly Western in his attitudes and ideas; but he was all for doubtful compromise. Whether his plunge to death a year later was accident, suicide or murder, he paid dearly for his ill-judgment. Vlado Klementis, Masaryk's deputy and later a powerful figure in the Communist regime, I despised.

The Communist pattern for power in Czechoslovakia was a carbon copy of that used in Poland and Rumania. I observed that the Social Democrats never had any difficulty getting such posts as minister of transportation, justice, and so on. But the Communists grabbed the strategic portfolios. Through the Ministry of the Interior, they obtained control of press, radio, and the internal police, and, through the Ministry of Education, of what was taught in the schools. General Ludwik Svoboda, a pro-Russian, was Minister of War, and thus in control of the Army.

An incident out of my experience illustrates how pro-Russians like Svoboda utilized their power. Attached to my command when I arrived in Czechoslovakia was a Czech armored brigade which had been organized in England and had fought with the British Army through France and Germany until the Czech frontier was reached. The troops numbered about 5,600, and some 1,500 of them, I remember, had English wives. Three or four months later, this brigade was absorbed by the Czech national army. Its personnel was promptly scattered to the four winds, and I never heard of any of its officers obtaining given posts of importance, despite the fact they were the most experienced and best trained men in the Czech military. They, like many Czech fliers who had

273

fought with the Royal Air Force, were on the wrong side of the political fence.

Despite the Communist intriguing and periodic Communist-inspired efforts to embarrass Americans, my relations with minor Czech officials and ordinary people were always warm. The mayor of Pilsen, who was a Communist, insisted on commissioning my portrait and then hanging it in the city hall. He also presided at a ceremony in which I was given the freedom of the city of Pilsen and he assured me that I could return to live there tax-free if ever I so chose. I have some doubts whether this writ of honorary citizenship would be honored today—if I sought to exercise it. I have heard that my portrait was quietly removed from the wall a year after I left Czechoslovakia.

I attended a steady round of local festivals. I recall one in Novahut, the little village outside Pilsen where I lived. I surprised and delighted the peasants by going out into the fields to scythe the grain with them. I had learned to handle a scythe as a boy on a Vermont farm, but I never expected to find it a skill useful to a general stationed in Czechoslovakia. I also had opportunity to brush up on my horsemanship, for the local men often made their way to fairs and carnivals on horseback; they got a great kick out of seeing the American military commander arrive by similar mode of transport.

In early autumn General Patton, at my urging, came to Czechoslovakia. He was given a tumultuous reception in Prague, and President Beneš decorated him with one of the republic's highest honors, the Order of the Red Lion, First Class. He was touched, but I think he got a bigger kick out of a brief hunting trip we arranged for him after the formal part of the visit was over. We stayed at a castle as guests of a Czech nobleman and had a wonderful time stalking through tidy woods in search for deer and Hungarian partridges.

I tried to talk business with Patton after we got back to my villa near Pilsen; he hadn't bothered to reply to a number of questions I had sent him by mail in preceding weeks. But Patton grumpily brushed off my inquiries. "Why do you

274

bother me with all these stupid questions when I came up here to go hunting?" he asked in an exasperated tone.

I was a little concerned by his brusqueness, and privately asked General Hap Gay, his chief of staff, whether Patton was displeased with the way I had been handling things.

"No," Gay replied. "If he was, you would have heard from him long ago. He just doesn't want to be bothered right now because everything is going well. I assure you that if he wasn't satisfied, you would know about it."

Things probably were going better for me than they were for Patton. A few days later Patton—not for the first time—brought down a storm of criticism on himself by hasty words. At a press conference George had been asked his opinion about employing Nazis in German government posts; he replied that he saw no objection to it, and he volunteered the opinion that the German political struggle was not much different from the American tug-of-war between Republicans and Democrats. That, plus George's bullheaded refusal to deal circumspectly with the hard-to-handle but politically well-connected Jewish D.P. camps, proved too much for Eisenhower. He turned command of the Third Army over to General Lucian Truscott and banished George to the Fifteenth Army, which had become a paper staff assigned to write a report on the campaign.

An incident in which I played the decisive role contributed—quite unfairly—to Patton's reputation for mistreating Jewish D.P.s. About the time I arrived in Czechoslovakia, after most of the confusion that followed V-E day had subsided, a steady stream of displaced persons, most of them Jews, began to pour out of Eastern Europe into the American Zone in Germany. No doubt the emigration was encouraged by the Russians, who found caring for refugees inconvenient and expensive. Finally I received word that Germany could absorb no more D.P.s at the time; the message was accompanied by orders to turn back the unhappy and often desperate travelers at the border.

I attempted to carry out the order, but it wasn't easy. One

275

rainy, nasty day the Czechs pushed a freight train full of Jewish refugees over the demarcation line into my zone. Then the train crew unhooked the locomotive, which was coupled to the rear of the train, and hastily backed it back across the line. There were several hundred refugees aboard, packed like sardines into the boxcars.

When I learned of what had happened, I immediately telephoned Major General John M. Devine, commander of the Eighth Armored Division, and instructed him to get the refugees off the train and to a reception center where they could be fed and given a chance to bathe. I also told him to assign crews to give the train a thorough cleaning, for the cars were of course without toilet facilities. We kept those poor people about a week.

But we were unable to house them indefinitely, there was no place in Germany to send them, and I was afraid that if the Czechs and Russians saw that their gambit was effective they would try it again. I issued the orders for the refugees to be put back on the freight train. Then we brought up one of our locomotives and pushed those sad travelers back across the line into the Russian zone. Patton was in London when the news of what XXII Corps had done was angrily reported in Western newspapers. Patton was my commander; he took all the blame. This episode was extremely painful to me. But to this day I don't know what other course I could have followed.

Two months after his relief, while he was driving from Mannheim to Heidelberg to join me on another hunting expedition, Patton was fatally injured in an automobile accident.

I went to Prague again on October 28 to join Ambassador Steinhardt in reviewing the joyous parade staged by the Czechs to commemorate their independence day. They put on a brave show that autumn day, the first time in seven years they could celebrate their independence day in freedom. But my own stay in Czechoslovakia was drawing to a close, and the days of free Czechoslovakia were numbered. Negotiators hammered out an agreement that American and Russian

276

troops would withdraw simultaneously and that all troops would be gone by December 1. At XXII Corps headquarters we began to pack for a move to Regensburg, Germany.

I had a final diplomatic problem with the Czechs. There were about 100,000 German prisoners of war under my command who had provided much of the manpower for the restoration of the Czech railroads and other forms of transportation and communication in my zone. The Czechs wanted to detain the Germans for a while longer after our departure—to get more work out of them, I assume. But I found out that they planned to limit the POWs to a diet of 800 calories a day, and I felt I could not leave prisoners who were my responsibility under the rules of war to the uncertain fate of a semi-starvation diet. I called for extra trains and shipped the entire 100,000 men back to their homeland before we left. Our own troops followed.

On December 1, I delivered a farewell speech in Pilsen's city square and departed with my staff for our new headquarters at Regensburg. As was agreed, the Russian military forces departed as well, but there was a difference. They left behind their political agents to cement the power of the Communist Party. As a result they captured full control of the government less than a year later.

Czechoslovakia is a manufacturing nation, and I have always felt that if trade with the United States could have been resumed immediately after the war, the parliamentary parties might have been able to withstand the Communist onslaught. But that is all ancient history now. There was nothing in our record I was ashamed of. Our Signal Corps helped reestablish the Czech telephone system and other communications. We gave captured German food, tobacco, and motor transportation to the Beneš government. We provided gasoline for tractors and other farm machinery. And when the farmers' crops were about to spoil in the field, we supplied fleets of Army trucks and strong-armed young men to save the harvest. We did not play politics.

I made one more trip to Czechoslovakia, in October, 1946,

to join the Czechs again in celebration of their independence day. What a difference! In 1945 the parade had blazed with the brilliant and variously colored flags of the Allied nations. This time phalanxes of Soviet flags went by; only my middle-aged farsightedness permitted me to glimpse the one American flag in the procession. It was small, and it was carried by a very small but determined Boy Scout. I appreciated his problem. Sixteen visiting Russian field marshals took up most of the room in the reviewing stand, and I had a hard time pushing myself between their medals to get a good seat. A life-size Russian tank sat on a pedestal in Prague's main square, and it had been covered with gold leaf.

I ran into my old friend Colonel General Zadov. "How come you haven't been made a field marshal?" I asked, gesturing at the squad in the reviewing stand.

Zadov leaned close to my ear. "Because I got along too well with you," he muttered.

278

1945 - August: General Harmon is greeted by children in Novahut, Czechoslovakia, after a speech presenting a German gun to the townspeople.

1945 - German prisoners of war in Pilsen.

1945 - August 15: At V-J day celebration in Pilsen, General Harmon, Czechoslovak and Russian leaders review troops.

1945 - August 15: Tanks and their crews pass in review in Pilsen.

1945 - August 15: With Russian General Zadov, General Harmon takes salute in Pilsen.

1945 - General Lebedenko, Commanding Russian Army Corps and a Hero of Stalingrad, in Pilsen.

1945 - General Harmon lunches with Russian General Baklanov in Pilsen.

1945 - General Harmon receives Order of the Red Banner from General Zadov.

1945 - Russian soldier is decorated by General Harmon.

1945 - President Beneš of Czechoslovakia reviews troops with General Harmon.

1945 - General Harmon displays gift from Czechoslovak glass industry.

1945 - General Harmon demonstrates his skills at mowing wheat to Czech peasants.

1945 - Reunion of old friends: General ("Uncle George") Patton and General Harmon.

1945 - General Harmon on reviewing stand with Ambassador Steinhardt and Jan Masaryck.

1945 - September 27: For the first time, flag-bearing American troops cross bridge at Prague, Czechoslovakia.

1946 - July 25: General Harmon arriving at Kassel, Germany, to inspect Constabulary.

1946 - Constabulary in Sandhofen, Germany, used this imposing building for the Constabulary school.

1946 - In rare moment away from military responsibilities, General Harmon bagged a wild boar in Germany.

1946 - October 14: In Munich Generals Eisenhower, McNarney and Keyes reviewed General Harmon's Constabulary forces.

1947 - June: Review honoring General Harmon's retirement from the Constabulary was attended by Ambassador Murphy, General Clay and General Burress.

1947 - June: Standing before massed colors, General Harmon takes salute from the Constabulary at retirement ceremony.

NINETEEN
★★
The United States Constabulary

EVERY ONCE IN a while the American public makes a mistake. In 1945, at war's end, it was guilty of a real lulu. We in the Army had the feeling that virtually every voter back home was shouting, "Bring the boys home." Congress, naturally, reacted to the desires of its constituents, and the War Department had no choice but to comply. In Europe, as relations with the Russians grew increasingly tense, American demobilization moved into high gear. But even that wasn't fast enough to satisfy the demand. Military morale plummeted.

After the Armistice of 1918, General Pershing insisted that every soldier overseas be assigned to drill every morning. He vigorously promoted organized athletics and planned recreation for those in uniform. He required that every man who contracted a venereal disease be held in detention until he was cured and sent home. These demands no doubt diminished his popularity, but they ensured that the force under his command was an Army and not a rabble.

Eisenhower as top commander took a quite different tack. He spent much of his time tinkering with the complicated point system that determined who got to go home when. He issued no directives about mandatory drill. Before long the Army found itself in a situation where more than two million men were roaming around Europe virtually as they pleased,

279

and many of them were getting into trouble. Whether it was so intended or not, it was a prudent decision toward the year's end that transferred Eisenhower home to succeed General Marshall as chief of staff. He left behind a prickly Christmas present for Lieutenant General Joseph McNarney, his successor as American military commander in Germany.

After XXII Corps' removal from Czechoslovakia back into Germany, it was clear that its disbanding was close at hand. I asked for and was granted a brief leave so I could spend Christmas at home. My three sons were still overseas and my elder daughter was in Argentina; but I had a joyful reunion at our home outside Washington with my wife and younger daughter.

I returned to Germany shortly after New Year's Day for a new assignment. I reported to McNarney, learned he had real trouble on his hands, and found I was to become one of the troubleshooters. Discipline had deteriorated so badly among some of the American troops that on at least one occasion a mob of brawling, catcalling GIs had marched on his Frankfort headquarters shouting "We wanna go home."

"Harmon," McNarney said to me, "you are going to be head of the Constabulary."

"What's that?" I asked. So far as I could recall, the only constabulary I had ever heard of was the Philippine Constabulary created after the Spanish-American War, and I was uncertain about what the responsibilities of that unit had been.

McNarney laid out the picture for me: I was to develop an elite force of about 35,000 men designated to exercise broad police powers over civilians and American military personnel. They would also set an example of soldierly dress and discipline. The deterioration in the behavior of the U.S. military was so severe that the existing military police forces no longer could cope with it. I had six months—till July 1—to get the Constabulary into operation.

My comrade from Anzio days, General Truscott, who now

commanded the Third Army, had recommended me for the post of Constabulary commander. It was at Truscott's headquarters at Bad Tölz—where Patton had once held sway—that I launched myself upon the complex task of organizing this new kind of police force. Until a German civilian police could be revived to take over part of the job, I was to be responsible for the operation of an outfit large and mobile enough to maintain law and order in an area the size of Pennsylvania, occupied by 16 million Germans, more than a half million refugees, and hundreds of thousands of our own soldiers.

We got a good start by securing elements of two distinguished armored divisions—my own First Armored and the equally capable Fourth Armored—to form the nucleus of the new organization. I successfully wooed Colonel Laurence Dewey, my one-time chief of staff, to take on the difficult assignment of operations officer of the Constabulary, and I named Colonel Harley Maddox to be chief of staff. Then I came up with a genuine find, Colonel J. H. Harwood, a former state police commissioner of Rhode Island. On the basis of his Rhode Island experience, Harwood handled the publication of a comprehensive "Trooper's Handbook" that gave our prospective policemen a step-by-step guide to their duties. Dewey, Maddox, and I drew up, from scratch, the Constabulary's tables of organization and equipment.

During the war, as I have already said, the niceties of military dress were of little concern to me. The pressures of combat kept discipline sufficiently taut in the units under my command, for I never let my men forget that such virtues as neatness, alertness, promptness, and swift, precise compliance with orders all helped them stay alive. But in postwar Germany, the temptations to a soldier to go soft and sloppy were great.

My staff and I set out to design a distinctive uniform for the Constabulary that would clearly mark our troopers as members of an elite force. The uniform became an important symbol, as it bespoke a worthy soldier's pride in his appearance. In my plans for the Constabulary, I suspect I may have been reacting to a preposterous decision by the War Department that gave General James Doolittle the job of revising the Army's system of discipline and military courtesy. Jimmy Doolittle was indeed a brave and much decorated flier; but he had a long record as a careless and indifferent officer. I have always regarded Doolittle's assignment to the chore of disciplinary revision as one of the General Staff's most ill-considered actions in the early postwar era.

The Constabulary uniform we came up with was a real eyecatcher. We designed a yellow and blue shoulder patch slashed by a red lightning bolt, drawing on the distinctive colors of the cavalry, infantry, and artillery to signify the military backgrounds of our troopers. In addition to the shoulder patch, we modified the standard uniform of the day by prescribing smooth-sided paratrooper boots, a Sam Browne belt, a brilliant yellow neck scarf, and a helmet liner bearing the Constabulary insignia and striped in blue and yellow. The bright Constabulary colors were to soon become a familiar sight on the highways and byways of the American Zone of Germany, for I saw to it that they were applied lavishly to every piece of our rolling equipment from my personal railroad train to our ubiquitous jeeps and motorcycles.

We devised a motto for the Constabulary also intended to instill pride in their unit among our troopers: "Mobility, Vigilance, Justice." We were to be fast moving to ensure that no part of the American Zone was without the police power it needed; we were to be ever alert for trouble, especially on the borders; and above all, we were to be fair and impartial in our dealings with everyone.

U.S.O. shows, canteens, and other "morale boosters" that became standard fixtures of the postwar Army are all very well. But I remain unconvinced that this kind of good "morale" contributes as much to building a well-knit military unit as does firm insistence on discipline and the provision of a set of principles for soldiers to live up to. With discipline and principles a man acquires that sense of contentment that comes only after a hard job is well done.

Within a month our staff plans were sufficiently advanced for us to move to Bamberg, our first headquarters, and to begin intensive training. In March, at Sonthofen in the Bavarian hills, we opened the Constabulary School, an institution that soon became known to the irreverent as "the West Point with the dehydrated curriculum."

Given the curious surroundings of the school, a touch of irreverence was appropriate. The school was housed in a former Ordensburg, or "Castle of the Order," a gray limestone relic of one of Hitler's weirdest dreams. At Sonthofen and at similar institutions in the other three geographical corners of "greater" Germany, Hitler planned to revive the tradition of the Teutonic knights. Through intensive indoctrination of suggestible adolescents at the Ordensburgs, the Führer hoped to raise up a new elite of soldier priests who would form the backbone of continued Nazidom. To Sonthofen and two other Ordensburgs that actually functioned had come eager twelve-year-old boys selected from the Adolf Hitler Schulen to begin the prescribed six-year course of study. Fortunately Germany's defeat put an end to the distasteful project before there were any graduates. When we assumed occupancy of the Sonthofen Ordensburg we took one look at the spacious courtyard where the downy-cheeked aspirants once assembled to worship the rising sun and promptly renamed it "Corregidor Quadrangle."

The most difficult problem we faced in the creation of the Constabulary—and one never completely solved—was to obtain qualified men, and, once they were fully trained, to hang on to them. Clearly the Constabulary was peculiarly dependent upon the good judgment, sensitivity, and honesty of the individual trooper, for much of the police work was to be carried on by groups of two or three men operating away from their headquarters. They were to possess unusual powers of arrest, search, and seizure. We could expect them to be tempted frequently by the possibility of bribes, for Europe was filled with desperate people willing to pay high prices for permission to cross borders illegally or to deal in black market goods. Mature combat veterans, those best qualified for Constabulary service, were increasingly hard to come by. The rotation system swept them home for discharge and most of their replacements were inexperienced 18- to 22-year-old draftees. In the early days especially, our need for competent junior officers was sometimes critical.

Despite these difficulties, the Constabulary went into operation on July 1 as scheduled. The American Zone was divided into three states, or *lander,* for administrative purposes; we tailored our commands to match the civil divisions. Each of the lander was the responsibility of a brigade, each brigade was composed of three regiments, and each regiment was subdivided into three squadrons. Every month the school at Sonthofen graduated about 650 students. But it was an uphill race to keep our ranks filled with properly trained men. In the first two months of operation we lost 14,000 men, nearly half our full complement of 32,750, and had to accept green troops as their replacements.

In the emphasis the Constabulary placed on discipline and the traditional forms of military courtesy, we found ourselves swimming very much against the current. Other commanders found it difficult to resist pressures from their drafted enlisted men and the voters back in the United States to relax customary Army standards. It is important to remember that before 1946 Americans had had no experience with operation of a peacetime army that was not composed entirely of volunteers, generally career men. Much of the restlessness of the postwar draftees in Europe was incited or at least amplified by the soldier newspaper, *The Stars and Stripes*. The paper carried a regular (and avidly read) column called "The B Bag," to which the editors invited discontented enlisted men to submit their gripes about their commanders.

Such a forum no doubt has great value in the give-and-take of civilian life, but in a military unit it can only wreak havoc.

284

From the Constabulary's first days I made it plain to the men under my command that I would permit no trooper to ventilate his gripes in "The B Bag." I reminded them that under the Military Code every man was entitled to send his commanding officer any complaint he might have.

"If you have a problem with a superior, you can write me personally and I will investigate," I promised.

Only one trooper ever violated the ban on "B Bag" letters, a man attached to the regiment stationed at Karlsruhe. I figured I had made my position clear enough, and I saw to it the penalty was swift and severe. As soon as I found out about the trooper's misstep, I rearranged my schedule and went down to Karlsruhe in person. A parade formation of his unit was called and, in the presence of his comrades, I took off the man's insignia and dismissed him from the Constabulary.

Predictably, the incident came to the attention of several American newspapermen. I suspect they were tipped off by *The Stars and Stripes* staff. In any event, the correspondents went to General McNarney and asked what he intended to do about a situation in which one of his commanders was curbing the right of free speech. McNarney gave them a brief answer: "Harmon can run his own show." I learned what he had said soon enough, though he never said anything about the matter directly to me. I think I appreciated the fact that McNarney saw no point in asking me for a private explanation as much as I appreciated the public vindication.

I should add that as many as thirty or forty Constabulary troopers a month took advantage of my pledge to give personal attention to beefs they sent me, and I kept my part of the bargain. I recall especially an appeal I received from a man who said he was being sent to radio school against his wishes. That complaint required no investigation. I shot back a reply assuring the trooper that if he didn't want to go to radio school, I didn't want him to go—because he would be useless when he got there.

"You got the school assignment because you've done well in

your unit. If you complete the radio course, you probably will be promoted," I added. I suggested he think the matter over further and let me know if he still preferred not to go to radio school, so that I could cancel the orders.

For some weeks I heard nothing from my correspondent. Then one day I received a note in which he wrote that he had decided to take the course after all and that he had just been made a technical sergeant. "Poor old Bill," he added, referring evidently to a buddy, "he's still washing dishes back at the old outfit."

We were fortunate in the colonels we recruited to command our brigades and regiments; most were extraordinarily good. I do recall, though, one regiment's colonel who complained that several of his company commanders didn't know much and were poor at administration. I happened to know that our company commanders almost without exception had distinguished war records as combat leaders; many of them had been promoted in the field.

"If they were good enough to advance like that in wartime," I told the complaining colonel, "they can handle Constabulary companies. It's up to you to set up classes, train them in the handling of their paperwork and administration. If you can't do it, I'll get another colonel who can." The complainer took the hint, and soon found himself to be a better teacher than he had realized. In time his company captains also became competent administrators.

But owing to the difficulty we had in obtaining expert junior officers in sufficient numbers and to the sensitive nature of the Constabulary's assignment, I decided early that the force would need constant close supervision by its commanding officer. I set myself the task of visiting each of the twenty-seven squadrons at least once a month. The incessant crossing and recrossing of southern Germany that this plan necessitated would never have been possible without Hermann Göring's three-car private train, to which I had happily fallen heir.

We painted the train's exterior in the Constabulary colors,

but the interior fittings Göring had left behind suited my purposes just fine. The first car contained a kitchen and dining room, the second provided sleeping berths for me and my staff, and the last included a conference room and our communications equipment. We always carefully timed our arrivals, loitering a bit in the countryside if necessary, so that the train could draw up with a flourish at the day's inspection site precisely at the appointed hour. This arrival ceremony was designed largely to be eyewash for the civilian populace, and they responded eagerly. Almost always a large crowd was clustered near the platform when the Constabulary commander's train drew into the station. I was delighted to learn later that the citizens of Munich habitually referred to the arrival of my train as "the Second Coming."

My subordinate commanders joined in the high ceremony of these inspections with gusto. I recall an arrival one bright morning in Augsburg. At precisely 8 A.M. I stepped from the train with every crease in my uniform in its exact place. The colonel in charge and I exchanged salutes with snaps so crisp that they should have been audible. Drawn up at attention just beyond were the troops called out for my examination. The force in review that day included a company of seventeen tanks.

After inspecting the men and finding every detail in order, my attention turned to the tanks. They were an impressive sight. Banished were the undistinguished hues of combat— these behemoths gleamed in the sunlight in their freshly applied coats of Constabulary blue and yellow. Their crews, equally gleaming, stood at attention in the cockpits.

I walked around the nearest tank, sniffed the air, and became suspicious. A tank is a marvelous weapon, but—to be blunt—it stinks. In proper running condition it is redolent with the stench of gasoline and lubricating grease, but the odor of these tanks was that of paint.

"Let's twist their tails and see how they go," I suggested to the colonel.

His face flushed as red as a spanked baby's. The tanks had

287

been driven up to the inspection site, drained of their gasoline, washed down from stem to stern, and painted inside and out. So far as their mobility at that moment was concerned, they might as well have been set into concrete and put on display in the city square.

A major project of the Constabulary's was to do what it could to cut down the number of highway accidents, which each month claimed between fifty and sixty lives in the American Zone. Most roads were narrow and twisting and offered few temptations to speeders. But Germany in that era also boasted some of the world's finest high-speed highways, the celebrated *autobahnen*. Something about those broad ribbons of concrete seemed to bring out the maniac in every GI who had access to a jeep.

Jeeps, those great World War II workhorses, were not designed for high-speed highway travel. Accelerated beyond forty miles an hour, they flipped over and killed their occupants with monotonous regularity. I saw no reason whatever to make the enforcement of traffic safety regulations the sporting proposition many foolhardy drivers in the United States demand that it be. The Constabulary unashamedly established speed traps along the autobahns and saw to it that speeders caught in them were punished severely. Mobile summary courts organized under Constabulary auspices roved up and down the highways and dispensed speedy judgments right at the roadside. A man convicted of driving more than ten miles an hour above the speed limit lost his driving permit on the spot; if he was speeding less than ten miles over the limit, a notation was made by the court officer on his permit and he got one more chance—but only one—before his permit also was revoked.

I recall a day on which I personally nabbed two GIs who were racing in 6 x 6 trucks. I ordered the pair over to the shoulder and out of their trucks. No doubt they had to contend later in the day with an angry commanding officer who was confronted with the necessity of finding two new

288

drivers in a hurry. But I like to think I may have made some small contribution to ensuring that those boys got home to their families in one piece.

Although generally German civilians caused fewer police problems than did displaced persons and American soldiers, the closing months of 1945 brought a disturbing rise in incidents that evidenced a resurgence—or possibly a last gasp— of Nazism. In most cases the incidents amounted to nothing more alarming than the display of swastika flags and emblems and the posting of derogatory notices. Of greater concern were reports of sabotage and attempted sabotage to communication and transportation lines, unprovoked attacks on American military personnel, and several instances of wires—designed to decapitate the unwary—being strung across roads.

Part of my responsibility—in addition to my Constabulary duties—was to build a new German police force organized in the manner of an American state police organization. With the assistance of an able German nobleman, Count von Henneberg, these civilian policemen were soon ready to go on the job. Their activation permitted the Constabulary to relinquish the routine policing of civilians and concentrate its efforts on border control and law enforcement among displaced persons and American servicemen.

But we remained on call to work with the German police when needed. Working jointly with von Henneberg's force, we devoted our most intensive antisubversion effort to the investigation of a series of three, possibly four, simultaneous explosions on the night of October 19, 1946, in Stuttgart and Backnang. The explosions caused extensive damage to the town halls in the cities and to a jail in Stuttgart. A small fire in a displaced persons camp in Backnang which broke out at the same time was believed to have been ignited by a similar explosion. A month later agents of our Stuttgart Counter-Intelligence Corps Detachment organized a raid on several homes that had been under surveillance and arrested eleven persons who subsequently confessed to the bombings. Sieg-

289

fried Kabus, the leader of the group, identified himself as a former commander of Storm Troopers; most of the others said they had been leaders of the Hitler *Jugend,* the Nazi youth movement.

Our principal weapon against criminal activity in the crowded refugee camps was lightning raids. These were staged in cooperation with the U.N. Relief and Rehabilitation Administration, the agency responsible for the camps. In November, 676 troopers swept through a D.P. camp at Bamberg and seized $45,000 worth of morphine, codeine, and penicillin for which the camp residents could not account satisfactorily, as well as a considerable quantity of GI clothing and live ammunition. We turned eighty-four persons over to the military government for trial on charges of black marketing and other offenses.

One of our most elaborate raids, though its results were inconclusive, was conducted in December at the Wildflecken D.P. Camp, which housed 15,000 persons, mostly Poles. The word had gone around that Wildflecken was providing a hiding place for numerous fugitives, in every category from thieves to murderers. In addition, the camp security officer in Landkreis Fulda told the authorities that he had seen men in the camp openly wearing sidearms in defiance of the prohibition against all firearms. We sent more than 1,600 troopers into the camp on the day of the raid, but the contraband we found was not impressive: one carbine, a few pistols, several liquor stills, and, inconveniently, a bull and a number of pigs and horses that appeared to belong to neighboring farmers. We detained 500 persons temporarily, but we found sufficient evidence to arrest only fifteen.

Our men were under instructions to look closely for refugee resentment about these raids, but we found almost none. One refugee explained it to an investigator by saying simply, "It's not the S.S." That wasn't a bad explanation. Driven by the urgencies of the time, the Constabulary did engage in procedures that probably are unacceptable in terms of American constitutional principles strictly construed. But the Constabulary was an American organization, staffed by men who all their lives had been steeped in democratic ideals and the understanding that government is the servant of the people, not the reverse.

Among the Constabulary's responsibilities was the policing of the 1,400 miles of international and interzonal boundaries that ringed the American sector, and the control of international travel through the Zone. Only two passenger trains crossed through the American sector in 1946. One of them was the Orient Express, that train beloved of detective-novel readers, which ran from Paris to Istanbul; the other ran from London (with boat connections across the English Channel) to Switzerland. We soon discovered that many of the trains' passengers were not properly documented to enter the American Zone. Ultimately we solved the problem not by prohibiting transit passengers but simply by assigning troopers to ride the trains as they passed through our sector. The troopers' job was to examine the papers of those who sought to board or alight at stops in Germany.

The American Zone was a powerful magnet to black marketeers and other criminals as well as to refugees simply seeking a better life. Illegal immigrants were a steady challenge to the Constabulary's honesty and patrolling skills. In the first six months of operation the Constabulary at border posts turned back 26,000 prospective entrants who lacked the correct papers. Another 22,000 persons who had slipped across our borders illegally were nabbed by troopers who intensively patrolled the ten-mile-wide belt immediately inside the boundary.

In all, the Constabulary operated 126 border posts. Determined that these installations would serve to command respect for the United States, I insisted that they be maintained with the same attention to appearance I demanded in troopers' uniforms. On my orders Colonel Dewey drew up a blueprint of how each post was to be laid out: there would be three

291

small quonset huts, one for sleeping, one for eating, and one to serve as an office; a neatly trimmed grass yard would surround the buildings; and the Stars and Stripes would fly proudly from the flagpole in each installation.

Three months after the plans were distributed I sent out word that I was coming to inspect the border posts and warned that they had better be in order when I arrived. Most of the posts were in fine shape, but I visited one post where subordinates had let down their regimental commander: the huts were in place, but there was no grass and no flagpole.

"Colonel," I said stiffly to the commander, "you are as close to being relieved as you ever have been. I am relieving the squadron and company commanders responsible for this post effective immediately.

"I will return here in forty-eight hours and I want to find this post conforming to the specifications in every detail."

This ultimatum presented the colonel with a considerable problem, since the required grass was normally grown from seed, but he knew I meant what I said. I suppose he assigned men to scour the countryside until they located someone who had sod to sell. When I returned two days later the flag was flying high and a fine green lawn carpeted the grounds.

Predictably, we encountered our stickiest border problems along those sections of the boundary where we faced areas under Communist control—the German provinces of Thuringia and Saxony, which lay in the Soviet Zone, and Czechoslovakia. Czech diplomats were a source of constant worry to me. I received, and had to investigate, what seemed like an endless stream of objections from them that Constabulary troopers at the crossing points had treated them discourteously. Frequently my inquiries revealed that the trooper's "discourtesy" had consisted of nothing more than pointing out to the diplomat that no one—including diplomats—was allowed to bring prohibited goods across the border.

The worsening of U.S.-Soviet relations was apparent in my many difficulties in reaching solutions to relatively simple

292

problems along the boundary between the Russian Zone and ours. Moscow had clearly decided that Germany was to be the main scene of the struggle for power between the East and the West, and Moscow gave the orders. Unlike what I had seen in Czechoslovakia the year before, Russian military men in Germany had almost no discretionary powers.

General Prosnick, commander of the Eighth Guards Army, was my opposite number at the frontier. It took weeks of parleying before I was able to arrange a conference with him. And when I did so, it was a grim affair. Prosnick met me at the Russian line, took me six miles back to a pleasant German house, where we sat at a long table surrounded by the unsmiling faces of Russian officers. I made proposals for straightening out border difficulties. A good deal of promiscuous shooting was going on and there were nervous trigger fingers on both sides. No one had yet been hurt, but at any moment it was possible that real trouble might break out. Our gloomy conversations were carried on entirely through interpreters. The interpreter for the Russians was a young, frowning major who, it developed, was a graduate of New York's City College. Prosnick said he agreed in principle to my proposals, but added that he needed to get final authority from his government.

I invited General Prosnick many times during later months to visit me on my side of the frontier, but, with one polite excuse after another, he was never able to make it. I discovered the reason in a rather amusing way during my second, and last, meeting with Prosnick. Two weeks after the original conference, I returned to his headquarters behind the lines.

Prosnick told me that the Soviet government had agreed to my program. Then we all had lunch. Everything was solemn, and pretty boring. I hadn't seen a grin, scarcely even a facial movement or a twitch, in two visits. Abruptly the young major from City College was called away by telephone to some other duty. When he left, the luncheon table abruptly came alive. There was laughter and animation. Everyone was friendly.

Officers who had professed not to speak my language suddenly broke out in torrents of English. As the vodka passed, Prosnick and I debated most amiably the virtues of collectivism and individual enterprise. I discovered that Prosnick, who was a native of the Caucasus, was a connoisseur of snakes and knew considerably more about poisonous snakes in the United States than I did. With some assistance from others at the table I saw the light—the frowning young major was Moscow's watchdog. He was the commissar.

In September the Constabulary had reached a point where it was running fairly smoothly, and I then cut back the number of hours in my working days to something approaching peacetime standards. I urged my wife to come over to join me at Bamberg and she did so. Not long thereafter the Third Army was transferred to Austria, and my headquarters was moved to Heidelberg so that supervision of certain operations previously a Third Army responsibility could be added to my duties. The move gave my wife and me a chance to live in a delightful chateau that had been the Third Army guest house.

But as July 1947 approached—the Constabulary's first anniversary—I pointed out to the Pentagon that I had been abroad almost five years and I asked for transfer in duty to an assignment in the United States. My request was granted, and General Lucius Clay, who had succeeded General McNarney as American commander in Germany, came to Heidelberg for my final review of the Constabulary. He used the occasion to present me with my fourth Distinguished Service Medal.

Our travel plans called for us to depart by ship from Bremerhaven, and it was arranged that my private train would carry us and our baggage to the port, which is in the north of Germany. Train departure time was set for 7:30 A.M. As we drove to the station at that early hour, I was astonished and delighted to see the streets of Heidelberg lined with Germans who had turned out to bid me a last farewell. That wholly spontaneous demonstration was, I thought, eloquent testimony that the Constabulary had done its job of bringing impartial justice to Germany, and that the effort was appreciated.

294

1948 - March 31: At Netherlands Embassy in Washington, D. C., General Harmon and other heroes of World War II received various military degrees of the Order of Orange-Nassau from Netherlands Ambassador E. N. van Kleffens.

1948 - February 28: Final retirement of General Harmon came at Fort Monroe, Virginia.

Retirement provided: a farm home, "Liberty Hall," at Woolford, Maryland...

relaxed and leisurely times with Mrs. Harmon . . .

fun with "General," the family pet . . .

a chance to use farm skills learned in childhood . . .

the pleasure of sailing a boat in peaceful waters...

and moments to recall the past with a grandson, Jon Roll.

TWENTY
★ ★
A New Career

THE MIDDLE OF 1947, I soon discovered, was not a good time for a professional soldier to be a returning hero. While I had been busy with the occupation of Czechoslovakia and subsequently with the organization and operation of the Constabulary, other generals—many of them junior to me and possessed of less extensive war records—had accepted the plaudits of the American public. The huzzahs had ended by the time I came home.

I reported to the Pentagon and was given a two-month leave. My next post, I was told, would be as director of Army instruction at the Air Force Tactical College, Maxwell Field, Louisiana, and liaison officer between Army and Air Force programs at the field. The more I thought about it, the more disappointed I was with the assignment. After my long experience as an armored commander and the heavy administrative responsibilities I had borne as commander of XXII Corps and of the Constabulary, I felt I should have been offered command of a unit of some kind.

I suppose that if I had been willing to plunge into military office politics, I could have wangled a spot of greater appeal, but that game wasn't to my taste. I went off on my leave, a little bitterly I confess, and began reflecting on other possibilities for the future. From my vantage point, the post-World War II era was beginning to resemble the days after World

War I, and the tedium of Regular Army life as I had experienced it with many of my military contemporaries in the 1920s was something I didn't care to repeat.

My financial situation was pretty good. My four older children were all on their own and my daughter Jeanne had just graduated from Duke University. I had completed my contract of thirty years' military service and was entitled to draw a full pension. Moreover, as my wife softly reminded me, we had moved sixteen times in those thirty years. She was looking forward to the time, she said, when she could settle down and no longer have to uncrate the furniture to discover that nails had once again been driven inadvertently through the slats into the dining room chairs.

She and I drove over to the Eastern Shore of Maryland. I had always had the idea I would like to live near the sea. Outside Woolford, a little village eight miles from Cambridge, we found a sixty-acre farm for sale. The farm bordered on the Little Choptank River, an estuary of Chesapeake Bay. The price tag was one we could afford. We bought the farm, naming it "Liberty Hall," and I informed the Pentagon that I had decided to retire in the near future.

My orders to Louisiana were then canceled and I was directed to report to Fort Monroe, Virginia, to become deputy to General Jacob L. Devers, who was at that time commander of Army Ground Forces. During the war, Devers had risen to become commander of the Sixth Army Group (U.S. Seventh Army and French First Army), which operated in southern France and ultimately drove into Germany through Alsace and Lorraine. It was a pleasure to wind up my Army career as deputy to Jakie Devers; he and I had become fast friends when I was his chief of staff before the war.

In late summer I began the routine of driving down the Delmarva peninsula Monday mornings and ferrying across to Fort Monroe for my week's work; on Fridays I retraced my steps to Liberty Hall. On February 28, 1948, I retired: I had been thirty years and ten months in service following the flag. I was fifty-four years old.

296

In the beginning, life at Liberty Hall was the purest pleasure. The farm's buildings and grounds had deteriorated over the years, and I laid out a schedule for myself with a view to putting the place back into first-class shape. I had been away from farming a long time, but day by day the skills I had learned as a boy returned. I was busy plowing, seeding, renovating the house, building sheds for my farm machinery, pouring concrete walks.

Two beef calves purchased in the spring and fattened until autumn, a few hogs whose hams and bacon we subsequently smoked in a smokehouse I built myself, and a well-stocked chicken house went a long way toward supplying our meats. Oysters, tonged by local oystermen, were plentiful and cheap. The pasture was overrun with rabbits, and crabs and fish could be gathered from the Bay.

For a time our neighbors regarded us with reserve, for we were newcomers—and New Englanders to boot—in an area that still recalls and clings to its Southern heritage. The day I was finally invited to participate in a local poaching party I knew I had been accepted into local society.

In the Bay near the mouth of the Little Choptank there was an island that several years earlier had been stocked with small Japanese deer and made into a game preserve. A game warden, who had several dogs, lived on the island, assigned to enforce the "no hunting" regulation. A group of local men asked me to accompany them on what they informed me was a traditional annual challenge to the warden's skill.

Cloaked in the early morning fog, we sidled close to the island in a fishing boat. A burly fisherman and I slipped overboard into four feet of water and waded quietly ashore. I soon spotted a deer and shot it. The crack of the rifle, of course, aroused the dogs, and the race was on. Hastily the fisherman and I gathered up the deer and splashed back to the boat, where waiting hands hauled us aboard. The skipper gunned the motor and we scudded off into the fog. The rest of us rapidly cut up the deer, packaged it, and placed the parcels under the floorboards.

297

Then, as custom dictated, the skipper swung the boat past the warden's landing pier. He hailed the warden, who by this time had returned quarryless to his house.

"We heard a shot," the skipper called. "Can we be of any help?"

"No," he called back, "we had poachers here, but the damnable bastards got clean away in the fog, and I don't know which way they've gone."

We solemnly expressed suitable regrets and turned our course toward the mainland. As soon as we passed out of earshot, we joyfully and noisily congratulated each other on our triumph.

At Liberty Hall my constant companion was one member of the family I have not yet mentioned, my dog General. We got the dog, a creature of doubtful antecedents who appeared to be a cross between a spitz and Labrador retriever, in the early 1930s as a companion for our children. I was most skeptical at that time that I would ever wear stars on my shoulder; I provided him his name so we could be sure to have at least one general in the family. But the children grew up and went off to make their own lives, and General made it clear he was now at my disposal.

After living through the war in the confinement of our house in Vienna, General found the pleasures of the country-side much to his taste. He became an especial devotee of the rabbit chase. So far as I know he never succeeded in capturing one of his quarry, although the rabbits—almost deliberately, it seemed—offered him a sporting chance at success. They would dawdle insolently in full view of the dog while he launched a frenzied charge in their direction; then when he had got within perhaps fifty yards of the goal, they would turn and, with a flick of their tails, depart at speeds he could not hope to duplicate.

General was a "talker." He and I fell into the custom of holding long conversations with each other. I would speak to him and he would reply in those curious musical sobs some

298

dogs develop that seem almost a form of communication we humans could comprehend if we only knew the vocabulary.

As often as not when I had an errand to run in my pickup truck, General would station himself firmly at the running board, indicating that he planned to accompany me. I recall that the day of my daughter Jeanne's wedding General rode with me to Cambridge to pick up the wedding cake. It was raining when we returned, and I had to put the cake on the seat between us. As we drove back General helped himself to a lick or two of the frosting, a liberty I regarded as justified by the dog's status as a member of the family. The ladies of the house reacted somewhat less charitably when the matter came to their attention.

But the pain of owning dogs is that they live briefer lives than we. General developed the habit of waiting for me when I was away where the lane to our farm joined the main road. One night in the spring of 1950, while he was standing sentinel there, a hit-and-run driver killed him. We brought him home, wrapped him in an Army blanket and buried him under the catalpa tree.

I can now look back at the years in Woolford as one of those idyllic interludes that too few of us ever get the opportunity to enjoy. My appreciation of it was somewhat different then, for I did not know that it was an interlude, that I had a whole new career ahead of me. The first flush of excitement at being retired and free to amuse myself was soon supplanted by boredom and increasing restlessness. I was uncomfortably aware of the excellence of my health and the midget challenge offered by my vest pocket farm.

One day when I was out plowing one of my fields I happened to look over the fence into a neighbor's field. An unlettered laborer was there plowing just as I was. I suddenly said to myself, "You're wasting your time here. There are many more important things than plowing that you're capable of, and you ought to be doing them." And in time the summons to service came.

299

Over the years I had kept in touch with the waxing and waning fortunes of little Norwich University; my years there as student and as Commandant of Cadets fathered a sentimental attachment that continued to burn bright. During the winter of 1947-48 I began to hear reports of unrest among the faculty members and many complaints about the administrative shortcomings of the University's president. As time passed, the reports multiplied. Like many small colleges in the immediate postwar period, Norwich was hard pressed to compete for teachers, who suddenly and happily found colleges bidding against each other for their services. But the problem of recruiting and retaining faculty at Norwich was particularly acute; one year a third of the teachers departed for other posts. Clearly a disproportionately large number of young faculty members were deciding after their first or second year that Norwich was not the place they cared to build their careers. The school's academic quality was falling, its financial outlook becoming increasingly grim; finally, in the fall of 1949, the trustees asked the president to resign.

The following February, a delegation of the trustees came to visit me at Liberty Hall. They asked me if I would accept an invitation to become President of Norwich. I found the possibility exciting and said so, but I warned my visitors I might not be the man they were looking for. I had never considered myself anything but a rough-and-ready soldier, certainly not an educator.

"Bad actors are hard to change late in life," I said. "You'll have to take me rough edges and all."

Neither that declaration nor my added comment that I knew no more about running a university than running a railroad served to dissuade them. I sat down behind the Norwich presidential desk for the first time on May 1, 1950.

The prospect from my office windows was dispiriting despite the clear spring weather, and I had discovered little that was encouraging in my talks with teachers and students. About the most positive thing that could be said about Norwich at that

300

moment was that there was a lot of room for improvement.

A few years later one of my colleagues offered this description of Norwich as it was when I took office:

> The morale of faculty and students was low, the students were overcrowded in the dormitories, three or four to a room. Academic facilities were limited; the sciences were down in the basements of the dormitories, where they had been for years. The pay of the faculty was low and the faculty lacked stability; there was a rapid turnover in personnel.
>
> The buildings and grounds were unattractive; much major repair was needed. In general there was little at Norwich to make one proud to have been a graduate, or to induce a graduate to send his son there, or to persuade a bright instructor to join the faculty. The military was one department which over the years had been kept at a high standard; the Department of the Army consistently sent able personnel to its Vermont outpost.

If anything, that analysis understated the gravity of the situation. One of the first areas I explored was faculty housing. I found eighteen of my junior faculty, already underpaid, living in University-supplied housing that I considered unfit for human habitation. It was no wonder that young instructors were unwilling to subject their wives to more than a year or two of that sort of home.

This survey was the beginning of an intensive examination of every aspect of the school's life. My lists of things that appeared to need correction, improvement, strengthening grew longer and longer. But as the lists grew, so did my confidence. I did not consider myself an intellectual, but I knew that I knew how to delegate responsibility and how to make decisions. I also knew I had plenty of energy..

So I sailed into the job. In my first months at Norwich I fully expected I would occupy the President's post only two or

301

three years before I either made so grave a mistake or so seriously offended one of the four groups that control a college—the students and their parents, the faculty, the alumni, and the trustees—that I would be called upon to resign. I only hoped I would remain at Norwich long enough to put the school back on the uphill path.

Although Norwich is a military college and its outstanding graduating cadets are offered commissions in the Regular Army, I was the first career Army officer to be elected president of the school in more than thirty years. Dr. Dodge, my immediate predecessor, was a physicist. Many of the professors in nonmilitary subjects were uneasy about my appointment: understandably, they assumed that I would tend to favor the military sciences at the expense of other elements of the curriculum.

They need not have been so apprehensive. I knew only too well that strengthening the school academically was a major essential. A quick review of the faculty had shown me it was composed of a few veteran full professors—many of them able but rapidly approaching the age of retirement—and a large number of newly arrived, inexperienced instructors. Sadly lacking was the interior ladder of assistant professors and associate professors that is a college's investment for the future. I also learned soon enough that the number of faculty members with Ph.D. degrees is one widely used benchmark of a college's quality. When I took office only seven of Norwich's forty-four teachers held the Ph.D., and ten lacked even a Master's degree.

I set down for myself a list of six basic objectives for my administration. At the head of my list was a pledge to recruit and maintain a stable, progressive, loyal, and competent faculty. Second was a commitment to achieve full academic accreditation for every department and the highest academic standing for the school as a whole.

The other objectives, directed at other aspects of the University's life, equally had as their intent the development of a full measure of excellence at Norwich:

302

To provide for the necessary quantity with the highest possible quality of personnel in the Corps of Cadets.

To maintain and develop the campus and its facilities so that both students and alumni will be proud to acknowledge Norwich as their alma mater.

To keep the college solvent, depending neither on a large endowment nor on substantial tax support.

To develop students mentally, morally, and physically with a view to producing balanced and responsible graduates.

Those who looked askance at my selection as President of Norwich were not limited to members of my faculty. When I attended my first national meeting of college administrators, I had the uncomfortable feeling of having wandered into the wrong private club. On the first or second day of the conference, which met in Philadelphia, a large luncheon was held for the participants. I can still remember the discomfort of wandering aimlessly through the banquet hall with Dr. Robert D. Guinn, Norwich's dean. None of the other heads of Vermont colleges made any move to invite us to join them at their tables. Finally I spotted a table occupied by a number of clergymen at which there were two vacant seats.

"Would you mind having a sinner sit among you?" I asked the group.

They all laughed and urged Dr. Guinn and me to sit down. I soon discovered that the clerics were the presidents of some of the nation's leading Catholic universities—Notre Dame, Catholic University, Holy Cross, and several others. During the meal I entertained them with some of my best Army stories. None seemed to be concerned that I was not a professional academician, and all wished me well in my new job. I was touched by their friendliness and good wishes. At that moment I felt badly in need of moral support.

Fortunately, this suspicion of me as an outsider did not last long among either my faculty or neighboring college officials. But even while others expressed their doubts, I was confident I knew what needed to be done at Norwich. First, we would concentrate on building faculty, new facilities, and a keener spirit among our students, with the goal of bringing a backward, dispirited school up to a par with other New England colleges of similar size. Then we would turn to adding one by one the "extras" that make a college a distinctive institution, that may catch a prospective student's eye and convince him to select one school over another.

But it was clear that this program would take a number of years and cost a great deal of money that Norwich at that moment certainly did not have. For me, it was time to set out on a kind of hunt with which I had no previous experience, the college president's hunt for friends with large bank accounts, open checkbooks, and restless fountain pens. In the meantime we needed a dramatic symbol that a new day had dawned for Norwich. The whole college needed confidence.

Visitors to Norwich's campus as it is today cannot overlook the fact that it is a university with a lot of history behind it. The building names and memorial plaques tell the story. The walls of the mess hall are lined with murals that depict the exploits of Norwich men of yesteryear: Admiral Dewey directing the Battle of Manila Bay; Edward Dean Adams harnessing the power of Niagara Falls to generate electricity; the death of Colonel Truman B. Ransom, second President of Norwich, during the assault upon Chapultepec; and numerous others. But in 1950 all Norwich had to remind it of its past were two decaying buildings that had outlived their usefulness (both have since been demolished)—and memories.

Founded in 1819 by Captain Alden Partridge, a former superintendent of West Point, Norwich University is unquestionably the nation's oldest private military college and the progenitor of the ROTC programs now found on college campuses across the country. Norwich men (and I count myself in their number) also affirm that Norwich was the first American college (1824) to offer courses in "civil" engineering as differentiated from military engineering; we amiably dismiss the counterclaim of Rensselaer Polytechnic Institute in Troy, New York, as unfounded.

What could have been more fitting as a symbol of Norwich's hoped-for renaissance, than the gesture we selected, a great celebration of the centenary of the graduation of Major General Grenville Dodge, the University's most famous early graduate. From Norwich, Dodge went on to the Regular Army and ultimately to the building of the Union Pacific Railroad. In May 1869 he participated in the driving of the gold spike into a laurelwood tie at Promontory, Utah, that marked the completion of the United States' first transcontinental railroad.

With the assistance of several railroad companies, the citizens of Northfield, and many other Vermonters, Norwich made the October 6, 1951, celebration of the centennial an unforgettable occasion. The old was mixed with the new. Suitably costumed members of the University's dramatics club, flanked by two ancient wood-burning locomotives that rolled towards each other on a track at the Northfield railroad station, re-enacted the driving of the spike; later in the day Mrs. Harmon christened as "Norwich University" a new diesel locomotive that belonged to the Central Vermont Railroad.

Bands played. Orators orated. Norwich University had gone a long way from the days when it was the American Literary, Scientific, and Military Academy. Now it took pride in assuring Vermont and the nation that it would be in operation for a long time to come as an institution of higher learning.

TWENTY-ONE
★ ★
The Years at Norwich

GENERALLY SPEAKING, BEGGING is frowned upon in our society—unless the beggar happens to be a college president. During my fifteen years as President of Norwich, the University spent something more than $8.5 million in the construction and equipping of new buildings and the renovation of existing ones. With the exception of about $2.7 million borrowed from the federal government in long-term, low-interest loans, almost every penny of those construction funds was given by contributors. The art of fund raising was outside my experience before I came to Norwich, but I attacked the new pursuit with gusto. Never before a public speaker by choice, I found myself addressing audiences at plush banquets, at Rotary and Kiwanis luncheons, at exclusive city clubs. And to my delight many of the men from whom I detached substantial sums of money became—and remained—some of my closest friends.

Usually those who became major benefactors of the University soon fastened upon specific areas to which they wished to direct their support. The special concern of Harry W. Patterson, a 1909 Norwich graduate and a trustee from 1950 until 1963, for example, was the faculty. Patterson, a Stowe, Vermont, farm boy who grew up to become an extraordinarily successful businessman in Buffalo, was the largest single

306

contributor to the cause of improved housing for the faculty. By 1962 the University had acquired more than thirty houses, some of them containing two or three apartments, at a cost of about $400,000. In addition, nearly half of the teachers owned homes of their own, many of them aided by loans from a fund created for that purpose with Patterson's gifts. Toward the end of my administration Norwich began to grant paid leaves of absence to selected professors so they could pursue advanced study; contributions from Harry Patterson paid the tab.

Major General A. Conger Goodyear, a New York industrialist and National Guard officer I met during the occupation of Germany, grew interested in Norwich through his friendship with me. He became a trustee of the University in 1950, and one day about that time he and I spent a few hours tramping around the campus looking over the situation.

"What do you think Norwich's greatest need is?" I asked him after our tour. I hoped he would say a library or a new academic building of some sort.

To my astonishment he replied, "A swimming pool."

I told him, as tactfully as I was able, that I had considered the need for a swimming pool, but had concluded that such a facility would better be deferred until we had dealt with the University's more urgent needs. Goodyear was obviously a little nettled by my response.

"If you ever decide you need a swimming pool, I'll build it for you," he said. He was as good as his word. Norwich swimmers plunged into the sparkling waters of the $346,000 Goodyear swimming pool for the first time in the spring of 1961.

But long before that, Goodyear's generosity rescued me from a very rash gamble. Not long after I took office at Norwich, Dr. Godfrey L. Cabot of Boston, a veteran trustee and great benefactor of Norwich, offered to finance a new science building for the University. I accepted his offer with alacrity, for both the sciences and engineering were in bad trouble at Norwich—primarily because of our inadequate

307

laboratory facilities. Several of our programs in these fields either had been reduced to temporary accreditation or had lost accreditation entirely.

Construction of the James Jackson Cabot Hall of Science was to cost $629,000, and I felt I could not ask Cabot to contribute the cost of equipping it as well. Meanwhile, my suppliers told me that the Korean War effort had resulted in long delays in the delivery of civilian laboratory equipment. They warned me I must contract to purchase all the equipment I needed at least eighteen months before the desired delivery date. I didn't want to see the new hall sitting around empty after construction was completed, so I crossed my fingers and signed the orders for $130,000 worth of equipment—without a cent in the bank to pay for it. After several sleepless nights, I went down to New York and confessed to Goodyear what I had done.

He paused to digest what I had told him, then said, "I believe in what you're doing."

In the next thirty minutes I had my first introduction to what is called "pool giving." Goodyear lifted his telephone and began calling wealthy friends. To each one he said, "I'll give $5,000 if you will." At the end of the half hour he had raised $65,000. With that lifesaving head start, I acquired time enough to raise the balance by more prosaic means. General Goodyear was a great friend to Norwich and many hearts were heavy when he died in 1964.

Trustee Godfrey Cabot also had his field of special interest—aviation. As early as 1935 he financed the creation of the James Jackson Cabot Fund for aviation studies, named for a son shot down over France in World War I. In 1951, again with Cabot's generous support, Norwich was able to open an academic department unique among American colleges, the Department of Aviation Administration. Cadets looking toward careers in the air transportation industry were able to major in the field and go straight from college to excellent jobs. But the rapid growth and change in aviation in the late

308

1950s made it impossible for the University to keep its teaching material up to date, and major airline companies indicated they regarded it more practical to provide on-the-job training in the distinctive aspects of aviation management. Reluctantly Norwich closed the department in 1960, and Dr. Cabot authorized the diversion of the funds that had supported it to general support of instruction in the sciences, particularly chemistry and physics.

Another good friend was Henry P. Chaplin of Windsor, Vermont. Chaplin, who was president of the Cone Automatic Machine Company until his death in 1962, was a leading member of a group called the Amphictyonic Society. The group, which combined elevated thoughts with pleasant recreation, normally held its meetings at Bailey's Island, a modest speck of land in the mouth of the harbor of Portland, Maine, that had been in Chaplin's family for many years. Early in my career at Norwich I was invited to attend one of the society's sessions. The agenda called for us to discuss world topics during the evening, then rise the following morning at 5 A.M. for a day of fishing. Our companions sensibly retired at 2 A.M., determined to get in a cat-nap before the fishing began, but Henry and I deemed the evening still young and recognized that many issues of grave import to mankind were still unresolved. We continued our talk, became fast friends, and Henry was recruited as a Norwich booster. When 5 A.M. chimed, he and I pushed off manfully in a rowboat to spend the day fishing near the Portland harbor lighthouse.

Not too long thereafter I paid a call on Henry. Norwich was renovating its library and I needed $110,000 to pay for the job. A foundation had offered $35,000 on a matching basis, but I still had to raise the balance. I laid out the situation to Henry.

"How much money do you want from me?" he asked.

"Fifty thousand dollars," I said. I saw no point in beating around the bush.

Henry rose, paced rapidly around his desk about four times.

309

Then he sat down heavily in his swivel chair.

"All right," he said. "If you will take $25,000 now and $25,000 on January 1 so that it falls in the next tax year, I'll give it to you."

I was only too happy to let Henry schedule the presentation of his gift to the library as he wished.

My greatest friend among the Norwich benefactors was J. Watson Webb of Shelburne, Vermont, who in his youth was one of America's greatest polo players. Webb had been a Norwich trustee in the 1920s and early 1930s, but had resigned in disgust in 1935. I persuaded him to rejoin the board in 1952. Almost every year during the 1950s I managed to go deer hunting with him on his estate in upstate New York. J. Watson insisted that the rules of sportsmanship be strictly observed by those he invited on these trips. On one such expedition when I was along, an unfortunate guest failed to make what J. Watson considered an adequate effort to track a deer the guest had wounded. A noticeable chill descended, and in later years that particular acquaintance was not invited back to Ne-ha-sa-ne Park.

The last time I went hunting with Webb, I shot a magnificent buck. It was Webb's custom to permit the rifleman to bring away the hide and meat of the deer he shot, but the head remained the property of the estate. I badly wanted the buck's head so I could have it mounted and hang it in my den; I haggled with J. Watson and we worked out a deal—he traded me the deer head for the dagger I had confiscated from General Borowietz during the German surrender outside Bizerte.

When Webb was dying, he called me to see him and gave me back the dagger. "It won't mean anything to my heirs," he told me, "and I know it means a lot to you." J. Watson Webb was that kind of friend. He made many generous gifts to Norwich, including a contribution of $500,000 for the construction of the classroom building now known as Webb Hall.

Building by building the new Norwich rose around us.

1950 - May: General Harmon's retirement was short-lived. His old alma mater, Norwich University, named him President.

This was not the first time Norwich had issued him a call to duty. From 1927 to 1931 Captain Harmon had served as Commandant of Cadets.

During the Norwich years, Commandant Harmon's favorite mount was "Diamond Dick."

1961 - October 6: The Dodge Celebration at which the student body reenacted the historic driving of the golden spike, was one of the first of a series of events aimed at reinvigorating the self-esteem of the college.

*1961 - At the Dodge Cele-
bration, Mrs. Harmon un-
veiled a new diesel
locomotive.*

*To keep in shape for his
administrative duties, General Harmon often worked
out on the University's ice-
skating rink.*

*1962 - General Harmon at
his desk in the President's
Office at Norwich.*

1966 - In 1965 General Harmon resigned the Presidency of Norwich, which in fifteen years had regained its position as one of the nation's great military colleges.

1969 - Norwich still figures importantly in General Harmon's life. As a trustee of the University, at the June graduation he sponsored Congressional Medal of Honor winner Captain Burt for an honorary degree. Captain Burt was a member of the 2nd Armored Division during the attack that cracked Seigfried line.

Beginning with the unromantic (but vital, in Vermont's bitter winter weather) new heating plant, we completed a new building—sometimes two—almost every year I was President. To the sentimentalists on our board of trustees and among the alumni, probably the most painful building decision of my administration was the decision, announced in 1964, to demolish Jackman Hall, Norwich's oldest building. Jackman had been occupied without interruption since the University had moved to Northfield in 1866 after a disastrous fire demolished the original campus in Norwich.

Jackman was a lovely building, it was old, but it was a firetrap, and horrendously expensive to operate. I had the building carefully gone over by architects with a view to renovating and fireproofing it. The report was that the project would cost at least $230,000. Moreover, the experts declined to guarantee that the building walls would not collapse while the renovations were under way. The ancient mortar was made of lime rather than cement, and time had taken its toll.

New federal legislation had made available long-term low-interest loans for the construction of college classroom and administration buildings. We successfully negotiated a loan of $1,000,000 from the federal government, added from our own funds, and began construction of a new main administration building. The structure now stands on the sites once occupied by Jackman and by Dodge Hall, a second (but ugly) nineteenth-century Norwich building. We tried to preserve at least a small measure of Norwich's past by naming the new building Jackman Hall for its predecessor and by lining its main lobby with brick salvaged from the original Jackman.

I had always admired the ivied walls so characteristic of the campuses of many New England colleges, and each year the current senior class dutifully set out ivy plants around one of the new buildings. Other new landscaping arrangements on the campus, designed by a firm I hired, flourished, but to my disappointment the ivy didn't seem to grow. One of my administrative colleagues, who considered himself an expert horticulturalist, advised me that the strain of ivy I had picked was too tender to survive the severe Vermont winters; I listened to his explanation, but remained skeptical. Several years after the ivy program began, I happened to take a close look at a building and grounds crew that was preparing to repaint the trim of one of the buildings. The foreman, shears in hand, was cutting down that year's growth of ivy. I angrily demanded an explanation, and the foreman told me that the ivy got in the painters' way.

"The painters will have to figure out a way to cope with it," I told him firmly. Since then ivy has flourished on the walls of Norwich just as it does at other colleges.

Some of the buildings that are now fixtures of the rebuilt Norwich campus started life devoted to another purpose, but judicious remodeling fitted them for continued usefulness. Prior to World War II, for example, Norwich specialized in training its cadets for cavalry service, and the Taylor Riding Arena was the pride of the campus. But military horsemanship passed into the history books, and the arena stood vacant until 1948, when it was converted into a makeshift hockey rink. It seemed appropriate to me to go all the way and remodel the arena into the real thing. In 1956 artificial ice equipment was installed, the rink was enlarged to regulation size, and the Taylor Hockey Arena went into service. The disused weather bureau building which the federal government deeded to Norwich in 1948 underwent a similar extensive face-lifting. In 1955 it was converted into the present Ainsworth Infirmary.

One present ornament of the Norwich campus had its origin in an event as slight as a chance conversation. Someone happened to mention to me one day that a set of Belgian bells had been stored unused for many years in a Cambridge, Massachusetts, warehouse. My mendicant instincts alerted, I investigated. Sure enough, the report was correct. The bells had been brought to the United States for the Chicago World's Fair and subsequently bought from the Belgian government by Mrs. Charlotte Greene of Boston. She had

312

intended to give them to Harvard, but Harvard, already equipped with a carillon, apparently felt one was enough. I investigated further and discovered that Mrs. Greene's son and daughter-in-law, Mr. and Mrs. Stephen Greene of Dover, Vermont, were willing to give the $25,000 set of bells to Norwich in Mrs. Greene's memory. The 36-bell carillon—subsequently enlarged to 47 bells—now hangs in a tower dedicated to the memory of Jeannie Porter Adams, mother of a former President of Norwich.

As much as a college president concerns himself with them, buildings of course only form a backdrop to what is truly important at a college—the students themselves, and what they learn (or fail to learn) during their student years.

In general I left strictly academic matters up to the faculty, feeling these should be the responsibility of the professional educators. I did, however, propose one mandatory course early in my administration that was speedily endorsed by the curriculum committee. I felt, and the committee agreed, that every student, no matter what his major, should be required to successfully complete at least one course in American history. It remains my conviction that no American citizen should be permitted to consider himself an educated man unless he has a college-level appreciation of the story of his own nation's origins and development.

Not too long after I took office, I found myself embroiled in a fracas over athletics. I suppose those responsible for the fracas, knowing that I played football at West Point, had typed me as a football nut. I'm not—at least not the kind they had in mind. That year's varsity team and the then-coach had dreams of playing the kind of semi-professional ball that has taken over the athletic programs of too many universities. They felt sure I would have no obejction to granting special privileges to the football team, including relief from certain cadet drill requirements. They were wrong. I did object, and I saw to it that Norwich got a new coach.

I believe that athletics are an important part of a student's development, but that they must be in balance with other essential activities. I was much more interested in developing intramural sports in which everybody could participate than in developing championship teams. We couldn't afford the championship policy, and I didn't believe in it anyway. Throughout my administration I was content to win half our athletic games and lose half, and I liked to schedule our games with other colleges that felt the same way.

During my one year as an underclassman at Norwich in 1911-12 I was a member of Alpha Sigma Pi (later a chapter of Sigma Alpha Epsilon), and I returned to the University disposed to be a supporter of the fraternity system. But I soon discovered both that fraternities had become a luxury Norwich literally no longer could afford, and that fraternities no longer placed their first loyalty in the University of which they were a part.

My survey of the University when I assumed office showed me that construction of a new student dining facility was imperative, and the new Student Union—named Harmon Hall by the trustees—opened for business in 1955. Accounting studies indicated plainly that the $700,000 initial cost of the building could not be amortized unless all cadets were required to take all their meals in the union. By tradition fraternity men had eaten in their off-campus houses, but I gritted my teeth and issued the regulation abolishing the privilege. There were protests, but many fraternity men understood that fraternity eating places were a burden on the University. One senior, for instance, said at the time, "We all realize that there was no alternative. As far as I personally am concerned, I put my University ahead of my fraternity. After a couple of classes graduate, no one will ever recall that the Greek-letter guys ever had those special privileges."

At that point, I still hoped that fraternities, shorn of their feeding responsibilities, could be worked into the fabric of the life of the new Norwich. But as the years rolled on I saw unmistakable evidence that the fraternities were becoming not

314

less but more divisive to the University student community. More and more cadets who chose to be Greeks—about half the student body—were using their houses as oases of alcohol in violation of Norwich rules. Too, fraternities were blatantly unmilitary. They encouraged the members to become slipshod about how they wore the cadet uniform and about performance at cadet parades. Many efforts were made by me and others to convince the fraternities' officers to mount a major housecleaning and overhaul of their procedures, but the conversations and warnings had no effect. Finally, in the fall of 1959, the Board of Trustees, acting at my request, voted to abolish fraternities entirely at the close of the academic year.

I didn't want to take such action, partly because of my respect for tradition, and partly because I knew it would infuriate many alumni. In retrospect, however, I believe that for the future of Norwich the abolition of fraternities was the most important single act of my fifteen years as President. The decision was announced only as a *fait accompli,* and no contrary opinions were sought or considered after the fact. I received a predictable number of alumni protests—about 200, as I recall. An abortive student protest strike was called on November 10, 1959; it consisted solely of a refusal by a large number of upperclassmen to fall in for reveille and an unmilitary march for lunch. We in the Administration got rather excited at the time but no one cut classes and the entire demonstration lasted only one day. I can laugh about it now; compared to the refinements of uproarious student protests we have seen on other campuses in the second half of the 1960s, the entire affair was child's play.

To replace the fraternities, the University bought three of the Greek-letter houses and converted them into clubhouses for the sophomore, junior, and senior classes, respectively. The top floor of Harmon Hall meanwhile was remodeled into a similar clubhouse for the freshmen. All students were welcome by their class' clubhouse. The first year after fraternities were eliminated the senior class, evidently still sulking over my decision, made little use of their new clubhouse. But student memories are short. Within another year or two fraternities were merely a note in the University's history so far as the students were concerned.

Although my decision to abolish fraternities at Norwich was based solely on our experience on our own campus, I learned that many of my fellow college administrators had come to the same conclusion. The late 1950s and early 1960s saw fraternities disappear forever from the campuses of many of New England's small private colleges.

Norwich had never had a chapel, an omission I was eager to correct in the course of the rebuilding of the college. The opening of new dining facilities in Harmon Hall in 1955 left its predecessor, White Hall, open for conversion to other uses; the building's high arched windows and raftered ceilings made remodeling it into a chapel relatively simple. As it was my custom to take a considerable personal interest in projects, I went down to New York to order the furnishings for the chapel when the necessary structural work was well under way.

Though I have sought to follow the ethical principles of religion, I have never been a frequent churchgoer. Accordingly, my tour of the religious supply house became an introduction to an unfamiliar field. Throughout my life, I must add, I have fought a largely unsuccessful battle against the vice (a minor one I hope) of profanity: during my inspection of the varieties of pews, pulpits, crosses, communion sets, and the like, I gave vent to at least a few of my saltier turns of phrase. As the wearying day drew to a close, I sank down on a chair and observed to the firm's sales manager, "Well, you certainly have taught me a new language today." His face crinkled into a grin. "You've taught me one too, General," he replied.

Year by year the improvement of the appearance of the Norwich campus and the expansion of the college's facilities erased the listlessness and gloom that had infected many of

316

the teachers and students when I first arrived. Together we were building a school of which all could be proud.

Norwich officials had periodically discussed introduction of a cadet honor system, but the idea had never been carried through. This seemed to me an unfortunate oversight for a military college. In the fall of 1951, at my urging and with the enthusiastic support of the cadet Corps, an honor system based on West Point's honor code was put into force.

From the beginning the Norwich honor system has been a student-run affair. It is administered by twelve seniors assisted by a junior and a sophomore representative from each cadet company. These students interpret the code, explain it to the new cadets, and manage its enforcement. Under the system, every student is honor bound not only to conduct his own affairs with honesty but also to report any infractions of the code by others.

From a practical point of view, the system has worked well. In the academic year of 1959-60, the year we suffered the most code violations during my administration, only twenty-five students were suspended or expelled. Most of those penalized suffered one-year suspensions. Under the code, only stealing and a few other very serious offenses are grounds for permanent expulsion; over the years 85 percent of those suspended returned to Norwich to become good and honorable cadets. More important than the practical aspect, however, the creation of a Norwich honor system provided the foundation for an intense student spirit that has well served both the students and their college.

Although most Norwich graduates do not plan Army careers, they take officers' commissions in the Reserve, and—after the customary three years' active duty—move on to other pursuits, I am satisfied that the college offers an excellent program in the military sciences. When I assumed the presidency, military specializations in armor and signal corps were offered, with an optional extra training course in mountain and winter warfare. During my administration, with the support of the Department of the Army, we added specialties in military engineering and flight training.

The mountain and winter warfare course always held my particular affection, partly because of my memories of the bitter weather we suffered through during the Battle of the Bulge. Students in the course (which is unique to Norwich) volunteer for an extra four hours of training a week. These hours are spent not in warm classrooms, but in climbing mountains on skis and snowshoes when the temperature is often below zero. The climax of the course is a winter bivouac: each student is required to carry in his rucksack all equipment necessary to sustain himself in deep snow and very cold weather, above timberline and below it. He climbs a minimum of 2000 feet vertical ascent and an overall distance of from six to twelve miles; he provides his own shelter and cooks his own meals, melts snow for water, finds wood for fire.

About 100 cadets a year take the training. Such an experience in triumphing over the harsher side of nature strengthens the spirit of any man. And should a Norwich man ever find himself in combat under such conditions, what he learned in the mountains near Northfield might very well save his life.

As President of Norwich I lived a double life: my job required that I bend every effort to build the college into an institution of excellence, but it also required that I keep an ever-wary eye on the account books. My first year we recorded a loss (of $22,580), but that never happened again. Every year thereafter we managed to tuck a little something into the sock, from $21,253 in 1951-52 to a high of $325,291 in 1963-64, for operating capital and expansion. After my second year, we no longer had to borrow from the bank to meet our summer payrolls.

In at least one area, my concern for my students' progress and my concern for the University's bankbook meshed neatly into a single policy decision. As a businessman, I was concerned that the Norwich plant stood largely idle during the summer months; as an educator, I was distressed that Norwich

318

freshmen were flunking out because they were inadequately prepared in mathematics and English. In 1956 we opened what became the pre-freshman remedial summer school. With this, and other more usual summer course offerings, the Norwich summer school became a paying proposition. Every year it earned the college at least $10,000 and in one bumper year, 1962, more than $40,000. It also enabled Norwich to admit many freshmen we would have otherwise rejected. We found that we could offer places in the freshman class to 80 percent of those applicants to whom we had suggested pre-freshman summer school because their high school records were not quite good enough to meet Norwich's entrance requirements.

Norwich had—and still has—an insignificant unrestricted endowment. Although, technically, it is the "military college of Vermont," it receives no aid from the state other than a $200 scholarship from the legislature for any Vermont resident who wishes to enroll. Consequently, the school must pay its way largely by student fees. It pained me during my administration that we were compelled to edge the tuition steadily upward. I was a poor boy once myself, and I was loath to price Norwich out of poor boys' reach. Although spiraling costs made tuition hikes unavoidable, the program of enlargement of the student body that I initiated—enrollment grew during my time from 574 to 1211—helped considerably to hold down the size of the increases.

As I looked about me in the fall of 1964, the beginning of my fifteenth year as President, the enlarged student body and the cornucopia of new, attractive buildings were only the most superficial indicators that this was a greatly changed college. Far more significant was what had happened among our teaching staff. The little band of seven professors with doctorates had grown to more than twenty; the faculty as a whole, which numbered forty-four when I took office, had grown to more than seventy. In 1950 the highest paid faculty member earned $4400; in 1965 every full professor was paid at least

$10,390. Perhaps even more telling was what had happened to the total faculty payroll: $141,250 in 1950, it now exceeded $600,000. And the problem of constant teacher turnover had vanished: in 1962 the turnover rate, once 33 percent a year, settled at 5 percent and stayed there.

I do not claim full credit for the renaissance that came to Norwich during my administration. It was the work of many dedicated people—generous trustees and benefactors, hard-working professors who caught the vision of what a revived Norwich might be and labored to make it so, and the students who passed through the college in those years and made the University's motto their own: "I will try."

One staunch supporter of Norwich whose contributions must not be overlooked is my wife Leona. One of my friends once observed that even my worst enemies worship the ground that my wife walks on. It must be so, if one can judge from the way Lybrand House, the Norwich presidential residence, was thronged with visitors during our years at the college.

But in that fall of 1964 it was clear to me that I had done what I could for Norwich. Given the growing national demand for college education. I could envisage a new expansion of the college to an enrollment of about 1800. But I knew the task would take between five and ten more years. I was seventy years old; that job belonged to another younger man. On October 17 I announced my intention to retire at the conclusion of the academic year, and turned my attention to winding up my second career.

Several years earlier my wife and I had bought a house at Grand Isle, Vermont, a village on one of the islands in Lake Champlain. It is there that we have lived since I became Norwich's President Emeritus in June 1965, and there that this book came to be.

I suppose all men fortunate enough to live to my age come ultimately to the time when they devote themselves to the effort of assessing the meaning and usefulness of what they

General Harmon's birthplace in Pawtucketville, a suburb of Lowell, Massachusetts.

The General's mother at age 18.

In this 1890 photograph, the future general is held by his father.

Etta, Charles and Ernest Harmon.

The General's mother and sister.

Mr. and Mrs. Durant of West Newbury who became Ernie Harmon's foster parents.

The General's Lady: Leona Harmon.

Family reunion after World War II. Standing: Robert, the General, Halsey and Ernest. Seated: Barbara, Mrs. Harmon, Jeanne.

1951 family reunion was attended by the Harmon children and grandchildren.

General Harmon and grandson 2nd Lieutenant H. Roll just before the latter left for duty in Vietnam.

General and Mrs. Harmon make their last official appearance at a Norwich formal dance in 1965.

Career summary: Mrs. Harmon created this hooked rug which details the General's military career and carpets the stairs of their home.

have done. There is much that I see about me in my country that I do not like, that seems to me an unthinking casting away of values I fought in two wars to protect. If our colleges are now to disintegrate into anarchy, if our cities are to become ungovernable and uninhabitable because Americans young and old, black and white, no longer can find a way to understand and trust each other, then it does not sadden me that I shall not be around to see the future.

Yet I have no regrets that I devoted my life to military service and the leadership of men. Everything I have seen suggests to me that men, when you dig beneath the slogans, are all pretty much the same. They want food, clothing, and shelter for themselves and their families, they hope for peace and freedom, and they try to provide for their children a life a little better than they had themselves. And it is on this conviction that I rest my hope.

Many of our troubles, I suspect, can be traced to failures of communication. My experience both as military commander and as college president taught me that support for unpopular decisions can best be won by honest explanations of why the decision has been made. I know also that hasty criticism of another man's actions is generally a mistake. People usually have reasons, frequently good reasons, for doing what they do, and it is best to seek out and weigh those reasons before making a judgment.

What we in the Army call morale has its application to civilian life and institutions. Good morale is built when men have confidence in their leaders and their comrades, when they understand and value the tasks that are set before them. Good morale depends, primarily, upon the exercise of effective leadership. And the key to effective leadership is painstaking and persistent attention to communication: learning the concerns and needs of those who work with you and for you; clearly explaining what should be done and why; conveying to others your own confidence that the task at hand can be done, and done well.

To the sophisticated, such a view may seem simple-minded, but I have found that it wears well. I have worked hard all my life at carrying out the missions that were given to me. Many of those tactical problems, and even the strategies of which they were a part, seem far away and little related to the questions that now confront us. But I always tried to do my best. I felt that anything worthwhile deserves one's best effort, and I am convinced that nothing worthwhile ever comes easy.

A long time ago I came upon a statement by Abraham Lincoln that strikes me as the essence of wisdom for any man who would devote his life to service:

"How much more good would be accomplished if men were not jealous of where the credit falls."

322

Maps

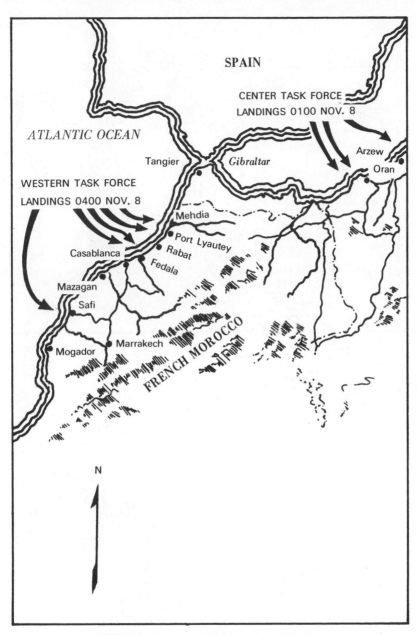

FRENCH NORTHWEST AFRICA

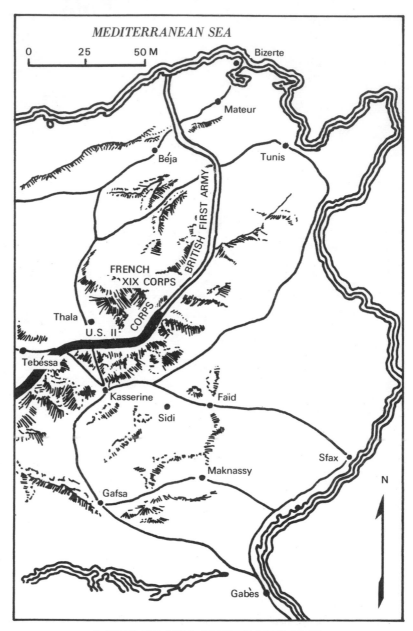

MEDITERRANEAN SEA

0 25 50 M

Bizerte

Mateur

Béja

Tunis

BRITISH FIRST ARMY

FRENCH XIX CORPS

CORPS

Thala

U.S. II

Tebéssa

Kasserine

Faïd

Sidi

Sfax

Maknassy

Gafsa

Gabès

N

TUNIS FRONT, FEBRUARY 1943

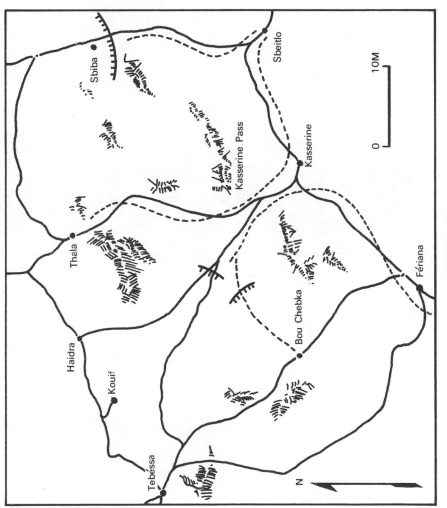

KASSERINE

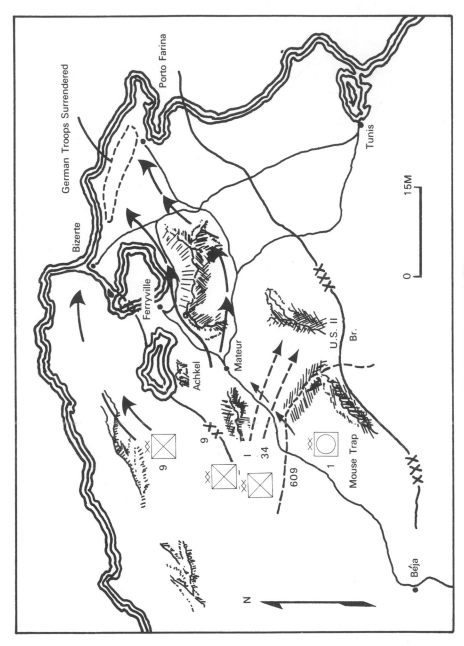

German Troops Surrendered

Porto Farina

Bizerte

Tunis

Ferryville

Achkel

Mateur

U.S. II

Br.

9

9

34

609

1

Mouse Trap

Béja

N

0   15M

MATEUR-BIZERTE

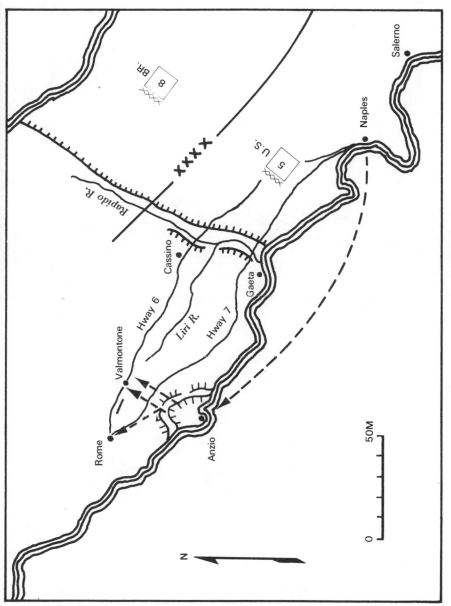

STRATEGY OF ANZIO CAMPAIGN

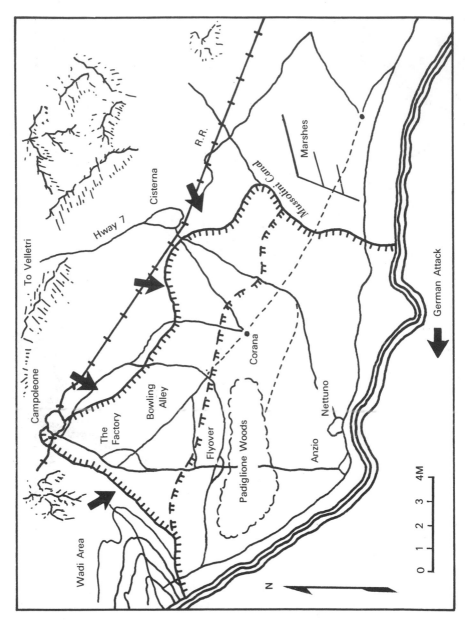

ANZIO

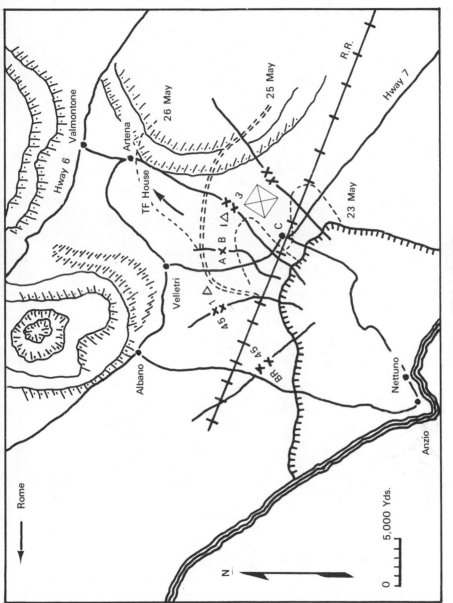

ANZIO BREAKOUT

30 MAY—ATTACK TOWARD ROME

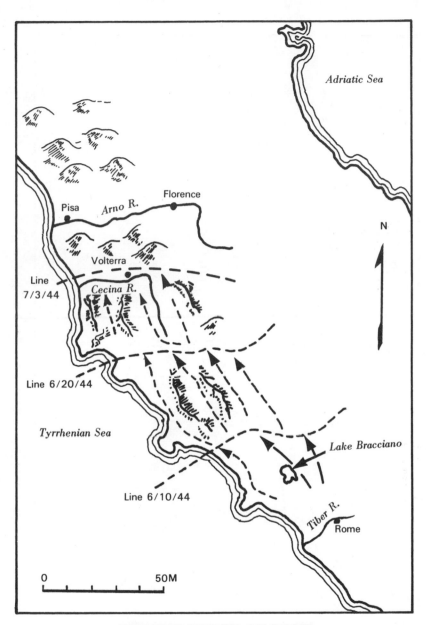

Adriatic Sea

N

Pisa *Arno R.* Florence

Volterra

Line
7/3/44 *Cecina R.*

Line 6/20/44

Tyrrhenian Sea

Lake Bracciano

Line 6/10/44

Tiber R.
Rome

0   50M

PURSUIT NORTH OF ROME

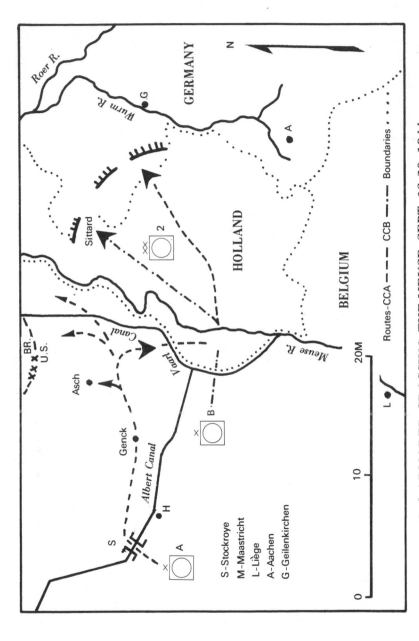

2nd ARMORED CROSSING THE MEUSE, SEPT. 13-20, 1944

GERMANY

Roer R.

Wurm R.

.G

A

HOLLAND

Sittard

2

BELGIUM

Meuse R.

Voorth Canal

BR.
U.S.

Asch

Genck

Albert Canal

B

H

S

A

Maastricht

N

20M

10

0

L

S - Stockroye
M - Maastricht
L - Liège
A - Aachen
G - Geilenkirchen

Routes - CCA · · · · · ·
CCB — · — · —
Boundaries · · · · · ·

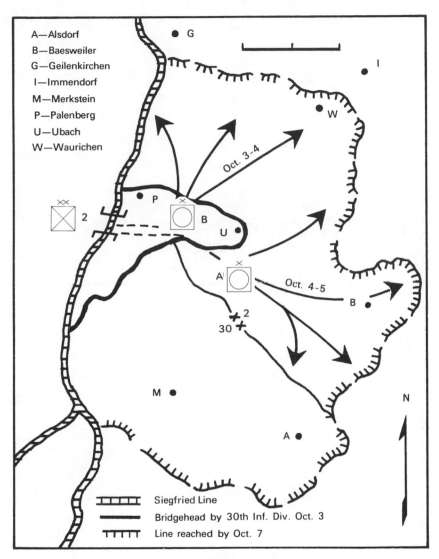

A—Alsdorf
B—Baesweiler
G—Geilenkirchen
I—Immendorf
M—Merkstein
P—Palenberg
U—Ubach
W—Waurichen

Oct. 3-4

Oct. 4-5

Siegfried Line
Bridgehead by 30th Inf. Div. Oct. 3
Line reached by Oct. 7

N

BREAKING THRU SIEGFRIED LINE OCT. 3-7, 1944

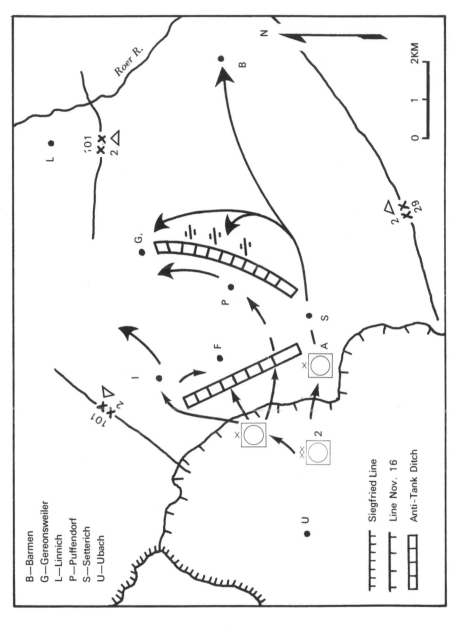

BATTLE OF THE ROER RIVER NOV. 16-28, 1944

B—Barmen
G—Gereonsweiler
L—Linnich
P—Puffendorf
S—Setterich
U—Ubach

Siegfried Line
Line Nov. 16
Anti-Tank Ditch

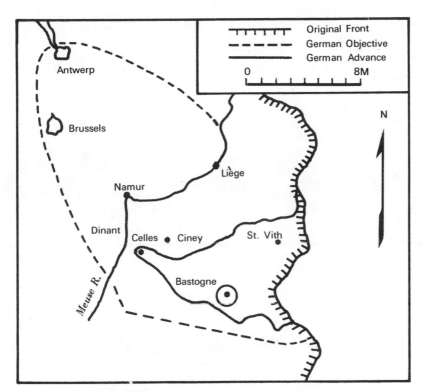

Original Front
German Objective
German Advance

0   8M

Antwerp

Brussels

Liège

Namur

Dinant

Celles   Ciney   St. Vith

Meuse R.

Bastogne

N

ARDENNES COUNTEROFFENSIVE

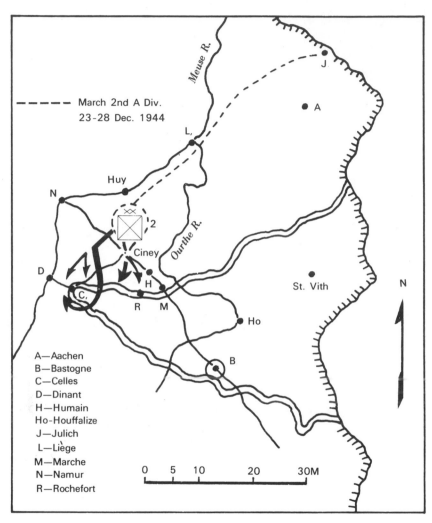

March 2nd A Div.
23-28 Dec. 1944

Meuse R.

Ourthe R.

J

A

L

Huy

N

2

Ciney

D

H

C

R   M

St. Vith

Ho

N

B

A—Aachen
B—Bastogne
C—Celles
D—Dinant
H—Humain
Ho-Houffalize
J—Julich
L—Liège
M—Marche
N—Namur
R—Rochefort

0   5   10   20   30M

1st PHASE BULGE BATTLE

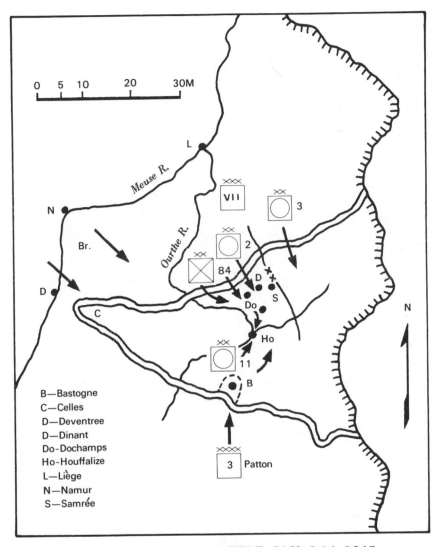

0 5 10   20   30M

L
Meuse R.
N
Br.
Ourthe R.
D
C

VII

⭕ 3

⭕ 2
84
D
S
Do
Ho
⭕ 11
B

B—Bastogne
C—Celles
D—Deventree
D—Dinant
Do-Dochamps
Ho-Houffalize
L—Liège
N—Namur
S—Samrée

3 Patton

N

**2nd PHASE BULGE BATTLE, JAN. 2-14, 1945,
REDUCING THE SALIENT**

WESTERN CZECHOSLOVAKIA

Index

INDEX

Aachen, Germany, 212, 231
  displaced persons camp at, 258
Adams, Edward Dean, 304
Adams, Jeannie Porter, 313
Adolf Hitler Schulen, 283
Aguinaldo, Emilio, 25
Ain Rebaou Pass, North Africa, 126
Air Force Tactical College, Maxfield, La., 295
Aire River, 38, 43
Albano Road, Italy, 155, 161, 163-65, 168-72,
  175, 183, 187
Albert Canal, Belgium, 208-10
Alexander, Gen. Sir Harold R. L. G., 127-28,
  130, 153
Algeria, 72
  See also North Africa, Allied invasion of
Algerian pirates, 1
Algiers, 100, 102, 103, 144
Allen, Gen. Frank A., Jr., 150, 154, 189
  Harmon's dissatisfaction with, 194
Allen, Gen. Terry, 100
Allied Expeditionary Force, Supreme
  Headquarters of (SHAEF), 207, 265
American armies
  First, 32, 207, 211, 229, 251
  Third, 209, 229, 236, 241, 265, 294
  Fifth, 59
  Ninth, 211, 215, 229, 252
  Fifteenth, 249-50, 275
American army group, 12th, 262
American battalions
  16th Armored Engineers, 132, 148
  27th Armored Field Artillery, 148
  91st Armored Field Artillery, 174-5
  82nd Armored Reconnaissance, 245
  48th Engineer Combat, 151
  1264 Engineers Combat, 222
  158th Field Artillery, 148
  189th Field Artillery, 148
American brigades
  150th, 227
  4th Mechanized Cavalry, 236
  Seventh Mechanized Cavalry, 57
American corps
  IV, 25, 197
  V, 262
  VI, at Anzio, 162-92
    Arno River, 193-203
  VII, 208, 229-30, 241
  XIX, 208, 212, 215-16, 220
  XXII, 249, 250, 277, 280
    Harmon given command of, 248
    Ruhr River, 252
  XXIII, 206
American divisions
  17th Airborne, 250
  82nd Airborne, 250-1
  101st Airborne, 250
  First Armored, 100, 112, 124, 149

    in battle, 134-35
    British assessement, 127
    Harmon takes command, 122
    Harmon's goodbye to, 203
    Italian campaign, 142-203
  Second Armored, 62, 145, 147
    advance to Roer River, 215-26
    Battle of the Bulge, 227-45
    in Europe under Harmon, 205-245
    Montgomery congratulates, 247
    North African campaign, 67-144
  Third Armored, 209, 212, 233, 251-2
  Eighth Armored, 276
  Ninth Armored, 62
  Eleventh Armored, 242
  20th Armored, 250
  First Cavalry, 54
  First Infantry, 28, 29, 34, 42, 100
    in Tunisia, 130
    leaves Tunisia, 144
  Second Infantry, 44, 225
  Third Infantry, 110, 176, 189-90
    at Cisterna, 155, 165, 180, 183
  Fourth Infantry, 225
  Ninth Infantry, 67, 133, 224
  26th Infantry, 270
  28th Infantry, 38, 40, 43, 225
  29th Infantry, 216, 218-19
  34th Infantry, 130, 141, 183, 191, 194, 197
  35th Infantry, 35-38, 41, 44
  36th Infantry, 153-4, 191-2
  42nd Infantry (Rainbow), 23, 34, 43
  45th Infantry, 159, 165, 171, 189, 191
  75th Infantry, 232
  84th Infantry, 232, 235
  88th Infantry, 202
  89th Infantry, 34
  94th Infantry, 250
  102nd Infantry, 218
American special service force, First, 181
  in Anzio breakout, 189
American industry, Allied invasion of North
  Africa and, 76
American regiments
  First Armored, 134, 202
  Sixth Armored Infantry, 150-51, 163, 170,
    183, 195, 202
  Thirteenth Armored, 202
  41st Armored, 248
  66th Armored, 216, 231
  67th Armored, 222
  Second Cavalry, 14, 17, 22-24
    Provisional Squadron of (Harmon's
    command), 22-24, 32-34
  Third Cavalry, 22
  Sixth Cavalry, 22, 48
  Eighth Cavalry, 54
  Fifteenth Cavalry, 22
  First Mechanized Cavalry, 57

343

345

347

INDEX

349